The Quest
for Loyalty

The Harvard Business Review Book Series

The Quest for Loyalty

Creating Value through Partnership

Edited with an Introduction by
Frederick F. Reichheld
Foreword by
Scott D. Cook

A Harvard Business Review Book

The *Harvard Business Review* articles in this collection are available as individual reprints. Discounts apply to quantity purchases. For information and ordering contact Customer Service, Harvard Business School Publishing, Boston, MA 02163. Telephone: (617) 495–6192, 9 a.m. to 5 p.m. Eastern Time, Monday through Friday. Fax: (617) 495–6985, 24 hours a day.

The paper used in this publication meets the requirements of the American National Standard for Permanence of Paper for Printed Library Materials Z39.48–1984

Library of Congress Cataloging-in-Publication Data

The quest for loyalty : creating value through partnership / edited with an
    introduction by Frederick F. Reichheld ; foreword by Scott D. Cook.
        p.   cm.—(A Harvard business review book)
    Includes index.
    ISBN 0-87584-745-5 (alk. paper)
    1. Customer relations.   2. Loyalty.   3. Employee loyalty.
    4. Corporations—Investor relations.   I. Reichheld, Frederick F.
    II. Series: Harvard business review book series.
    HF5415.5.Q47   1996
    658.8′12—dc20   96-22727
                                                                         CIP

Contents

the wheel and missed the turnoff for the future. The
authors sound a wake-up call to those managers who
are devoting too much energy to preserving the past
and not enough to creating the future. Any company
that is a bystander on the road to the future will
watch its structure, values, and skills become
progressively less attuned to industry realities.

improvement, and matrix management ignore the human need for predictability. The authors discuss how, to help employees focus and create value, managers must clarify for their employees the courses of action that will affect and improve their lives.

Part III   Investor Loyalty

The U.S. system of allocating investment capital is failing, putting American companies at a serious disadvantage and threatening the long-term growth of the nation's economy. Based on a two-year research project sponsored by the Harvard Business School and the Council on Competitiveness, the author recommends five far-reaching reforms to restructure both external and internal allocation of corporate investment capital.

The author offers new perspectives on one of the most startling power shifts in economic history—the rise of pension funds as major shareholders of large companies. He looks to Germany and Japan to outline the answer to the critical questions: For what should corporate management be held accountable, and how should accountability be structured?

Part IV   Customer Loyalty

Companies that want to improve their service quality should aim for "zero defections"—keeping every

customer they can profitably serve. Defection rates
are not just a measure of service quality; they are also
a guide for achieving it. The authors describe how, by
listening to the reasons why customers defect,
managers learn exactly where the company is falling
short and where to direct their resources.

Many managers assume that there is a simple linear
relationship between general customer satisfaction
and loyalty. But in exploring that relationship in a
broad range of industries, the authors found that the
difference between loyalty of *completely* satisfied and
merely satisfied customers is tremendous. Providing
customers with outstanding value may be the only
reliable way to achieve sustained customer satisfaction.

Just because competition in the airline industry is
tough, that's no reason to be tough on customers,
says Sir Colin Marshall, the chairman of British
Airways. In this interview, Marshall speaks about the
challenges and rewards of delivering consistent,
high-quality services in a complex, people business.

In this related article to "Competing on Customer
Service," the author provides a first-hand account of

how British Airways analyzed customer defections and invested in people and systems to pursue a radically different approach to customer relations: championing the customer as opposed to defending the company.

Foreword

Scott D. Cook

My business philosophy is simple: If you can't keep the customers you have, you don't deserve any new ones. Thirty years ago, it would have been unnecessary to point that out. Pleasing customers was something of a given in those days. But the logic of customer retention has fallen into such baffling disfavor over the past few years that we have to look at loyalty today as if it were a brand new business idea. This book is an effort to do that, and to take a good look at the various loyalties—employee loyalty, investor loyalty, customer loyalty—that skillful managers use to build loyalty-based strategies and business systems.

Yet the starting point must always be customer loyalty, for customer loyalty is gold. When good customers hang around, they become *better* customers. They buy more, take less time, and deliver more profit. Most important, delighted customers are one of the best means of acquiring new customers because they spread such positive word of mouth about your business. They also help you grow in another important way—they're not leaving through the back door while you're welcoming new customers at the front. The question, of course, is how to earn such customer loyalty. The answer is by delivering value. At Intuit, the value goal we've set for ourselves is to make the most effective and user-friendly products on the market and provide the best customer service in consumer software.

Some people think customer service is essentially janitorial—cleaning up messes, placating malcontents. But at Intuit, we take it more seriously than we take any other business function except product design. More than half our employees are in customer service, and we tell new people, "Your goal here is not just to field phone calls. Your goal is to create apostles, to do whatever it takes to make customers very glad that they use our products and absolutely tickled that they called. Your job is to make them feel *so* good about working with us that they'll go out and tell five friends." Support staff who come to us from other companies often think their job is to be an all-knowing expert. But as we're fond of pointing out, customers won't care how much we know until they know how much we care.

Value is not just wonderful products and terrific service, however. Value also means first-rate, highly motivated employees. To get good employees to stay, we reward them with evergreen stock options and what we call a performance-sharing bonus that's based on growth as well as profits. To get them to stay *enthusiastic*, which is even more important, we've found that a sense of mission matters more than money. Great people want to do great work.

Let me tell a story that illustrates how all this can come together. In 1984 Intuit launched a personal financial software program called Quicken. Its ease of use and our great customer service made it a big success. Over the next few years, we produced a string of improvements and new products, including tax software, that won us a strong position in a variety of personal finance markets. Then, in 1992, we introduced QuickBooks, a software package for small business accounting that we had spent several years developing. We thought QuickBooks was a decided improvement on competing systems because we'd made it so much easier to understand and use, but all the same we were entering what was widely considered a mature market, and we had a lot riding on the outcome.

The launch went well. Better than well. In the first month, we captured market leadership. But then our technical support people started getting reports of a problem, bugs in the system that could lose all of a customer's data, and the problem quickly spread. In accounting, few things matter more than data integrity, so these complaints were like a fire alarm. Suddenly, we had one of those problems that can wipe out a new business. The bugs seemed likely to kill the product and prevent us from ever reentering that market segment.

What saved us was the quick, overpowering reaction of our technical service team—supported by a company culture built from the ground up to do right by the customer. Without having to be told or managed or motivated—and without having to ask for direction or permission—our technical service people mobilized an avalanche of appropriate responses. They assembled cross-functional teams that worked night and day to solve the technical problem. As quickly as possible, they sent every customer a letter explaining the problem along with a temporary fix disk. They hired 40 new people and set up special procedures to deal with the flood of service calls. They contracted with temp agencies to provide extra help where needed. Once the problem had been corrected, they sent every buyer a thoroughly tested new release of the software. Furthermore, where customer data had been lost, they hired bookkeepers to reenter it. And where bugs had caused users to understate their state sales taxes, they negotiated with state governments for waivers of potential penalties. They were everywhere and did everything, anticipating customer concerns and spending whatever it cost to ease customer difficulties.

Their response overwhelmed the potential damage. The company could have used that same time and energy to figure out how to *minimize* our costs and liabilities. Instead, our employees ignored costs and set out to *maximize* our response to the mischief the bug in the product had created. Altogether, our service people spent $1.5 million to fix the problem. And they did fix it. They did better than fix it. Not only did they debug the software and rescue its reputation, they actually improved our credibility and our overall customer loyalty, not in spite of the problem but *because of the way they dealt with the problem.*

The lesson here is not that "loyalty" pulled us through. The lesson is that dedicated employees knew the meaning of loyalty when it came down to how we were going to treat our customers in a crisis. They focused relentlessly on the service and value we could deliver.

There is also a second lesson, which is that loyalty *to* the customer creates loyalty *from* the customer. Since its near-death experience in 1992, QuickBooks has outsold its closest competitor by a margin of two to one.

If all this sounds like idle boasting, let me point out that the payoff on this kind of customer loyalty is anything but idle. What it can mean in terms of growth and profits is deeply impressive. And while it takes concentration and tenacity and genuine commitment to make a loyalty-based system work, the secrets to success are not really secrets. Fred Reichheld gives many away in the introduction, and the excellent articles he's collected here reveal a dozen more. Basically, however, the secrets to loyalty are two: value creation and the realization that loyalty is a two-way street. Let me illustrate with another quick example from my company.

At Intuit, 52% of our employees are in customer service and a little more than 1% are in sales, but our growth rate is roughly 40% per year. The key to this improbable equation is word of mouth. To see what our customers really think of us, we ask them if they have recommended the product to their friends. We want to know if we've actually created apostles so dedicated that they'll do our marketing for us. So far the answer is yes. Some 71% of our Quicken customers tell us they have recommended the product to an average of seven people each. For our tax programs, that number is 82%; for QuickBooks, 86%. Putting all those numbers together, we come up with a part-time sales force of nearly seven million people! And friends telling friends have more credibility than any professional sales staff. That's the secret to growth.

Almost any company can grow the way we've grown if it will make the effort. Part of what it takes is a messianic devotion to creating value for customers and employees. But it also takes practical applications like managing customer retention, which you'll learn more about in this book. This collection gives managers an opportunity to hear some top-notch thinking about loyalty as a "new" business idea and to visit some of the systems and techniques that put flesh on that thinking and make it work.

Introduction

Frederick F. Reichheld

Loyalty seems to be dying in our society. Look at the way we treat friendships, community organizations, even marriage. You would think we were renting cars or motel rooms instead of making commitments. And it's not just our social lives that seem to be less permanent. As the *Financial Times* pointed out recently, business too seems to have entered the age of the one-night stand.[1] The average U.S. company now loses half its customers in five years, half its employees in four, and half its investors in less than one. Layoffs, stock-market churn, fickle customers, executive job surfing—all signs seem to point toward opportunism and disloyalty as the governing principles in commerce as well as in society. Worse yet, a lot of business leaders accept this state of affairs with a shrug of the shoulders. Loyalty is not fashionable, lucrative, or relevant, they think, and anyway they have more urgent problems to worry about—for example, growth, productivity, and profits.

The problems that concern them are certainly urgent. In recent decades, annual rates of real growth at large companies have run only 2–3%; productivity has risen at an average rate of little better than 1% per year over the past ten years (despite *trillions* of dollars spent on productivity-enhancing technology); and profits as a percentage of sales have declined in every decade since the 1940s. But ignoring loyalty in order to focus on these "more pressing" problems may be exactly the wrong fix. A few large companies have managed to buck the depressing trends of the past couple of decades and have grown their revenues, profits, and productivity at rates as robust as those we're used to seeing only in start-ups—and virtually all these large but swiftly growing organizations are companies that place a heavy emphasis on customer and employee loyalty.

In short, loyalty is *not* dead. Nor is it irrelevant or unrewarding. It is, however, a different kind of loyalty than that of our parents and grandparents, and the difference is critical to understanding how modern loyalty-based business systems work. Fifty years ago, loyalty played a much larger part in everyday life than it does today. People were deeply loyal to their families, of course. But people also displayed unquestioning loyalty to a long list of civic, religious, and professional authorities and even to the companies they bought from and worked for. Many people made a profound commitment to an employer, for example, and many employers repaid them with a promise of job security that was normally unspoken but nevertheless kept.

Nearly all these unconditional loyalties have followed the whooping crane into virtual extinction. It's probably safe to say that none of us feel an absolute obligation to anything anymore except ourselves and our children. We're still fairly loyal to kin and country (though not as loyal as we used to be), and some of us are still somewhat loyal to a community, say, or a school, but very few of us feel *unconditional* loyalty to anyone or anything. The very idea of blind, unquestioning loyalty toward a company, whether we are its employees, its customers or, for that matter, its owners, seems frankly alien.

In other words, old-fashioned, "yes sir" loyalty *is* hard to find, especially in business. Some people claim to mourn its loss, but that oversimplifies the reality. Loyalty itself is not gone, only the unqualified, hierarchical loyalty that looked so much like obedience. Free markets have replaced it with something far superior—mutual, earned loyalty; loyalty that works in two directions. What we now say to the corporations we buy from or work for is, in effect, this: "I will invest my loyalty in businesses that can deliver superior value. When value is insufficient, and when a reasonable effort to fix the problem fails to produce results, I will defect to a business where my loyalty can create better value."

Few people would be satisfied to make so conditional a commitment to their families, but in the business marketplace this kind of loyalty is not only appropriate but constructive. Loyalty is in fact as basic a virtue as it ever was. But today, in business, there is a critical difference between blind trust and eyes-wide-open loyalty. The former *is* out of date and unproductive. The latter, properly understood and managed, can mean great value for customers and employees and, for the corporation, a long life of sustained growth and profit.

Back at the turn of the century, a Harvard philosopher named Josiah Royce outlined a hierarchy of loyalties. At the lowest level was loyalty to individuals. Next came groups. At the highest level he placed practical devotion to a set of values and principles. Since time and information have stripped away most of our old, blind loyalties, we are left with loyalty to principles, and we give our loyalty to people and organizations only when they live up to the principles we prize. In the case of a business, that practical principle is the creation of value in whatever form we seek it—quality, money, security, speed, whatever. As customers, employees, and investors, it is value we're after and value we reward. As business leaders, therefore, it is the *creation* of value that will keep our businesses healthy, growing, and profitable by inspiring loyalty in all the participants in our business systems—customers, employees, and investors.

Let's look at how a loyalty-based business system actually works. At its core—indeed, at the core of *every* successful business system—is the creation of value for one constituency, customers. While profit has always occupied center stage in conventional thinking about business systems, profit is not primary. Profit is indispensable, of course, but it is nevertheless a consequence of value creation for customers. The implicit business model behind most present-day strategic plans and budgeting procedures begins with a *profit target* and works *backward* to arrive at required revenue growth and cost reduction. But my view of business economics was radically altered by the ten years I spent studying companies that begin instead with *value* and *loyalty targets* and work *forward* to realize the growth and profits that these bring with them.

In fact on the basis of what we learned, my consulting colleagues and I developed a new business model based on these two principles—value creation, which generates the forces that hold these businesses together, and loyalty, which is inextricably linked to value creation as both a cause and an effect. As an effect, loyalty reliably measures whether or not the company has created and delivered superior value. Customers either come back for more or they go elsewhere. As a cause, loyalty initiates a series of economic effects that cascade through the business system as follows:

1. Revenues and market share grow as superior value sweeps *the best customers* into the company's business system, building repeat sales and referrals. A strong value proposition allows the company to be more selective in new customer acquisition, which further stimulates sustainable growth.

2. Sustainable growth also enables a company to offer rewards and careers that attract and retain *the best employees*. Delivering consistently superior value to customers increases employee loyalty still further by giving people pride and satisfaction in their work. Finally, as long-term employees get to know their long-term customers, they learn to deliver still more value, which further reinforces both customer and employee loyalty.

3. Motivated, long-term employees learn how to reduce costs and improve quality, and this in turn builds more customer value and generates *superior productivity*. The company can then use this productivity surplus to fund superior compensation and better tools and training, all of which reinforce the productivity, compensation growth, and loyalty of employees.

4. Upwardly spiraling productivity (coupled with the fact that loyal customers do business more efficiently) generates the kind of cost advantage that is very difficult for competitors to match. *Sustainable cost advantage* (coupled with the fact that customer retention means a more rapidly growing customer inventory) generates the growth and profits that make it easier to attract and retain loyal investors.

5. Loyal investors behave like partners. They stabilize the system, *lower the cost of capital*, and allow surplus cash to flow back into the business to fund customer and employee investments that increase the company's potential to create new and still greater value.

Profits are not at the heart of this new model. They are critically important, of course, as an end in themselves and because they are the source of the incentives that keep employees, investors, and customers loyal. But the source of all cash flow, including the cash flow that eventually becomes profit, is the rising spiral of value that springs from the creation of superior value for customers but that soon comes to involve employees, investors, managers, suppliers, communities, and all the other constituencies that every business touches.

Mutual, earned loyalty is a powerful, business-building force. The 14 articles in this book make that point again and again, though rarely in so many words. Instead, each of these articles has its own points to make about what the role loyalty plays in business, about the way it works, and about what it means for the businesses that have adopted it, or are adopting it, or would very much like to adopt it if only they had a better understanding of how it helps to address the perpetual problems of productivity, growth, and profit. The fact is that while a few companies—the ones we call loyalty leaders—have pursued loyalty-based strategies for decades (with remarkable but largely unpublicized results), and while the principal ramifications of customer and employee retention have been identified and analyzed, nevertheless loyalty-based business systems are still relatively unfamiliar. My book on loyalty—*The Loyalty Effect: The Hidden Force Behind Growth, Profits, and Lasting Value* (HBS Press 1996)—examines loyalty-based management in depth and lays out its economic benefits in hard numbers. But much research on loyalty's third- and fourth-order effects is needed, especially regarding the question of investor loyalty, where we know less than we'd like to.

The first article in this book, "Loyalty-Based Management," is one I wrote more than four years ago, while working on my book. It gives too little attention to the subject of investor loyalty, but it is still a good overview of what an integrated system of customer and employee loyalty looks like in practice. It also helps to emphasize another critical point, namely that loyalty is a *system*. All companies would prefer to have loyal customers, and all companies make some effort to find them and win their hearts. But how many companies have understood that employee loyalty is a vital component of customer loyalty, or that investor loyalty is critical to both? It is the *system* that works, not isolated bits and pieces of best practice.

The second introductory article, Gary Hamel and C. K. Prahalad's "Competing for the Future," argues that the companies that compete successfully over the coming decades will be those that think clearly and carefully about the future. For example, return on investment has two components—a numerator made up of net income and a denominator comprised of assets, costs, and head count. The companies that succeed into the future will be those that focus on increasing the numerator, not those that spend their energies on downsizing and divestitures in order to decrease the denominator. In other words, the winners will be the companies that grow their revenues by delivering outstanding value to their customers and earning their loyalty.

People often suppose that loyalty as a management approach gives little thought to the future but concentrates all its attention on the past. How loyal has this customer or segment been? But in fact loyalty-based management, while it measures past behavior, looks relentlessly forward. Its goal is to build Hamel and Prahalad's numerator into the future by targeting the right customers and mapping out strategies for future value creation. (Of course it also lowers the denominator by targeting the right employees and earning their loyalty in order to increase productivity.) One result is that a loyalty-based business system can predict future cash-flow and profitability with an accuracy that accounting—which *does* focus on the past—can hardly dream of.

After "setting the stage," the collection is arranged in sections that deal with employees, investors, and customers. I have put employees and investors ahead of customers because they are the less obvious pieces of the puzzle. As it happens, the three articles in the employee section also help to illuminate some of the basic principles underlying loyalty-based management in its broadest sense.

For example, Charles Handy's "Trust and the Virtual Organization" does a good job of pointing out that as organizational structures grow more and more "virtual," values and standards grow more and more important. The advantages of developing networks and flexible, ad hoc arrangements with employees and contractors are potentially great, but to realize those advantages, the company and the people who do its work need to align their guidelines, goals, methods, motivations, and decision making. Such alignment requires a high level of mutual trust, best achieved by means of shared loyalty to a clear set of principles.

Integration of principles, people, systems, and technology has probably never reached greater heights than at USAA. Thomas Teal's interview in 1991 with then CEO Robert McDermott, "Service Comes First," is a study in how to build customer loyalty by focusing on employee loyalty. When McDermott took over in 1968, employee turnover was prodigious, productivity abysmal, and technology nearly nonexistent. The chances of finding any particular customer's service file on any given day were about 50/50. McDermott decided to enrich the jobs with training, mobility, compensation, cutting-edge technology (which was never used to create or justify a layoff), better working conditions (including a companywide four-day work week), better promotion prospects, country-club benefits, and the satisfaction of providing the best customer service and value creation the company could invent. The program has probably worked better than McDermott himself imagined. Today the company invests 7% of its revenues in technology, and job satisfaction and productivity have made phenomenal gains. The 1960 employee turnover rate of 43% is down to 6%, and while the company's financial assets have grown 100-fold over 30 years, employment has grown by a factor of only five. To top it all off, customer churn is under 2%, about as close to perfect as nature will allow.

The last article in this section, "The Power of Predictability" by Howard H. Stevenson and Mihnea C. Moldoveanu, carries the message on beyond insurance and technology and applies it to any work force struggling with change and uncertainty. No one can guarantee a company's future, but people need a fairly high level of predictability if they're to concentrate not on protecting their own skins but on the only question that really matters: What can I do to create value? So managers need to give people a predictable relationship with the company, a predictable agenda, predictable ways to succeed, and predictable rewards if they do. Mutual, earned loyalty is by definition a two-way street. What the company gives employees is a sense of order, mission, and credibility. What the employees give back is commitment to the vital task of building customer loyalty and the cash flow, growth, and profit that go with it.

Predictable relationships have benefits that extend into almost every corner of a business system. The trick, in this chaotic world, is how to create them. Part of the answer lies with investors, who are in an excellent position to put the right partnerships in place among employees, managers, and owners. In fact, *loyal* investors are well placed to do an immense amount of good in the companies they own. They can align the interests of managers and owners, and they can press management to engineer a similar alignment of interests with employees. They can also stabilize the cost of capital and encourage management to make thoughtful investments in long-term value creation.

In practice, of course, few investors do any of these things because they are not committed to the long-term welfare of the companies they own. This is another way of saying they are not loyal to their own investments, which sounds illogical. The fact remains that while loyal, involved investors (like Warren Buffett) make *far* more money than opportunistic investors (like most pension and mutual funds managers), stock market churn is rising steeply. As Michael Porter points out, we are moving in the wrong direction and crippling our nation's economic capacity as we do so. But as Peter Drucker observes, at least the larger institutional investors will soon have no choice but to become more involved in corporate governance. The funds they administer are becoming so large and unwieldy that they can no longer churn their holdings. You can buy a thousand or even ten thousand shares of any company as a pure speculation, because you can sell whenever the price reaches your target. But a 5% ownership interest in a large corporation is not a thing you can sell without disastrous effects on the price you wanted to get. The only realistic alternative these pension funds have is to abandon the idea that they are speculators and turn their attention instead to what Drucker calls maximizing the wealth-producing capacity of the enterprise—a fair definition of what investor loyalty means.

The two articles included here—Michael Porter's "Capital Disadvantage: America's Failing Capital Investment System" and Peter Drucker's "Reckoning with the Pension Fund Revolution"—deal with the broad social and policy implications of investor shortsightedness. Investor disloyalty also impairs a company's ability to retain its human assets and therefore has a negative effect on growth and profits. As I pointed out in *The Loyalty Effect,* the root of the problem is the failure of corporate leaders to think of investor loyalty the same way they're beginning to think of customer and employee loyalty—as a two-way street. Company executives are experts at measuring and managing the value that they deliver *to* stockholders. They must now begin measuring and managing the benefits, net of the costs incurred, which they receive *from* investors. They will discover that some investors soak up more value than they help to create. This is especially true of investors who urge expedient action to boost short-term reported earnings. It is also true of investors who pressure managers to embrace management fads and fashions instead of focusing on superior long-term return on investment. If a set of loyal owners would increase the company's long-term earnings trajectory by, say, 5% per year, then that opportunity cost should be loaded back onto the shoulders of the high-churn investors to find the real cost of their capital. This analysis sheds startling light on the actual price of short-term capital, confirms the arguments made here by Michael Porter and Peter Drucker, and will give anyone who carries it out a new appreciation of the value of low-cost, loyal capital.

Having looked at the two dimensions—employees and investors—that are the least obvious and have the least spontaneous appeal, we can now move on to customer loyalty, the loyalty that every company wants but few understand how to earn. As I have already said, customer loyalty is the key to growth and profit, and the key to customer loyalty is value. Since value creation is the key to growth and profit, we must therefore figure out a way to measure it. What we want to measure is not necessarily quality, or quantity, or price, or any other number that we could derive from ledgers or statistics or even standard deviations, though all these factors play a role. What we want to measure is value as the customer perceives it. Happily, even though value in this sense is subjective, we can measure it objectively by measuring customer behavior, that is to say, by measuring repurchase loyalty.

"Zero Defections," the first article I wrote on this subject (in 1990, with Earl Sasser) is a primer on the subject of defections as a litmus test of whether the value you're offering your customers is adequate. Zero *defects* revolutionized manufacturing. Zero *defections* is a way of thinking about and managing value creation that can eradicate the root causes of customer dissatisfaction. Again, not in theory but in practice, because the great companies, the loyalty leaders, really think this way and come as close to zero defections as anyone can get. USAA, remember, has customer retention above 98%.

Satisfaction surveys can be useful tools in this effort, but as Thomas Jones and Earl Sasser point out in "Why Satisfied Customers Defect," they are riddled with shallow and misleading indicators. Companies that take satisfaction surveys at face value are certain to stumble into one or more of their abundant pitfalls.

One of these traps is mistakenly to see a loyal customer in the customer who does not have the option of defecting—for reasons ranging from lack of competition to, say, a rewards program that holds the customer captive. Another is the common failure to distinguish between the right customers and the wrong ones. Not all customers are created equal, but many companies give equal weight to first-class and third-rate customers in allocating resources to counteract defections, and some overzealous customer-recovery units spend money to save unprofitable customers or customers that actually cost the company money. Companies with high fixed costs, like automakers and telephone companies, fall easily into this trap. Every customer brings in revenue that helps offset fixed costs, so every customer looks like a good customer.

Airlines are a good example. Every time an airplane leaves a gate, its precious empty seats are rendered instantaneously worthless, so all customers, including last-minute bargain hunters, seem attractive. But Steven Prokesch's interview with British Airways' Sir Colin Marshall, "Competing on Customer Service," shows how important it can be to target customers even in an industry with high fixed costs and a commodity-like product. The goal need not be the 100% of target segment that some insurance companies shoot for. If an airline can enrich its mix from 20% target customers to 40%, it is off to the races.

The Marshall interview should be required reading for managers in all the industries—banking and automaking leap to mind—that have failed to focus on target customers, and for that matter, to grasp the concept of loyalty-based management in general. When this interview was first published, I wrote a letter to the *Harvard Business Review* to praise British Airways and, in passing, to lay out the basic principles of loyalty-based management in case anyone had missed them. I've included that letter here, partly because I think it makes a good introduction to the book's final section about the ins and outs of making customer loyalty work.

The first of these four articles, Charles Weiser's "Championing the Customer," is also about British Airways, and it originally appeared as an appendage to the Colin Marshall interview. Here it gets the spotlight it deserves. It is one of the best short descriptions I have yet read of how to move beyond customer "satisfaction" and turn service complaints into opportunities for the creation of lasting customer loyalty.

Weiser's primer on fielding service complaints leads nicely into another long-standing question about customer relations, "Do Rewards Really Create Loyalty?" by Louise O'Brien and Charles Jones. The answer is no if all a company can do is offer gimmicks or some second-generation version of S&H green stamps. But the answer is yes if a company can learn to do three things: design rewards that *create* value instead of merely transferring it; measure the value and the loyalty thus created; and devise ways to align the interests of all the players, including the interests and goals of different functions within the company itself.

"Do You Want to Keep Your Customers Forever?" by B. Joseph Pine II, Don Peppers, and Martha Rogers is about the mass customization of goods and services to satisfy individual customers—a neat trick but one that is now well within the capacity of many companies. The key is to build what is called a learning relationship with customers, who teach the company more and more about their particular needs and preferences. As the relationship grows closer, the company develops a unique ability to create more and more value for the customer, customers get better and better goods and services, and the company's competitive advantage—at least with its current customer inventory—becomes nearly unassailable.

The last article in the book, "Learning from Customer Defections," is my attempt to integrate everything I know about the cause-and-effect relationship between value creation, customer loyalty, and financial success. It also provides some practical tools for carrying out improvements. Many businesses fail because too much of their measurement, analysis, and learning revolves around profit and too little around value creation. This article's powerful preferred approach is the deep strategic learning that can come from analyzing customer defections.

When CEOs see falling short-term profits as the only critical problem worth struggling to repair, they concentrate on a symptom and miss the underlying breakdown in the value-creation system. When CEOs see customer issues as secondary to profits and delegate them to the marketing department, they are misreading their own responsibility. Questions about customer value are questions about basic company strategy. As a consequence, decisions about value creation and customer loyalty must be cross-functional, far-sighted, and fundamental. They are the province of CEOs and other senior executives. In fact, unless senior executives are involved, the analysis of customer defections is likely to be as ineffective as satisfaction surveys. The moment defection analysis is dished off to the lower levels of the organization, it becomes routine and trivial and ceases to be the exercise that can move a company toward robust growth, vigorous cash flow, and sturdy profits.

For all the companies we call loyalty leaders, the road to zero defections began at the top, with leaders like Robert McDermott, Sir Colin Marshall, Scott Cook, and a few dozen others. These CEOs never assigned a loyalty project to marketing or anyone else. They never thought of loyalty as a project, much less as a project they could delegate. They committed themselves and their organizations to a higher mission than profits: the creation of so much value for customers that there would be plenty left over for employees and investors. They recognized that loyalty was not only an important means of accomplishing this mission but also the best measure of their progress. They understood that losing half their customers every five years—the dismal average at most American companies—would be irresponsible management, indeed, that as a test of value creation, it would be a failing grade. And they realized that long-term superior performance *without* loyal customers, employees, and investors was a virtual impossibility.

The tendency to regard short-term profits as the primary business objective has become more and more pronounced. Fickle customers, fast-buck speculators, disposable employees, and an emphasis on expansion by means of slick marketing and massive new-customer conquest are some of the norms of modern business practice. But these norms are beginning to display a kind of mettle fatigue. Business leaders who want the leveraged advantages of sustained growth and profit must begin to measure and nurture their human assets as carefully as they do their financial assets. They must renegotiate their partnerships with investors, employees, and customers. Otherwise they're doomed to an uphill struggle against the low-growth economics of disloyalty and perpetual churn.

Note

1. *Financial Times,* 12 April 1996, p. 3.

The Quest
for Loyalty

PART

I

Setting the Stage

1
Loyalty-Based Management

Frederick F. Reichheld

Despite a flurry of activities aimed at serving customers better, only a few companies have achieved meaningful, measurable improvements in customer loyalty. In manufacturing as well as services, business leaders intuitively know that when customer loyalty goes up, profits do too. Yet few companies have systematically revamped their operations with customer loyalty in mind.

Instead, most companies adopt improvement programs on an ad hoc basis. Hearing about the success of a loyalty leader such as MBNA's credit card business, which loses customers at half the industry rate, companies copy one or two of MBNA's practices. They set up customer-recovery units, for instance, that try to save defecting customers—who, because they are probably less homogeneous than MBNA's customer base, may or may not be profitable. Or they adopt MBNA's policy of delivering employee paychecks in envelopes labeled "Brought to You by the Customer"—while failing to base the bonuses inside those envelopes on incentives that enhance customer value and loyalty. Not surprisingly, payoffs don't materialize.

Building a highly loyal customer base cannot be done as an add-on. It must be integral to a company's basic business strategy. Loyalty leaders like MBNA are successful because they have designed their entire business systems around customer loyalty. They recognize that customer loyalty is earned by consistently delivering superior value. By understanding the economic effects of retention on revenues and costs, loyalty leaders can intelligently reinvest cash flows to acquire and retain high-quality customers and employees. Designing and managing this self-reinforcing system is the key to achieving outstanding customer loyalty.

The economic benefits of high customer loyalty are considerable and, in many industries, explain the differences in profitability among competitors. When a company consistently delivers superior value and wins customer loyalty, market share and revenues go up, and the cost of acquiring and serving customers goes down. Although the additional profits allow the company to invest in new activities that enhance value and increase the appeal to customers, strengthening loyalty generally is not a matter of simply cutting prices or adding product features. The better economics mean the company can pay workers better, which sets off a whole chain of events. Increased pay boosts employee morale and commitment; as employees stay longer, their productivity rises and training costs fall; employees' overall job satisfaction, combined with their knowledge and experience, leads to better service to customers; customers are then more inclined to stay loyal to the company; and as the best customers and employees become part of the loyalty-based system, competitors are inevitably left to survive with less desirable customers and less talented employees.

The forces in a loyalty-based system are cumulative. The longer the cycle continues, the greater the company's financial strength. At MBNA, a 5% increase in retention grows the company's profits by 60% by the fifth year. And at State Farm Insurance Companies, another champion of customer loyalty, small increases in retention create substantial benefits for the company and its policyholders.

Learning how to compete on the basis of loyalty may be complex, but it is not mysterious. It requires, first of all, understanding the relationships between customer retention and the rest of the business and being able to quantify the linkages between loyalty and profits. Only then can daily decisions reflect systematic cost-benefit trade-offs. It involves rethinking four important aspects of the business—customers, product/service offerings, employees, and measurement systems. To get the full benefit of a loyalty-based system, all these facets must be understood and attended to simultaneously because each is essential to the workings of the whole. If any area is overlooked or misunderstood, the system will underperform. When all areas are aligned, they reinforce each other, and the results are outstanding.

The "Right" Customers

Customers are obviously an essential ingredient of a loyalty-based system, and success depends on their staying with the company a long time. But not all customers are equal. Companies should target the "right" customers—not necessarily the easiest to attract or the most profitable in the short term but those who are likely to do business with the company over time. For various reasons, some customers don't ever stay loyal to one company, no matter what value they receive. The challenge is to avoid as many of these people as possible in favor of customers whose loyalty can be developed.

Demographics and previous purchase history give some indication of a customer's inherent loyalty. People who buy because of a personal referral tend to be more loyal than those who buy because of an advertisement. Those who buy at the standard price are more loyal than those who buy on price promotion. Home owners, middle-aged people, and rural populations also tend to be loyal, while highly mo-bile populations are inherently disloyal because they interrupt their business relations each time they move.

But generalizing about the right customer fails to take into account the fact that a customer who is disloyal and therefore expensive for one company may be valuable for another. USAA, a loyalty leader with a remarkable 98% retention rate in its field of auto insurance, has created a steady client base among military officers, a group known for frequent moves. Military officers are not very profitable for most insurers, but by developing a system tailored to that group's particular needs, USAA has made it possible and economical to keep them.

The heart of USAA's system is a centralized database and telephone-sales force that customers can access from anywhere in the world. The system itself rather than the insurance agent provides continuity with the customer. That continuity works to the customer's and company's advantage. The military officer doesn't have to find a new agent every time he or she is redeployed, and USAA doesn't have to transfer records or create new ones. More important, USAA avoids having to lure a new customer to replace the one it would have lost.

Finding loyal customers requires taking a hard look at what kinds of customers a company can deliver superior value to. If the analysis is done well, that customer segment will be fairly homogeneous, and that homogeneity improves the economics of serving the segment. MBNA, a loyalty leader in the credit card business, provides cards primarily to members of affinity groups such as the American Dental Association or the Georgetown University Alumni Association. Be-cause members in these groups share important qualities, MBNA has been able to understand their common needs and has made adjust-ments to serve them well. Its data-processing systems are designed so every group can receive customized packages of services. As a result,

MBNA keeps its customers once it gets them. When AT&T introduced its Universal Card, other credit card companies lost market share, but MBNA held its ground.

Historical attrition rates can also point the way to the most promising customer segments. Direct marketers such as L.L. Bean have accounting systems that track individual customers year by year. Other companies can get similar information by asking a sample of customers to reconstruct their purchase patterns from various suppliers over the past five years. This will reveal attrition rates and lifetime value for each type of customer.

With knowledge of which customers are likely to be loyal comes knowledge of which customers are not. Companies can then direct resources away from customers who are likely to defect and toward those likely to stay. Special promotions and other kinds of pricing strategies aimed at acquiring new customers often backfire. Companies typically use pricing as a blunt instrument to bring customers in indiscriminately, when instead, they should use pricing to filter out precisely the customers unlikely to be loyal. Cable television companies talk about increasing retention rates but then recruit new customers via price promotions and free sampling—techniques that draw out of the woodwork precisely those customers hardest to keep. Those recruitment efforts merely load the pipeline with people who are inherently disloyal.

Even attempts to recover customers who threaten to leave are often a waste of resources. Investments in service-quality improvements may be counterproductive when they are focused on customers the business actually should get rid of. Auto insurers discovered that certain segments of young drivers were a drag on profits. It took ten years to break even on them, but due to high attrition, only 10% to 15% would stay that long. The industry also realized that it took at least four years before most companies could break even on the average customer, in part because of the high front-end commission paid to salespeople for signing new customers. If the customer didn't stay with the same insurer for four years, the company never recouped those costs.

Lifetime Products and Services

Once a company has identified the customers it *should* keep, it has to go about the business of keeping them. Often that means adding new products and services to meet customers' evolving needs. Companies that fail to use their knowledge of customers to develop the product or service those people will need next are leaving the door open for another company to lure them away. Although it is tempting to use new products to win whole new markets, it almost always makes better sense to stick with existing customer segments. Over time, the company develops intimate knowledge of those people, and then can make good intuitive market judgments. Also, it is easier to build sales volume with customers who already know the company than it is with newcomers. USAA, for example, having come to understand one narrow market segment inside and out, found it relatively easy to go beyond auto insurance to offer mutual funds, life insurance, health insurance, and credit cards.

When Entenmann's of New York, a loyalty leader in specialty bakery products sold through grocery stores, saw its sales leveling off, it monitored customer purchase patterns in each local market. It discovered that as its core customers aged, they were looking for more fat-free and cholesterol-free products. Through direct contact with customers via telephone surveys and focus groups, the company found that consumers would buy those products from Entenmann's if they were available.

So the company had a choice. It could create a new line of products to serve those customers, or it could search for a whole new market segment. Ultimately, the company determined that it was much more economical to develop new fat-and cholesterol-free products than to go with another group of customers. Entenmann's new product line has been highly successful. It addressed the changing needs of the company's core clientele and even attracted new customers.

In yet another industry, Honda has emerged as the loyalty leader in the midpriced U.S. auto market. Life-cycle marketing has helped propel Honda's owner repurchase rate to 65%, versus an industry average of 40%. After the success of the subcompact Civic, Honda's next car, the Accord, was designed to meet the needs of Civic owners, who continued to care about reliability, conservative design, and value as they moved from their early twenties to marriage and family. Honda added the Accord wagon when it noticed customers defecting to other brands as their families grew.

By growing through the repeat purchases of its core customer base, Honda has maintained a relatively simple product line, and its manufacturing economics have benefited from this low product complexity. Honda's dealer and distribution system also benefits from low customer complexity in equally important, if less well-understood, ways.

One of the largest multifranchise dealers in the United States described this advantage as he saw it: "My Honda dealership is my most profitable because the company makes it so simple. There are fewer models and option packages. The key is the customers, who are very similar to one another." His sales and service operations are geared to the "Honda" customer. In contrast, he described his Mitsubishi dealership as a real challenge: "Salespeople have to deal with a lawyer buying a $30,000 Diamonte one minute, a construction worker buying a pickup truck the next." How can one salesperson (or service representative) develop proficiency with such customer complexity?

Curiously, Honda has had a tougher fight in Japan, where it remains a small player. Even though Honda had the same product advantages that resulted in its strong U.S. position, Toyota remains the dominant player in Japan because of its strong dealer network. In Japan, dealers don't have a lot of showrooms but instead rely on a direct sales force. Because sales-force turnover is low (less than 10% per year for Toyota), they get to know customers very well. It is this enduring bond that has outmuscled Honda. In the United States, where car salespeople turn over quickly (60% to 100% annually) and customers have virtually no relationship with the sales force, Honda's product advantage blasted right through to put it out ahead.

Loyal Employees

Many companies diminish their economic potential through human resource policies that ensure high employee turnover, in part because they can't quantify the economics of retaining employees. Executives might say they want to keep employees, but if doing so means raising salaries, their conviction soon fades. They question the wisdom of increasing pay by, say, 25% in order to decrease employee turnover by 5%. Yet the fact is that employee retention is key to customer retention, and customer retention can quickly offset higher salaries and other incentives designed to keep employees from leaving.

The longer employees stay with the company, the more familiar they become with the business, the more they learn, and the more valuable they can be. Those employees who deal directly with customers day after day have a powerful effect on customer loyalty. Long-term employees can serve customers better than newcomers can; after all, a customer's contact with a company is through employees, not the top executives. It is with employees that the customer builds a bond of trust and expectations, and when those people leave, the bond is broken.

Companies wanting to increase customer loyalty often fail because they don't grasp the importance of this point. While conducting customer focus programs, they may be terminating or rotating the people who have the most influence on the customer's experience. While they are reengineering their business processes, they are failing to reengineer career paths, job content, and compensation so that employees will stay with the company long enough to learn the new processes.

Just as it is important to select the right kinds of customers before trying to keep them, a company must find the right kinds of employees before enticing them to stay. That raises the issue of hiring. The goal is not only to fill desks but also to find and hold onto workers who will continue to learn, to become more productive, and to create trusting relationships with customers. State Farm, the loyalty leader among auto insurance companies that sell through agents, has a distinctive agent-appointment strategy. Prospective agents may spend a year or more in a recruiting and selection process. During this time, they are in competition with several other well-qualified candidates. The lengthy process enables the company's field managers to select the best qualified person. State Farm often looks for candidates with roots in the community who are already likely to have long-term relationships with prospective customers.

One way for any company to find new hires who will likely stay is to look at the patterns of their own employees who defected early. Had they found the job at your company through newspaper ads, college recruiting, or personal referrals? Equally important, how long had they stayed with employers before coming to you? In a loyalty-based system, skills and education are important, but not as important as how long a prospective worker is expected to stay and grow with the business.

Although longevity deepens familiarity, some company policies render familiarity useless. Banks, for instance, are notorious for offering branch managers career paths that rotate them through a series of branch offices. Each time managers move, they take with them the knowledge learned at the branch where they put in their time. They have to start over again in each branch, building a network with the customers and the other employees. Their incentives to acquire the right customers and employees are reduced since it is their replacements who will reap the benefits. In a major bank with several hundred branches, branch managers who had been in the system an average of 12 years stayed at a given branch for only 2 years. Only one branch manager had remained in place and, not surprisingly, his office had the highest customer-retention rate in the entire system. It's worth noting that most banks have 50% to 100%-a-year teller turnover, which is also costly. Because most bankers cannot quantify the systems costs of these policies, they cannot justify the investments required to fix the situation.

But not all businesses follow those practices. The highly successful Olive Garden restaurant chain goes against the industry norm of moving successful managers to open new restaurants or to run bigger ones every few years and letting assistants take over. The chain hires local managers whose major asset is that they are known and trusted in the community. These managers are then kept in place so their asset appreciates in value. Learning accumulates as people stay on the job. By becoming intelligent about the business, getting to know customers, and providing the advantages knowledge gives, long-time hires add value to the company.

Leo Burnett Company's strong position in the advertising industry is largely attributable to its slavish devotion to employee retention. Most advertising firms experience high turnover of their creative people, and they make a point of rotating people through various accounts. They also experience constant client churn accompanied by massive layoffs and severe downturns in revenues and profits. At Leo Burnett, in contrast, new staffers are assigned to their first account "for life," in the words of one executive. Layoffs are rare, and customer retention is high.

Even businesses that don't rely on direct relationships between customers and employees can benefit from boosting employee retention. USAA has an information system that lets any employee pull up a customer's records instantly, so customers don't have to speak with the same employee every time. But USAA's employee turnover of around 7%—one-third the industry average—is one of the most important reasons its productivity is the best in the business. The learning unleashed by employee retention helps in other ways. When the marketing department wants to know more about customer needs or reactions to a new product, they can hold a focus group meeting of employees whose daily customer contact provides powerful insight.

Of course, employees won't stay and apply their knowledge unless they have an incentive to do so. All other things being equal, the best people will stay with the company that pays them the most. Loyalty leaders know this, and they share their "loyalty surplus" with employees as well as stockholders. They view their best employees as they do their best customers: once they've got them, they do everything possible to keep them. And they provide incentives in the form of higher salaries or bonuses and commissions that align the employees' self-interest with the interests of the company. Bonuses can be based on aggregate customer retention rates, and commissions can be designed to be small initially but grow the longer the customer stays with the company.

There are many ways reward programs can be structured to recognize loyalty. Olive Garden found that its experienced waiters and waitresses resented the fact that new hires were receiving the same base wage as they did, so management established a slightly higher base wage for employees who had served $25,000 of meals.

If employees are expected to be long-termers, companies can justify investing more in them. It becomes worthwhile to teach employees to do the right thing for the customer, which in turn leads to happier customers and ultimately to increased profits, which can be put toward the higher salaries of long-term employees. And the commitment to creating a loyalty-based system has spillover effects. Employees take pride in delivering value to a customer time and again. Their satisfaction in contributing to a positive goal is another thing that induces their loyalty to the company.

Measures of Loyalty

Even the best designed loyalty-based system will deteriorate unless an effective measurement system is established. Competitors, customer preferences, technologies, and employee capabilities are constantly changing. Measures establish the feedback loops that are the foundation of organizational learning. Only through effective learning can an organization consistently deliver value in an ever-changing world.

Unfortunately, most accounting systems do not measure what drives customer value. They can show the benefits of the one-year magic cure but not of programs and practices that take three to five years or longer to affect profits. Managers who have a year to earn a bonus or two years to turn a business around are forced to think of the usual shortcuts to higher profits: raising prices and cutting costs. Those actions alone rarely create value for customers, and although customers don't all leave at once, if they are not getting the best value, they will eventually turn to a competitor. To make matters worse, the best customers are often the first ones to go.

The first step in developing effective measures is to understand the cause-and-effect relationships in the system. The primary mission of a loyalty-based company is to deliver superior value to customers. Success or failure in this mission can be clearly measured by customer loyalty (best quantified by retention rate or share of purchases or both). Customer loyalty has three second-order effects: (1) revenue grows as a result of repeat purchases and referrals, (2) costs decline as a result of lower acquisition expenses and from the efficiencies of serving experienced customers, and (3) employee retention increases because job pride and satisfaction increase, in turn creating a loop that reinforces customer loyalty and further reducing costs as hiring and training costs shrink and productivity rises.

As costs go down and revenues go up, profits (the third-order effect) increase. Unless managers measure and monitor all of these economic relationships, they will default to their short-term, profit-oriented accounting systems, which tend to focus on only the second-and third-order effects. Focusing on these symptoms—instead of on the primary mission of delivering superior value to customers—often leads to decisions that will eventually reduce value and loyalty.

In the life insurance business, for instance, a five percentage point increase in customer retention lowers costs per policy by 18%. However, very few companies have quantified this relationship, and as a result, they focus their cost-reduction efforts on process reengineering and layoffs, which appear to lower costs but in fact lower employee motivation and retention, leading to lower customer retention, which increases costs!

When life insurers want to grow, they hire more agents, raise commissions, drop prices (to new customers only, if possible) and/or add new products. The result: more inexperienced salespeople (low productivity and high cost) bringing in the wrong kind of customer (disloyal price shoppers) with escalating costs of product-line complexity. The only way to avoid these mistakes in insurance, or any business, is to develop systems that allow employees to track and understand the cash-flow consequences of changing customer loyalty.

It is only the true defection of the target customer that should be of concern because that means something may have gone wrong, and if it has, it's worth a considerable amount of effort to find out what. It could mean that another company has done something innovative that gives customers a better value.

It is important to define customer retention carefully and what it means in a particular industry. In the auto business, for instance, a manufacturer should worry about a customer who switches to another brand—but not about a customer who sells his or her car and takes public transportation. In an industrial setting, customers might shift a percentage of their purchases to competitors, so changes in purchase patterns should be watched as carefully as customer defections.

Customer satisfaction is not a surrogate for customer retention. While it may seem intuitive that increasing customer satisfaction will increase retention and therefore profits, the facts are contrary. Between 65% and 85% of customers who defect say they were satisfied or very satisfied with their former supplier. In the auto industry, satisfaction scores average 85% to 95%, while repurchase rates average only 40%. Current satisfaction measurement systems are simply not designed to provide insight into how many customers stay loyal to the company and for how long.

State Farm's Loyalty-Based System

State Farm insures more than 20% of the nation's households. It has the lowest sales and distribution costs among insurance companies of its type, yet its agents' incomes are generally higher than agents working for the competition. Its focus on customer service has resulted in faster growth than most other multiple-line insurers, but rather than being consumed by growth, its capital has mushroomed (all through internally generated surplus) to more than $18 billion, representing the largest capital base of any financial services company in North America. Because of careful customer selection and retention, State Farm is able to price below the competition and still build the capital necessary to protect its policyholders in years such as 1992 when they incurred $4.7 billion in catastrophe losses.

These impressive achievements can be traced to State Farm's well-designed loyalty-based system. State Farm began by choosing the right customers. The company was founded more than 70 years ago to serve better than average drivers, first in farming communities and now throughout suburban and urban markets across the United States and in three Canadian provinces. State Farm agents work from neighborhood offices, which allows them to build long-lasting relationships with their customers and provide the personal service that is the basis of the corporate philosophy.

This kind of personal service can start at an early age. Teenagers in State Farm households are usually written while still under the umbrella of their parents' policies. Many State Farm agents routinely sit new drivers down in their offices for a "dutch uncle" speech about the responsibilities of driving and the impact an accident or ticket—particularly for drunken driving—would have on their rates. Also, in an effort to educate all teens on safe driving, agents have available company-produced safe-driving materials for high schools. All these efforts tend to make the young drivers that State Farm insures more careful, and their parents grateful for the interest and help.

When agents are rooted in the community, they often know who the best customers will be. For example, they can scan the local newspaper for the high school honor roll and be sure that their young customers' good grades are recognized with premium discounts. Agents make it their business to get to know the people they insure. The most powerful computer and the brightest underwriter at headquarters simply can't compete with that level of customer insight.

Pricing policies work as a magnet to retain good customers. At the end of three years, accident-free customers get a 5% discount, followed by another 5% decrease three years later. The discounts make customers feel they've earned special status and value, and they create a disincentive to jump to another company, where they might have to start all over again.

State Farm agents not only want to attract and keep good customers, they also have the incentive to do so. Commissions are structured to encourage long-term thinking. Agents receive the same compensation rate on new auto and fire policies as for renewals, thus rewarding agents for serving existing customers, not just for drawing in new business. Unlike organizations that say retention is important while pushing salespeople to find new customers, State Farm consistently conveys the message that both are important.

Remaining focused on its target customers, State Farm provides a full life-cycle product line. Rather than bringing in lots of new customers, the company's marketing efforts encourage existing customers to buy additional products, like home and life insurance. The homogeneity of their market means that one agent can sell and service everything. The full product line preserves the agent's relationship with the customer and allows the agent to learn more about the customer's needs. In addition to benefiting the policyholder and company, this approach serves the agent well, as multiple-line customers are less expensive for the agent to service than are single-line customers. Multiple-line customers have also proven to stay with the agent longer.

State Farm agents are also loyal. According to industry studies, more than 80% of newly appointed agents remain through their fourth year, compared with 20% to 40% for the rest of the industry. And the average agent at State Farm has 13 years of tenure, compared with 6 to 9 years for the industry. This retention advantage can be attributed both to the lengthy recruiting and selection process before appointment and to the fact that State Farm agents are independent contractors who sell and service State Farm products exclusively. Because agents have built and invested in their own businesses, they are more likely to remain with State Farm than their counterparts representing other companies. In return, State Farm is loyal to its agents and distributes its products only through them. The company has built a marketing partnership with its agents and involves them in key decisions that affect them or their customers.

Agent retention and customer retention reinforce one another. The agent who is committed to a long-term relationship with the company, and indeed, to his or her own business, is more likely to build lasting relationships with customers. In addition, loyal customers make life easier for the agents, who spend more time working with people they know and like and far less time chasing new customers. Finally, agents like being part of a system that consistently delivers superior value to customers. Agents' experience, plus the fact that they spend more time servicing and selling to proven customers, raises agents' productivity to 50% above industry norms.

State Farm's business systems support its focus on loyalty. Measures of customer retention and defections are distributed throughout the organization. Agents and employees at all levels know whether the system is working and can adjust their activities. Agents find a list of their nonrenewing customers each morning when they switch on their computers, which they can use to prompt telephone follow-ups to try to retain the account. And management can use the same kind of information as a check against policyholders' satisfaction with the service, product, and price they receive.

State Farm's success in building customer loyalty is reflected in retention rates that exceed 90%, consistently the best performance of all the national insurers that sell through agents. State Farm agents make more money by operating in a business system engineered for superior loyalty. And they are more productive, which makes it possible for them to earn superior compensation (after adjusting for the fact that State Farm agents pay their own expenses) while the company actually pays lower average commission rates. The result is a 10% cost advantage. The company also keeps its costs relatively low because it avoids excessive administrative and claims costs associated with acquiring and servicing a large percentage of new customers. State Farm's system provides outstanding value to its customers, benefits for its agents, and has created a company that is a financial powerhouse.

Managing for Loyalty

The success of State Farm and other loyalty leaders shows the direct linkages between providing value for customers and a superior financial and competitive position. Doing the right thing for customers does not conflict with generating substantial margins. On the contrary, it is the only way to ensure profitability beyond the short term.

Creating a loyalty-based system in any company requires a radical departure from traditional business thinking. It puts creating customer value—not maximizing profits and shareholder value—at the center of business strategy, and it demands significant changes in business practice—redefining target customers, revising employment policies, and redesigning incentives.

Most important, if companies are really serious about delivering value and earning customer loyalty, they must measure it. And while senior executives may be daunted by the time and investment required to engineer an entire business system for high retention, they may have no alternative. Customer loyalty appears to be the only way to achieve sustainable superior profits.

Managing for loyalty serves the best interests of customers, employees, and investors. The only losers are the competitors who get the leftovers: an increasingly poor mix of customers and employees and an increasingly less tenable financial and market position. As loyalty leaders refine their ability to deliver value by more effectively harnessing the economics of loyalty, their advantages will multiply. Competitors must respond, or they will find it increasingly difficult to survive on the leftovers of the marketplace.

2
Competing for the Future

Gary Hamel and C.K. Prahalad

Look around your company. Look at the high-profile initiatives that have recently been launched, the issues preoccupying senior management, the criteria and benchmarks by which progress is measured, your track record of new-business creation. Look into the faces of your colleagues, and consider their ambitions and fears. Look toward the future, and ponder your company's ability to shape that future in the years and decades to come.

Now ask yourself: Do senior managers in my company have a clear and shared understanding of how the industry may be different ten years from now? Is my company's point of view about the future unique among competitors?

These are not rhetorical questions. Get a pencil and score your company.

How does senior management's point of view about the future compare with that of your competitors?
Conventional and reactive   Distinctive and farsighted

Which business issue absorbs more senior-management attention?
Reengineering core processes   Regenerating core strategies

How do competitors view your company?
Mostly as a rule follower   Mostly as a rule maker

What is your company's strength?
Operational efficiency   Innovation and growth

What is the focus of your company's advantage-building efforts?
Mostly catching up   Mostly getting out in front

What has set your transformation agenda?
Our competitors   Our foresight

**Do you spend the bulk of your time as a maintenance engineer
preserving the status quo or as an architect designing the future?**
Mostly as an engineer   Mostly as an architect

If your scores fall somewhere in the middle or off to the left, your company may be devoting too much energy to preserving the past and not enough to creating the future.

When we talk to senior managers about competing for the future, we ask them three questions. First, what percentage of your time is spent on external rather than internal issues—on understanding, for example, the implications of a particular new technology instead of debating corporate overhead allocations? Second, of this time spent looking outward, how much do you spend considering how the world may change in five or ten years rather than worrying about winning the next big contract or responding to a competitor's pricing move? Third, of the time devoted to looking outward *and* forward, how much do you spend working with colleagues to build a deeply shared, well-tested perspective on the future as opposed to a personal and idiosyncratic view?

The answers to these questions typically conform to what we call the "40/30/20 Rule." In our experience, about 40% of a senior executive's time is devoted to looking outward and, of this time, about 30% is spent peering three, four, five, or more years into the future. Of that time spent looking forward, no more than 20% is devoted to building a collective view of the future (the other 80% is spent considering the future of the manager's particular business). Thus, on average, senior managers devote less than 3% (40% x 30% x 20%) of their time to building a *corporate* perspective on the future. In some companies, the figure is less than 1%. Our experience suggests that to develop a distinctive point of view about the future, senior managers must be willing to devote considerably more of their time. And after the initial burst of energy that they must expend to develop a distinct view of the future, managers must be willing to adjust that perspective as the future unfolds.

Such commitment as well as substantial and sustained intellectual energy is required to answer such questions as: What new core competencies will we need to build? What new product concepts should we pioneer? What alliances will we need to form? What nascent development programs should we protect? What long-term regulatory initiatives should we pursue?

We believe such questions have received far too little attention in many companies, not because senior managers are lazy—most are working harder than ever—but because they won't admit, to themselves or to their employees, that they are less than fully in control of their companies' future. Difficult questions go unanswered because they challenge the assumption that top management really is in control, really does have more accurate foresight than anyone else in the corporation, and already has a clear and compelling view of the company's future. Senior managers are often unwilling to confront these illusions. So the urgent drives out the important; the future is left largely unexplored; and the capacity to act, rather than to think and imagine, becomes the sole measure of leadership.

Beyond Restructuring

The painful upheavals in so many companies in recent years reflect the failure of one-time industry leaders to keep up with the accelerating pace of industry change. For decades, the changes undertaken at Sears, General Motors, IBM, Westinghouse, Volkswagen, and other incumbents were, if not exactly glacial in speed, more or less linear extrapolations of the past. Those companies were run by managers, not leaders, by maintenance engineers, not architects.

If the future is not occupying senior managers, what is? Restructuring and reengineering. While both are legitimate and important tasks, they have more to do with shoring up today's businesses than with building tomorrow's industries. Any company that is a bystander on the road to the future will watch its structure, values, and skills become progressively less attuned to industry realities. Such a discrepancy between the pace of industrial change and the pace of company change gives rise to the need for organizational transformation.

A company's organizational transformation agenda typically includes downsizing, overhead reduction, employee empowerment, process redesign, and portfolio rationalization. When a competitiveness problem (stagnant growth, declining margins, and falling market share, for example) can no longer be ignored, most executives pick up a knife and begin the painful work of restructuring. The goal is to carve away layers of corporate fat and amputate underperforming businesses. Executives who don't have the stomach for emergency-room surgery, like John Akers at IBM or Robert Stempel at GM, soon find themselves out of a job.

Masquerading behind terms like refocusing, delayering, decluttering, and right-sizing (Why is the "right" size always smaller?), restructuring always results in fewer employees. In 1993, large U.S. companies announced nearly 600,000 layoffs—25% more than were announced in 1992 and nearly 10% more than in 1991, the year in which the U.S. recession hit its lowest point. While European companies have long tried to put off their own day of reckoning, bloated payrolls and out-of-control employment costs have made downsizing as inevitable in the old world as it is in the new. Despite excuses about global competition and the impact of productivity-enhancing technology, most layoffs at large U.S. companies have been the fault of senior managers who fell asleep at the wheel and missed the turnoff for the future.

With no growth or slow growth, companies soon find it impossible to support their burgeoning employment rosters and traditional R&D budgets and investment programs. The problems of low growth are often compounded by inattentiveness to ballooning overheads (IBM's problem), diversification into unrelated businesses (Xerox's foray into financial services), and the paralysis imposed by an unfailingly conservative staff. It is not surprising that shareholders are giving moribund companies unequivocal marching orders: "Make this company lean and mean;" "Make the assets sweat;" "Get back to basics." In most companies, return on capital employed, shareholder value, and revenue per employee have become the primary arbiters of top-management performance.

Although perhaps inescapable and in many cases commendable, restructuring has destroyed lives, homes, and communities in the name of efficiency and productivity. While it is impossible to argue with such objectives, pursuing them single-mindedly does the cause of competitiveness as much harm as good. Let us explain.

Imagine a CEO who is fully aware that if he or she doesn't make effective use of corporate resources, someone else will be given the chance. So the chief executive launches a tough program to improve return on investment. Now, ROI (or return on net assets or return on capital employed) has two components: a numerator—net income— and a denominator—investment, net assets, or capital employed. (In a service industry, a more appropriate denominator may be head count.) Managers know that raising net income is likely to be harder than cutting assets and head count. To increase the numerator, top management must have a sense of where new opportunities lie, must be able to anticipate changing customer needs, must have invested in building new competencies, and so on. So under intense pressure for a quick ROI improvement, executives reach for the lever that will bring the fastest, surest result: the denominator.

The United States and Britain have produced an entire generation of managers obsessed with denominators. They can downsize, declutter, delayer, and divest better than any other managers. Even before the current wave of downsizing, U.S. and British companies had, on average, the highest asset-productivity ratios of any companies in the world. Denominator management is an accountant's shortcut to asset productivity.

Don't misunderstand. A company must get to the future not only first but also for less. But there is more than one route to productivity improvement. Just as any company that cuts the denominator and maintains revenues will reap productivity gains, so too will any company that succeeds in increasing its revenue stream atop a slower-growing or constant capital and employment base. Although the first approach may be necessary, we believe the second is usually more desirable.

In a world in which competitors are capable of achieving 5%, 10%, or 15% real growth in revenues, aggressive denominator reduction under a flat revenue stream is simply a way to sell market share and the future of the company. Marketing strategists term this a *harvest strategy* and consider it a no-brainer. Between 1969 and 1991, for example, Britain's manufacturing output (the numerator) went up by only 10% in real terms. Yet over this same period, the number of people employed in British manufacturing (the denominator) was nearly halved. The result was that during the early and mid-1980s, the Thatcher years, British manufacturing productivity increased faster than that of any other major industrialized country except Japan. Though Britain's financial press and Conservative ministers trumpeted this as a "success," it was, of course, bittersweet. While new legislation limited the power of trade unions, and the liberalization of statutory impediments to workforce reduction enabled management to excise inefficient and outmoded work practices, British companies demonstrated scant ability to create new markets at home and abroad. In effect, British companies surrendered global market share. One almost expected to pick up the *Financial Times* and find that Britain had finally matched Japan's manufacturing productivity—and that the last remaining person at work in British manufacturing was the most productive son of a gun on the planet.

The social costs of such denominator-driven job losses are high. Although an individual company may be able to avoid some of those costs, society cannot. In Britain, the service sector could not absorb all the displaced manufacturing workers and underwent its own vicious downsizing in the recession that began in 1989. Downsizing also causes employee morale to plummet. What employees hear is that "people are our most important asset." What they see is that people are the most expendable asset.

Moreover, restructuring seldom results in fundamental business improvements. At best, it buys time. One study of 16 large U.S. companies with at least three years of restructuring experience found that while restructuring usually did raise a company's share price, such improvement was almost always temporary. Three years into restructuring, the share prices of the companies surveyed were, on average, lagging even further behind index growth rates than they had been when the restructuring effort began.

Beyond Reengineering

Downsizing attempts to correct the mistakes of the past, not to create the markets of the future. But getting smaller is not enough. Recognizing that restructuring is a dead end, smart companies move on to reengineering. The difference between restructuring and reengineering is that the latter offers at least the hope, if not always the reality, of getting better as well as getting leaner. Yet in many companies, reengineering is more about catching up than getting out in front.

For example, Detroit automakers are catching up with Japanese rivals on quality and cost. Supplier networks have been reconstituted, product-development processes redesigned, and manufacturing processes reengineered. However, the cheerful headlines heralding Detroit's comeback miss the deeper story—among the losses have been hundreds of thousands of jobs, 20-some percentage points of market share in the United States, and any hope of U.S. automakers beating Japanese rivals in the booming Asian markets anytime soon.

Catching up is not enough. In a survey taken at the end of the 1980s, nearly 80% of U.S. managers polled believed that quality would be a fundamental source of competitive advantage in the year 2000, but barely half of Japanese managers agreed. Their primary goal was to create new products and businesses.[1] Does this mean that Japanese managers will turn their backs on quality? Of course not. It merely indicates that by the year 2000, quality will be the price of market entry, not a competitive differentiator. Japanese managers realize that tomorrow's competitive advantages will be different from today's. It remains to be seen whether Detroit will set the pace in the next round of competition and produce vehicles as exciting as they are fuel efficient and reliable or will once again rest on its laurels.

We come across far too many top managers whose advantage-building agenda is still dominated by quality, time-to-market, and customer responsiveness. While such advantages are prerequisites for survival, they are hardly a testimony to management foresight. Though managers often try to make a virtue out of imitation, dressing it up in the fashionable colors of "adaptiveness," what they are adapting to all too often are the preemptive strategies of more imaginative competitors.

Consider Xerox. During the 1970s and 1980s, Xerox surrendered a substantial amount of market share to Japanese competitors, such as Canon and Sharp. Recognizing that the company was on the slippery slope to oblivion, Xerox benchmarked its competitors and fundamentally reengineered its processes. By the early 1990s, the company had become a textbook example of how to reduce costs, improve quality, and satisfy customers. But amid all the talk of the new "American Samurai," two issues were overlooked. First, although Xerox halted the erosion of its market share, it has not fully recaptured share lost to its Japanese competitors: Canon remains one of the largest copier manufacturers in the world. Second, despite pioneering research in laser printing, networking, icon-based computing, and the laptop computer, Xerox has not created any substantial new businesses outside its copier core. Although Xerox may have invented the office as we know it today and as it's likely to be, the company has actually profited very little from its creation.

In fact, Xerox has probably left more money on the table, in the form of underexploited innovation, than any other company in history. Why? Because to create new businesses, Xerox would have had to regenerate its core strategy: the way it defined its market, its distribution channels, its customers, its competitors, the criteria for promoting managers, the metrics used to measure success, and so on. A company surrenders today's businesses when it gets smaller faster than it gets better. A company surrenders tomorrow's businesses when it gets better without changing.

We meet many managers who describe their companies as "market leaders." (With enough creativity in delimiting market boundaries, almost any company can claim to be a market leader.) But market leadership today certainly doesn't equal market leadership tomorrow. Think about two sets of questions:

Today	In the Future
Which customers do you serve today?	Which customers will you serve in the future?
Through what channels do you reach customers today?	Through what channels will you reach customers in the future?
Who are your competitors today?	Who will your competitors be in the future?
What is the basis for your competitive advantage today?	What will be the basis for your competitive advantage in the future?
Where do your margins come from today?	Where will your margins come from in the future?
What skills or capabilities make you unique today?	What skills or capabilities will make you unique in the future?

If senior executives don't have reasonably detailed answers to the "future" questions, and if the answers they have are not significantly different from the "today" answers, there is little chance that their companies will remain market leaders. The market a company dominates today is likely to change substantially over the next ten years. There's no such thing as "sustaining" leadership; it must be regenerated again and again.

Creating the Future

Organizational transformation must be driven by a point of view about the future of the industry: How do we want this industry to be shaped in five or ten years? What must we do to ensure that the industry evolves in a way that is maximally advantageous for us? What skills and capabilities must we begin building now if we are to occupy the industry high ground in the future? How should we organize for opportunities that may not fit neatly within the boundaries of current business units and divisions? Since most companies don't start with a shared view of the future, seniors managers' first task is to develop a process for pulling together the collective wisdom within an organization. Concern for the future, a sense of where opportunities lie, and an understanding of organizational change are not the province of any group; people from all levels of a company can help define the future.

One company that developed a process for establishing a point of view about the future is Electronic Data Systems (EDS), based in Plano, Texas. In 1992, EDS's position seemed unassailable. With $8.2 billion in sales, EDS had recorded its thirtieth consecutive year of record earnings and looked forward to the ever-growing demand for computer-services outsourcing. EDS expected to become at least a $25 billion company by the year 2000.

But some top executives, including Chairman Lester Alberthal, foresaw problems. Margins were under intense pressure from new competitors, such as Andersen Consulting. Customers were demanding hefty discounts in their long-term service contracts. Fewer new customers could be found among leading-edge IT users in the United States. And future business needs would involve desktop computers, not the mainframes EDS specialized in, while the most exciting new information-network services would focus on the home, not the office.

The company's top officers, known as the Leadership Council, concluded that EDS was no more immune from "great company disease" than any other successful enterprise. Council members committed themselves to rebuilding industry leadership for the 1990s and beyond.

As it happened, others in the company were already thinking along similar lines. Back in 1990, a small band of EDS managers, none of them yet corporate officers, had created a Corporate Change Team. Despite their lack of an official charter, team members believed EDS needed to rethink its direction and its deepest assumptions. They soon realized this would require far more resources, both temporal and intellectual, than could be mustered by one small team.

After talking with the Leadership Council about its goals, the Corporate Change Team developed a unique approach to company renewal. From across the company and around the world, 150 EDS managers—key resource holders as well as less-senior managers who were known to be challenging, bright, and unconventional—gathered in Dallas, 30 at a time, to begin creating the future. Each of the five "waves" considered in detail the economic threats to EDS and the opportunities afforded by the digital revolution. Each wave was given an assignment. The first wave studied the discontinuities that EDS could use to change the shape of the industry. The second and third waves tried to develop a view of the company's competencies that was substantially independent from current definitions of EDS's served markets. They then benchmarked those competencies against EDS's strongest competitors. Drawing on the work of the previous waves, wave four explored opportunities on the horizon. And wave five considered how to devote more company resources to building competencies and developing opportunities.

Each wave's output was thoroughly debated by the other waves and with the Leadership Council. Finally, a team composed of members from all the waves produced a draft corporate strategy, which, again, was debated throughout the company.

EDS's new strategy is captured in three words: globalize, informationalize, and individualize. The strategy is based on the company's ability to use information technology to span geographical, cultural, and organizational boundaries; to help customers convert data into information, information into knowledge, and knowledge into action; and to mass-customize and enable individuals to mass-customize information services and products.

The process of developing this strategy for the future was full of frustrations, surprises, unexpected insights, and missed deadlines. More than 2,000 people participated in the creation of EDS's new strategy, and nearly 30,000 person-hours were devoted to the exercise. (More than one-third of the time investment was made outside the company's normal business hours.)

EDS emerged from the process with a view of its industry and its role that was substantially broader, more creative, and more prescient than it had been 12 months earlier. This view was held not only by a few technical gurus or corporate visionaries but by every senior EDS manager. Indeed, those who participated in the process thought it contributed as much to leadership development as it did to strategy development.

The Quest for Foresight

To create the future as EDS has done requires industry foresight. Why do we talk of foresight rather than vision? Vision connotes a dream or an apparition, and there is more to industry foresight than a blinding flash of insight. Industry foresight is based on deep insights into trends in technology, demographics, regulations, and lifestyles, which can be harnessed to rewrite industry rules and create new competitive space. While understanding the potential implications of such trends requires creativity and imagination, any "vision" that is not based on a solid foundation is likely to be fantastical.

For this reason, industry foresight is a synthesis of many people's visions. Often, journalists or sycophantic employees have described foresight as the "vision" of one person. Much of the credit for NEC's visionary concept of "computers and communication" may have gone to Akira Kobayashi, but the idea of exploiting the convergence between the two industries synthesized the thinking of many in the company. Senior executives are not the only ones with industry foresight. In fact, their primary role is to capture and exploit the foresight that exists throughout the organization.

Given that change is inevitable, the real issue for managers is whether that change will happen belatedly, in a crisis atmosphere, or with foresight, in a calm and considered manner; whether the transformation agenda will be set by a company's more prescient competitors or by its own point of view; whether transformation will be spasmodic and brutal or continuous and peaceful. Palace coups make great press copy, but the real objective is a transformation that is revolutionary in result and evolutionary in execution.

Developing a point of view about the future should be an ongoing project sustained by continuous debate within a company, not a massive one-time effort. Unfortunately, most companies consider the need to regenerate their strategies and reinvent their industries only when restructuring and reengineering fail to halt the process of corporate decline. To get ahead of the industry change curve, to have the chance of conducting a bloodless revolution, top managers must recognize that the real focus for their companies is the opportunity to compete for the future.

Note

1. Donald Hambrick, *Reinventing the CEO: 21st Century Report* (New York: Korn Ferry International and the Columbia University Graduate School of Business, 1989).

PART

II

Employer/Employee Loyalty

1
Trust and the Virtual Organization

Charles Handy

Not long ago, I found myself in the Laurentian Library, which Michelangelo built in Florence for the Medicis nearly 500 years ago. It is a special place, filled with the scent of learning; a place more restful and more uplifting, in many ways, than the Church of San Lorenzo, in whose cloister it stands. The Laurentian is no longer used as a library, however. It is visited only by tourists, and, as for its contents, they could all be fitted onto one CD-ROM disc.

Was this, I wondered, a symbol of what was coming to all our organizations? Their buildings turned into museums for tourists, their work on discs? And would we not lose something thereby, because, for all their probable efficiency, videoconferencing and cruising the Internet are not the same as working in Michelangelo's library?

Only the week before, in fact, I had been with a group of librarians, discussing the future of their modern-day libraries. Computer screens and keyboards, they agreed, were taking over from shelves of books and journals. A publisher revealed that he was no longer going to print and publish his journal but would instead enter it into the database of subscribing organizations. In that case, said one of those present, we need never visit a library again; we can get all that we want from the screen in our room. At the University of Virginia, added another, the change is already happening; all you need to access the library is a password and a modem. The library of the University of Dubrovnik was destroyed, someone else reported, but the gift of a computer terminal, linked to a host of foreign databases, more than compensated.

I watched the expressions of those in the room as they took in the implications of what was being said. They were coming face-to-face with the idea of the virtual library: a library as a concept, not a place; an activity, not a building. For the librarians, who were accustomed to seeing themselves as guardians of a special place, the idea was either frightening or exciting, depending on their ages and attitudes.

Libraries, whose lifeblood is information, were always likely to be among the first to confront the challenge and opportunity of virtuality, but as businesses become ever more dependent on information, they come up against the same dilemmas. An office is, at heart, an interpretative library geared to a particular purpose, and more and more of our economic activity is a churning of information, ideas, and intelligence in all their infinite variety—an invitation to virtuality.

It is easy to be seduced by the technological possibilities of the virtual organization, but the managerial and personal implications may cause us to rethink what we mean by an organization. At its simplest, the managerial dilemma comes down to the question, How do you manage people whom you do not see? The simple answer is, By trusting them, but the apparent simplicity disguises a turnaround in organizational thinking. The rules of trust are both obvious and well established, but they do not sit easily with a managerial tradition that believes efficiency and control are closely linked and that you can't have one without a lot of the other. Organizationally, we have to wonder whether a company is, in the future, going to be anything more than the box of contracts that some companies now seem to be. Is a box of contracts a sustainable basis for getting the work done in our society, or is it not, in fact, a recipe for disintegration? For society as a whole, the challenge will be to make sure that virtuality brings benefits to all and not just to a favored few. Organizations and, in particular, business organizations, are the linchpins of society. That gives them responsibilities beyond themselves, responsibilities that virtuality throws into high relief.

The Virtuality Dimension

If one ignores the technology, there is nothing new, conceptually, in the idea of an activity without a building as its home. Where information is the raw material of work, it has never been necessary to have all the people in the same place at the same time. A network of salespeople is the most common example—so ordinary and everyday an example that we would not think of giving it such a grandiose title as a virtual organization. Yet salespeople operate on their own, out of no common place—out of sight but not, one hopes, out of touch or, for that matter, out of line.

Journalism provides other examples. I myself fill an occasional slot on the BBC morning radio program *Today.* For many years, I did not meet my director, nor have I ever met any members of the production team. I communicate by telephone from wherever I happen to be, and my contributions are often broadcast from remote, unmanned studios. It is not in any way unusual.

The Open University in Great Britain, with counterparts all over the world, is perhaps the most ambitious example of a concept without a place. The Open University has a home base, to be sure, but none of the students and few of the faculty are to be found there. Its home base is merely the administrative hub of an unseen and sprawling empire. Its business school is already the largest in Europe, although few of the students have ever met any of the faculty or any of the other students. They used to meet at short residential summer schools, using the campuses of more traditional universities. This year, however, the university has created its first truly virtual summer school. The students will participate from their homes or places of work via E-mail, mobile phone, and videoconferencing. They will never be together in the same place at the same time. The technology has been provided by the university, which has thoughtfully included the mobile phone for students so that, as they sit with their computers beside them, still connected to their land telephone lines, they may converse with supervisors.

In my part of Great Britain, the central library in Norwich, serving the eastern region of the country, burned to the ground last summer. The librarian is considering replacing the grand building with a network of tiny libraries in every hamlet and town throughout the region, each linked to a central facility and, indeed, to every library in the world if need be. As in Dubrovnik, disaster can help us leap into the future before we ever intended. What will hold our librarian back, however, is not the technology or the money—both are potentially available—but the hearts and minds of his staff and his political masters. That's because what people cannot see they often cannot contemplate.

Business is creeping along behind such exemplars from the public sector. Large parts of organizations are now made up of ad hoc miniorganizations, projects collated for a particular time and purpose, drawing their participants from both inside and outside the parent organization. The projects often have no one place to call their own. They exist as activities, not as buildings; their only visible sign is an E-mail address. Inside the buildings that *do* exist, so-called hot-desking is increasingly common. In international business, videoconferencing is the norm. The trains in Great Britain double as mobile offices, with the commuter's doze interrupted by the ringing of personal phones and the bleeping of portable computers.

One day soon, when everyone has a personal phone, the phone will no longer belong to a place. That will be more dramatically different than it sounds. We will be able to call anyone without knowing where they are or what they are doing. The office as the home of our telephone—with a secretary to answer it and a line plugged into the wall—will become an antiquated and very expensive notion. An office that is available 168 hours a week but occupied for perhaps 20 is a luxury that organizations can ill afford. If there is an office in the future, it will be more like a clubhouse: a place for meeting, eating, and greeting, with rooms reserved for activities, not for particular people.

Virtuality, however, isn't always as much fun as it is supposed to be. A room of one's own, or at least a desk of one's own, has been the executive security blanket for a century or more. A sense of place is as important to most of us as a sense of purpose. E-mail and voice mail have many attractions, including immediacy, but they are not the same as watching the eyes of others. The loneliness of the long-distance executive is well documented. Even office politics and gossip have their attractions, if only as an antidote to the monotony of much of what goes on in the name of work. Few are going to be eager advocates of virtuality when it really means that work is what you do, not where you go.

The Managerial Dilemmas

Like it or not, the mixture of economics and technology means that more and more of us will be spending time in virtual space—out of sight, if not out of touch. No longer will our colleagues be down the corridor, available for an unscheduled meeting or a quick progress check. Most meetings will have to be scheduled, even those on video, and will therefore become more infrequent. We will have to learn how to run organizations without meetings.

We will also have to get accustomed to working with and managing those whom we do not see, except on rare and prearranged occasions. That is harder than it sounds. I once sat with a features writer of a daily paper. She was interviewing me in the newsroom, a place filled with smoke, noise, telephones, and the sweat of 100 journalists. I had to perch on the edge of her desk—there was nowhere else.

"Couldn't we have done this somewhere else?" I said over the hubbub. "Like at your home?"

"I wish we could," she said. "Indeed, I would do so much of my work a lot better if I could do it where it suited me. I could send it down the wire just as easily from home, or wherever, as from here."

"Why don't you, then?" I asked with surprise.

"Because *they* want me where they can see me." And she pointed down the long room to where two men sat behind large plateglass windows. They were the editors, she explained, and they liked to be able to see what everyone was doing, to check the work, or to interrupt it whenever they needed to give out a new assignment.

"The truth is," she said, "they don't trust us."

Trust is the heart of the matter. That seems obvious and trite, yet most of our organizations tend to be arranged on the assumption that people cannot be trusted or relied on, even in tiny matters. Oversight systems are set up to prevent anyone from doing the wrong thing, whether by accident or design.

The other day, a courier could not find my family's remote cottage. He called his base on his radio, and the base called us to ask directions. He was just around the corner, but his base managed to omit a vital part of the directions. So he called them again, and they called us again. Then the courier repeated the cycle a third time to ask whether we had a dangerous dog. When he eventually arrived, we asked whether it would not have been simpler and less aggravating to everyone if he had called us directly from the roadside telephone booth where he had been parked. "I can't do that," he said, "because they won't refund any money I spend." "But it's only pennies!" I exclaimed. "I know," he said, "but that only shows how little they trust us!"

Writ large, that sort of attitude creates a paraphernalia of systems, checkers, and checkers checking checkers—expensive and deadening. Some commentators have argued that *audit mania* (the urge to have some independent inspection) is a virus infecting our society. It exists, they suggest, because we no longer trust people to act for anything but their own short-term interests. That attitude becomes a self-fulfilling prophecy. "If they don't trust me," employees say to themselves, "Why should I bother to put their needs before mine?" If it is even partly true that a lack of trust makes employees untrustworthy, it does not bode well for the future of virtuality in organizations. If we are to enjoy the efficiencies and other benefits of the virtual organization, we will have to rediscover how to run organizations based more on trust than on control. Virtuality requires trust to make it work: Technology on its own is not enough.

The Rules of Trust

Common sense tells us that there are seven cardinal principles of trust we should keep in mind:

Trust is not blind. It is unwise to trust people whom you do not know well, whom you have not observed in action over time, and who are not committed to the same goals. In practice, it is hard to know more than 50 people that well. Those 50 can each, in turn, know another 50, and so on. Large organizations are not therefore incompatible with the principle of trust, but they have to be made up of relatively constant, smaller groupings. The idea that people should move around as much and as fast as possible in order to get more exposure and more experience—what the Japanese call the horizontal fast track—can mean that there is no time to learn to trust anyone and, in the end, no point, because the organization starts to replace trust with systems of control.

My title in one large organization was MKR/32. In that capacity, I wrote memos to FIN/41 or PRO/23. I rarely heard any names, and I never met the people behind those titles. I had no reason to trust them and, frankly, no desire to. I was a "temporary role occupant," in the jargon of the time, a role occupant in an organization of command and control, based on the premise that no one could really be trusted. I left after a year. Such places can be prisons for the human soul.

Trust needs boundaries. Unlimited trust is, in practice, unrealistic. By trust, organizations really mean confidence, a confidence in someone's competence and in his or her commitment to a goal. Define that goal, and the individual or the team can be left to get on with it. Control is then after the event, when the results are assessed. It is not a matter of granting permission before the event. Freedom within boundaries works best, however, when the work unit is self-contained, having the capability within it to solve its own problems. Trust-based organizations are, as a result, reengineering their work, pulling back from the old reductionist models of organization, in which everything was divided into its component parts or functions. At first sight, the new holistic designs for the units of the organization look more expensive because they duplicate functions and do not necessarily replicate each other. The energy and effectiveness released by the freedom within boundaries more than compensates, however. To succeed, reengineering must be built on trust. When it fails, it is because trust is absent.

Trust demands learning. An organizational architecture made up of relatively independent and constant groupings, pushes the organization toward the sort of federal structure that is becoming more common everywhere. A necessary condition of constancy, however, is an ability to change: If one set of people cannot be exchanged for another set when circumstances alter, then the first set must adapt or die. The constant groups must always be flexible enough to change when times and customers demand it. They must also keep themselves abreast of change, forever exploring new options and new technologies. They must create a real learning culture. The choice of people for these groups is therefore crucial. Every individual has to be capable of self-renewal. Recruitment and placement become key, along with the choice of group leaders. Such topics will require the serious attention of senior management. They should not be delegated to a lower echelon of human resources.

Trust is tough. The reality is, however, that even the best recruiters and the best judges of character will get it wrong sometimes. When trust proves to be misplaced—not because people are deceitful or malicious but because they do not live up to expectations or cannot be relied on to do what is needed—then those people have to go. Where you cannot trust, you have to become a checker once more, with all the systems of control that involves. Therefore, for the sake of the whole, the individual must leave. Trust has to be ruthless. It is incompatible with any promise of a job for life. After all, who can be so sure of their recruitment procedures that they are prepared to trust forever those whom they select? It is because trust is so important but so risky, that organizations tend to restrict their core commitments to a smaller group of what I call *trusties*. But that policy in turn pushes the organization toward a core/periphery model, one that can, if practitioners are not careful, degenerate into a set of purely formal contractual relationships with all the outsiders. Nothing is simple; there is paradox everywhere.

Trust needs bonding. Self-contained units responsible for delivering specified results are the necessary building blocks of an organization based on trust, but long-lasting groups of trusties can create their own problems, those of organizations within the organization. For the whole to work, the goals of the smaller units have to gel with the goals of the whole. The blossoming of vision and mission statements is one attempt to deal with integration, as are campaigns for total quality or excellence. Such things matter. Or rather, if they did not exist, their absence would matter. They are not, however, enough in themselves. They need to be backed up by exhortation and personal example. Anita Roddick holds her spreading Body Shop together by what can best be called "personal infection," pouring her energies into the reinforcement of her values and beliefs through every medium she can find. It is always a dangerous strategy to personalize a mission, in case the person stumbles or falls, as the Body Shop nearly did last year after unfavorable publicity, but organizations based on trust need that sort of personal statement from their leaders. Trust is not and never can be an impersonal commodity.

Trust needs touch. Visionary leaders, no matter how articulate, are not enough. A shared commitment still requires personal contact to make it real. To augment John Naisbitt's telling phrase, high tech has to be balanced by high touch to build high-trust organizations. Paradoxically, the more virtual an organization becomes, the more its people need to meet in person. The meetings, however, are different. They are more about process than task, more concerned that people get to know each other than that they deliver. Videoconferences are more task focused, but they are easier and more productive if the individuals know each other as people, not just as images on the screen. Work and play, therefore, alternate in many of the corporate get-togethers that now fill the conference resorts out of season. These are not perks for the privileged; they are the necessary lubricants of virtuality, occasions not only for getting to know each other and for meeting the leaders but also for reinforcing corporate goals and rethinking corporate strategies. As one who delivers the occasional "cabaret" at such occasions, I am always surprised to find how few of the participants have met each other in person, even if they have worked together before. I am then further surprised by how quickly a common mood develops. You can almost watch the culture grow, and you wonder how they could have worked effectively without it.

Trust requires leaders. At their best, the units in good trust-based organizations hardly have to be managed, but they do need a multiplicity of leaders. I once teased an English audience by comparing a team of Englishmen to a rowing crew on the river—eight men going

backward as fast as they can without talking to each other, steered by
the one person who can't row! I thought it quite witty at the time, but
I was corrected after the session by one of the participants, who had
once been an Olympic oarsman. "How do you think we could go
backward so fast without communicating, steered by this little fellow
in the stern, if we didn't know each other very well, didn't have total
confidence to do our jobs and a shared commitment—almost a pas-
sion—for the same goal? It is the perfect formula for a team."

I had to admit it—he was right. "But tell me," I said to him, "who
is the manager of this team?" "There isn't one," he replied, after
thinking about it. "Unless that is what you call our part-time admin-
istrator back in the office." Manager, he was reminding me, is a
low-status title in organizations of colleagues.

"Well, then, who is the leader?"

"That depends," he said. "When we are racing, it is the little chap
who is steering, because he is the only one who can see where we are
going. But there is also the stroke, who sets the standard for all of us.
He is a leader, too, in a way. But off the river, it's the captain of the
crew, who selects us, bonds us together, builds our commitment to our
goal and our dedication. Lastly, in training, there is our coach, who is
undoubtedly the main influence on our work. So you see," he concluded, "there isn't a simple answer to your question."

A rowing crew, I realized, has to be based on trust if it is to have
any chance of success. And if any member of that crew does not pull
his weight, then he does not deserve the confidence of the others and
must be asked to leave. Nor can all the leadership requirements be
discharged by one person, no matter how great or how good.

The Organization's Dilemma

Racing crews row for the sake of glory, but it is not as clear what
motivates the people in the virtual organizations of business. Why
should the now smaller core of trusted individuals give so much of
their lives and time and talent to an organization that they work for
but do not live in, an organization that, significantly, someone else
owns, someone whom they almost certainly do not know and have
never met, because, for the most part, that someone is not an individual at all but an institution owned, in turn, by other anonymous
people?

That question had a clear answer in times past. The organization was the instrument of its owners, and the individual was the instrument of the organization. The implied and the legal contracts were both instrumental. The individual was a hired hand, a human resource, employed to work the assets of the organization. Good pay, good prospects, and a challenging job were enough for most. The human resource, however, is now the human asset, not the human cost. That is not just refined semantics, it is the literal financial truth. The market value of the top 200 businesses on the London Stock Exchange is on average three times the worth of the visible fixed assets. In the case of the high-tech high fliers, it can be up to 20 times. If that means anything, it means that the market is valuing the intangible assets many times higher than the tangible ones. Whether those intangible assets are the research in a company's pipeline, the brands, the know-how, or the networks of experience, they amount in the end to one thing: the people.

Those people can and often do walk out the door. Whole teams of analysts nowadays shift themselves from one financial institution to another at the glint of a golden handshake or the lure of new pastures. If laborers are worthy of their hire, there is no reason to suppose that they won't go where the hire looks better. The assets of the new information-based corporations are, as a result, increasingly fragile. It is hard to measure assets in the present, harder still to gauge their future. Investing in information-based businesses will be even more of a gamble than it has been in the past.

The consequences of increased gambling are predictable: Investors will be in more of a hurry to get their money back; managers will be under pressure to milk their assets while they still have them; horizons will shrink; and the result will be that, even if the assets don't walk, they will wilt. Under those pressures, even inspired, articulate leaders will be hard-pressed to hold the virtual corporation together.

When laborers become assets, the underlying contract with the organization has to change. Trust inevitably requires some sense of mutuality, of reciprocal loyalty. Virtual organizations, which feed on information, ideas, and intelligence (which in turn are vested in the heads and hearts of people), cannot escape the dilemma. One answer is to turn the laborers into members; that is, to turn the instrumental contract into a membership contract for the smaller core. Members have rights. They also have responsibilities. Their rights include a share in the governance of the community to which they belong. No one can buy a club against the wishes of its members. Major capital investments and strategic initiatives require the agreement of the members. The terms and conditions of membership require members' agreement. Their responsibilities center on the need to make the business grow, because without growth there will be no striving and, ultimately, no point. Growth, however, can mean growth in quality, size, profitability, or desirability, and maybe in all four. People who think of themselves as members have more of an interest in the future of the business and its growth than those who are only its hired help.

Giving membership rights to key people is not the same as giving them ownership, but those membership rights inevitably diminish the powers of the owners. Shareholders become investors rather than owners. They are entitled to a reasonable return on their money—a return that takes the risk into account—but they are not entitled, for instance, to sell the company over the heads of its members or to dictate to management, unless the financial returns start to evaporate. Major investors, however, who tend to be long-term investors, might also be included in the extended family of the business. Such a shift in the governance of the corporation would bring Anglo-American businesses more into line with the businesses of continental Europe or Japan. Companies there, paradoxically perhaps, are seeking to give more power to the investors as a discipline for the members and their management and as a way of increasing the financial base. The principle of requisite balance would suggest that all groups should meet halfway, and they probably will, as the world of business becomes increasingly linked and interdependent.

The concept of membership, when made real, would replace the sense of belonging to a *place* with a sense of belonging to a *community*, even if that community were a largely virtual one. A sense of belonging is something humans need if they are to commit themselves to more than simple selfishness. Families and family businesses know something about the sense of belonging and the motivating force of collective pride in the family tradition, as well as the responsibilities that go with belonging. Families, at their best, are communities built on mutual trust. If the family could be extended to include key contributors, the sense of belonging would be properly inclusive. Without some real sense of belonging, virtuality looks like a very precarious state and a perilous base for the next phase of capitalism, whatever the economic and technological advantages.

Society's Dilemma

An economy that adds value through information, ideas, and intelligence—the Three I Economy—offers a way out of the apparent clash between material growth and environmental erosion. Information, ideas, and intelligence consume few of the earth's resources. Virtuality will redesign our cities with fewer skyscrapers and fewer commuters, making a quieter and perhaps a gentler world. Our aspirations for growth in a Three I Economy would increasingly be more a matter for the mind than for the body. The growth sectors would be education in all its varied forms, health care, the arts and entertainment, leisure, travel, and sports. As the economic statistics show, the new growth is already happening, and the organizations that deliver it tend to be small groups of colleagues united by mutual trust. Small, growing companies often serve today's young people, who aspire to better music systems and computers rather than to faster cars or flashier clothes. The younger generation also relishes employment in the new and freer organizations.

Not all people do, however. If the Three I Economy is to take off in the First World and thus give hope of a sustainable future to others, everyone needs to be able to participate. Currently, there is in every country of the First World a growing underclass that knows little about the concepts behind the Three I Economy. For members of that underclass, such concepts are a joke. They want hamburgers and heating, not computers. In the short term, maybe, they should be helped with their hamburgers and heating, but they also need a hand up into the Three I Economy. Virtuality will be a recipe for a divided society unless we help everyone, and a society divided will not long survive. We have to take from the present to ensure our future, instead of borrowing from the future to ensure our present, as most countries do today.

Everyone has something to contribute to a Three I Economy. There is no unteachable group. Talent in some form or another exists in all human beings; it only needs to be detected and developed. Naturally, early education is crucial, but our future should not be determined by the time we are 16. Work can be a great laboratory of learning, and organizations, therefore, hold one of the keys to the future of society. But if they concentrate their efforts only on their core members, they will be throwing away that key. Who else will help those who are outside the organization—the independents, the part-timers, and the small contractors and suppliers?

Already, in the European Union, one half of the available workforce is outside the organization, not in full-time jobs. If organizations do not embrace the concept of an extended family and include their associated workers in their plans for their human assets, the workforce will become increasingly useless to them and to themselves. If a trust-based organization means trust for some and the old instrumental contract for the less able, then trust will become a dirty word, a synonym for selfishness. Some see the peripheral workforce as the responsibility of government—to train, to employ, or, if all else fails, to support. Governments, however, have their limits. They can pass laws, they can regulate, and they can sometimes find money to empower others; but they cannot and should not try to do it all themselves. They need help from the rest of society.

The hope for the future that is contained within the virtual organization will end in disillusionment unless we can mobilize society to think beyond itself to save itself. Governments in a democracy can move only as fast as the opinion leaders in society. Business has always been a major leader of opinion, but if business minds its own business exclusively or if it takes virtuality to extremes and becomes a mere broker or box of contracts, then it will have failed society. In the end, its search for wealth will have destroyed wealth.

2
Service Comes First: An Interview with USAA's Robert F. McDermott

Thomas Teal

In his 22 years as CEO of the United Services Automobile Association (USAA), Robert F. McDermott has built a company with a reputation for superb service in an industry infamous for its indifference to the customer.

USAA is the nation's fifth largest insurer of privately owned automobiles and homes and is expanding rapidly into the field of financial services. Its 14,000 employees now serve more than 2 million customers and policyholders and manage $20.7 billion in assets. By focusing single-mindedly on service quality—and on its three component parts: customers, work force, and technology—McDermott has revolutionized USAA's approach to its business and to its customers' financial needs.

USAA was formed in 1922 by 25 army officers who wanted to provide one another with reciprocal auto insurance at a time when most local insurance companies saw military personnel as too mobile—and as living lives too full of risk—to be good bets. To this day, most of USAA's policyholders are its military and ex-military member-owners: about 95% of active-duty U.S. military officers are USAA members. To this day, too, the company uses no outside agents but does all its own sales and marketing.

McDermott has expanded USAA's market by taking in his members' children and grandchildren as associate members (with no ownership rights). And by law, the financial services the company sells must be offered to the general public. But the distinctive needs of USAA's military niche have been an important stimulus for the company's service focus.

USAA's origins also shape the company's approach to its work force—emphasizing a quasi-military esprit de corps and the continuous development of human resources. The company has an unmistakable military bearing. Of the 11 people who report to McDermott directly, 8 are ex-military officers. There is a strict dress code, employee performance is carefully measured, and the company's large, open bays allow for little privacy (even McDermott's office has one glass wall).

At the same time, USAA has pioneered progressive employment practices like the four-day workweek, spends $19 million annually on employee training (2.7% of its annual budget and double the industry average), and is a leader in integrating minorities into its work force. The company's 286-acre headquarters complex in San Antonio, Texas, includes tennis courts, softball diamonds, jogging trails, three artificial lakes, and 75 classrooms.

The third and final element of USAA's service recipe is technology. At a time when many service companies are discovering that their heavy investments in technology do not translate into productivity gains, USAA has used technology not only to increase productivity but also to improve the quality of service. For example, USAA's state-of-the-art electronic imaging system means that each day some 30,000 pieces of mail never leave the mailroom. Instead, an exact image of the correspondence is placed electronically in the customer's policy service file and, simultaneously, in a sort of electronic in-basket where it will be handled by the first available service representative anywhere in the building.

McDermott is a retired U.S. Air Force brigadier general and former World War II fighter pilot. A graduate of the United States Military Academy and the Harvard Business School, he has taught at West Point and served as the first permanent dean of faculty at the Air Force Academy. This interview was conducted at USAA's San Antonio headquarters by *Harvard Business Review* associate editor Thomas Teal.

HBR: *USAA limits the sale of its principal financial products to a customer base comprising no more than 2% or 3% of the U.S. population. You do little or no national advertising, you refuse to sell through the thousands of independent insurance agents in this country, and yet your growth and profitability are among the highest in your industry. What's your secret?*

Robert McDermott: The mission and corporate culture of this company are, in one word, service. As a company objective, service comes ahead of either profits or growth.

Now, profits and growth do matter. In 1987, Ernst & Young surveyed 154 CEOs about their top priorities. Profits was first on their list, and growth wasn't far behind. Service came in eleventh. But I submit that it's because service comes first at USAA that profits and growth have been so healthy. We've grown from $200 million to $20.7 billion in total owned and managed assets in 22 years. Our profits are among the highest in the insurance industry. But service comes first.

Is it really as simple as that?

No, not quite. If you want me to describe our mission in several words instead of one, I'd have to say it's service to a particular community of customers and members, because our niche in the market is very important to us. Our members started this company and own it, so this company exists to serve their needs.

Let me give you an example. Whenever a war starts, most insurance companies are quick to invoke the war clause in their life insurance policies so they won't have to pay off on people killed in combat. Since we serve military officers, we have no such clause. So, for example, we're one of only a few companies that didn't invoke a war clause as soon as Desert Storm began. On the contrary, we sold new life insurance to people who'd just been called up.

If an officer had a $100,000 policy with us and he got orders for Desert Storm, we not only kept the full $100,000 in force, we let him increase his insurance. We didn't suggest it, exactly, but we allowed it. We even sold new policies to people who suddenly panicked when they got their orders and realized they might need some protection for their families. We put a $50,000 limit on increases and new policies, but we were the only insurance company I know of that sold those people any new coverage at all.

We also encouraged them to leave a power of attorney with someone at home. And we set up a hotline—the Desert Storm Assistance Center—so that should a member be killed, the survivors could call in and we'd take care of everything: life insurance, bank account, investment management, property insurance—everything with one phone call. When they mobilized, we mobilized. But that's how we see our mission. We insure fighter pilots and tank commanders. We sell life insurance to astronauts. We insured those guys on the moon.

Did you have losses in the Gulf?

Well, of the 263 Americans who died in the course of Desert Storm, 55 were officers, and all of those were USAA members, though not all of them had life insurance. Now, those 55 deaths are a terrible loss in human terms, but in purely financial terms, the loss to the company was not significant—altogether about $800,000.

As a matter of good service, on the auto side, we encouraged members sent to the Gulf to downgrade their insurance and save themselves money. For example, if their cars were just going to sit in garages while they were gone, they wouldn't need liability coverage. And when two-car families had one spouse in the Gulf, we gave them the rates for a single person with two cars, which of course are lower than for a couple with two cars, since one person can't drive two cars at the same time. Moreover, we went out of our way to make sure people understood that we wouldn't cancel their insurance because of late payments due to the war.

How do you justify to member-owners such generosity toward member-policy-holders—even if they are the same people?

In the case of auto insurance, we didn't need much justification. In spite of all our efforts to reduce premiums and save our members money, losses were so much below normal that we declared a 25% dividend—a rebate—on auto insurance for everyone who served in the Desert Storm combat area during hostilities. So everyone came out ahead. In this company, service isn't a matter of generosity, it's our daily bread.

As I understand it, however, service wasn't always USAA's strong suit.

Well, yes and no. I think the company always tried to give good service, it just didn't always succeed.

When I arrived here in 1968, I had six months to look around before I took over as CEO. And what I saw gave me second thoughts. We were good on claims, we were good on price, we were honest and honorable. In most other categories, we fell short.

A lot of our problems were the same ones other bureaucracies face. The company was divided into two divisions: auto and what we called the multiple-line division, which handled all property insurance—homeowners, renters, farm, boat, and so forth. There were also a lot of smaller departments, and these were mostly run by warlords who didn't communicate with one another. They fought perpetual turf battles. Actuarial didn't speak to underwriting, and claims didn't speak to either one. No horizontal communication. No one knew how the whole thing fitted together, they just knew and cared about their own little piece of the company.

There was paper everywhere. We had 650,000 members at that time and 3,000 employees. Every desk in the building was covered with stacks of paper—files, claim forms, applications, correspondence. You can't imagine how much paper. Stacks and piles and trays and baskets of it. And of course a lot of it got lost. On any given day, the chances were only 50–50 that we'd be able to put our hands on any particular file.

In fact, so much of it got lost that, depending on the season, we had from 200 to 300 young people from local colleges who worked here at night finding files, just going around searching people's desks until they found the ones they were looking for. Every night.

When I first started, I would often stay late and go around putting little marks on papers and files, then I'd check the next night to see if they'd been moved. A lot of people moved no paper at all.

Did your members know how bad the situation really was?

We constantly got letters and phone calls about poor service. Most of our members were sticking with us because our premiums were lower than anyone else's and because we were good on claims. It certainly wasn't because of our prompt and dependable service in any other area. Anyway, most of them had auto insurance only. Penetration in the property market was poor.

One old friend told me he'd bought a new car 18 months earlier and insured it with us, but when the insurance didn't come up for renewal a year later, he began to wonder. He discovered that the policy had never been issued. Another old friend said he'd applied for homeowner's insurance, and 90 days later he still hadn't heard anything.

You took over in 1969. What steps did you take to get the company back on track?

By the time I took over, I had already made four basic decisions. First, we were going to automate our policy-writing system.

Second, we were going to reduce the number of employees and do it by means of attrition—we weren't going to fire anyone. Turnover was very, very high at the time, so it wasn't a difficult promise to keep.

Third, we were going to have an education and training program to upgrade employee quality and enrich the jobs. "Enriched" was a word

I'd seen on a loaf of bread, where it meant they'd added something to improve the nutrition. I wanted to add interest and challenge to our jobs.

Fourth, we were going to decentralize. The decisions about how to serve our 650,000 members had to be made on the front line. To get that ball rolling, I divided our policy-writing and servicing people into five groups and assigned each of them a fifth of our members at random, so each group had a cross section geographically and actuarially. Then I put the five groups into competition with one another. Not only was that a good way of motivating people, it was a great way of identifying people with imagination and drive, because competition makes those people stand out like light bulbs.

And did it work? Did service improve?

It worked so well, it changed this company forever. It worked so well, it convinced me that the further down you decentralize, the better run your organization is going to be, provided of course you have the necessary education and training base. "Empowerment" has come to be a buzzword recently. I don't suppose I'd ever heard it in 1969, but it describes what we set about doing almost as soon as I took over. We empowered our employees.

How do you empower people in actual practice?

Well, first of all, we empower them with knowledge. We've got a training and education budget of $19 million, with 211 full-time instructors and 75 classrooms. Before our service representatives start answering phones, they get at least 16 weeks of training and job simulations. We're very proud of the fact that when members or customers ask questions, our service reps know the answers. They don't have to call in the supervisor every time something comes up that's just a little off the beaten track.

We also developed a tuition program. We pay the fees for anybody studying for a business degree or taking a college course relevant to their job, providing they get a grade of C or better, B or better for graduate work. We make it not just possible but easy for people to take courses. For example, this building turns into a college campus at night. We bring teachers here from six local colleges and universities, and on a typical evening, all 75 classrooms are in use. We also introduced training programs for professional designations, of which the insurance industry has quite a few. Today almost 30% of our people are in education and development programs—one of the highest percentages in the country.

Second, we empower them with technology—information, expert systems, image processing—that allows them to serve the customer better than any other insurance company. The image-processing system alone has totally changed the way we do business.

Can you give me an example?

Suppose Colonel Smith has sent us a letter asking for a change in his homeowners insurance, and he calls and wants to know if we've received it. The service representative says, "Yes, sir, I've got it right here." "You do?" he says. "Yes," the rep says, "I have it right in front of me. What can I do for you?"

The colonel's impressed. We received his letter only that morning, but it's already been imaged, so it's instantly available to every service representative in the building.

Now, let's say Colonel Smith calls back the next day with some additional information we've asked him for and talks to a different service rep who also has his letter "right here in front of me." Now the colonel's impressed and amazed.

Let's also say that the service rep, who has not only Colonel Smith's letter but his entire file available on the screen, goes on to explain how the change Smith wants to make in his homeowner's coverage may reduce his need for umbrella liability and thus lower the cost of that policy. Now the colonel's impressed and amazed and very pleased. And so are we, because the whole transaction's taken five minutes. And so is the service representative, because serving people better is fulfilling and fun.

And gives people a sense of power.

That's right. The third way we empowered them was in the literal sense of the word—with delegated authority. Our service representatives can make policy changes on the spot, just as a claims representative can authorize certain payments without an inspection and have a check in the mail the same day you phone in the claim. Our people can also invent new improvements to the system. I can't sit here at this level and dream up ways of improving service. It's got to come from the people on the front line.

Let me go back to education and training for a moment. If 30% of your people are involved in training in any given year, that suggests a lot of movement inside the company. Either that, or people get more and more training but stay in the same old jobs.

We don't want anyone to get stuck in a job, especially in a job perceived as repetitive or boring. So we do our best to get people to sign up for training, apply for new positions, learn more jobs—as you say, move around inside the company. Every year, 45% of our people get a promotion, and every year 50% of our people change their jobs. We want people who know what the people in other departments do, we want our managers to have the broadest possible experience of the company, and we want to be able to fill key vacant positions quickly. In other words, we want flexibility, and we want functional integration. A company full of people who've worked in lots of different jobs and divisions has both.

What about the people who didn't want to learn new skills, who wanted to stay in easy jobs?

When I took over, I promised everyone change. That scared some people away. Another group left when the jobs got harder. Of the old warlords who refused to change with the company, most left when I transferred them—at no cut in pay, incidentally—to jobs with less responsibility. All in all, the work force changed a great deal over those first few years.

For example, when I arrived at the company, USAA had a work force that was mostly white female and a management that was mostly white male. But San Antonio was 45% minority—so it didn't make sense. I took steps to make the work force better represent the labor force in our community.

Why? There were no quotas. Why was that important to you?

I'd come from the military, where integration worked. It was shocking to come out of the military and see how poorly it worked in the rest of society.

During World War II, the services limped along with a kind of halfhearted integration—separate black units fighting alongside white ones. But it wasn't fair, it wasn't right, and it didn't work. Truman saw that and ordered full integration, and the military carried it out more quickly and completely than most people expected. After all, the professional officer corps was largely Southern.

But the army had an additional motive on top of the president's order. The military always resists lack of flexibility in the management of its people, and a segregated work force is just one more complication. Military people get occupation specialties so they'll be interchangeable and mobile. The air force can take a hydraulic mechanic at Kelly Field and move him to Japan for a three-year tour, and when he arrives he just goes to work. That was the practical argument that gave traction to the moral argument. Segregation is immoral, but if that's not good enough for you, it's also inefficient.

Did you see gains in efficiency at USAA?

What I discovered when we started hiring minorities was that they were excellent employees and very conscientious. The jobs meant a lot to them. They were hungry for opportunities.

But I also discovered that our merit system wasn't totally objective. So I said, "OK, let's start all over again," because it was clear that there was bias in the system. I put everyone in the same job on the same pay, which meant 25% raises for some people.

But what kept favoritism from simply reasserting itself?

The problem wasn't so much open favoritism as it was the preservation of old inequalities based on seniority and habit. So we did several things. First, we created a forced distribution system. The old way, supervisors could give raises anywhere within a certain range, let's say, 0% to 8%, and they'd often sidestep the issue by giving everyone, say, 4%, which perpetuated earlier inequities—in fact made the actual dollar gaps bigger. We now said they had to identify 20% at the top level, 40% at the next level, and so forth, which forced them to make decisions and encouraged them to give pay for actual performance.

At the same time, we put in a new merit evaluation system and then worked with supervisors until they understood it. It took us about three years to change the system all through the company, a few jobs at a time. [For a fuller discussion of USAA's performance appraisal systems, see "Merit Evaluation and the Family of Measures."]

Merit Evaluation and the Family of Measures

USAA uses several tools to track employee performance. First, supervisors conduct annual evaluations of all individual employees on a range of performance and behavioral skills. They consider such factors as how well employees know their jobs, how they relate to others, the way they organize their work, and they rate qualities like judgment and initiative. For employees whose work is more discretionary, a goal-setting discussion and periodic reviews supplement the annual evaluation scorecard. The company uses all these evaluations to determine performance-based pay increases and to help establish promotion eligibility.

At the same time, USAA has developed a separate tool called the Family of Measures (FOM) to track the quality of individual and unit performance to answer a different basic question: Is this person or group showing improvement, and if not, what areas need training and attention? Because USAA's goal is continuous improvement, FOM's principal function is to measure progress, not to give grades. Individual and group results are compared only with themselves over time, never with other units or individuals.

FOM is based on USAA's belief that judging individual and group performance is an indispensable first step to learning and improvement. The company believes that people want an ongoing picture of how they're doing, that they want to be measured in accordance with standards they themselves have helped to set, and that they value the opportunity to improve performance without direct reference to compensation.

FOM is a flexible, continuous evaluation process rather than a static inventory of numbers such as sales volumes or customer contacts. Its results are not used to determine pay. And workers themselves have developed the grading formulas, determined the relative difficulty of tasks performed, and agreed on how to weight each score in accordance with each individual employee's experience level.

Each monthly FOM report tracks five areas: quality, quantity (of work completed), service timeliness, resource utilization (the percent of available hours that the group actually spends working), and customer satisfaction. The system tracks individual performance in some categories and overall group performance in others. Employees receive an individual report each month showing monthly and year-to-date results.

The FOM for each work unit is developed by a representative group of employees who decide which key aspects of the job they should track and who ask themselves four questions about each potential measure: Is the activity under our control? Is it significant? Does it involve some form of data that we can collect? Can we easily analyze the results? They vote on which measures to include and on their relative weight in the system. Finally, they pass these recommendations along to managers, who do their own fine-tuning before implementation.

To see how FOM operates in practice, we can look at the policy service function for property-and-casualty insurance. (Since USAA has no agents in the field, policy service representatives are the people who deal with customers, by letter or by phone, on all issues not involving claims.) To measure quality, managers audit telephone calls, correspondence, and computerized business transactions in order to identify both exceptional performance and areas of potential improvement. The focus is on communication, accuracy, and knowledge.

FOM defines quantity as the number of telephone and business transactions handled (USAA now does 90% of its business by phone). The different kinds of policies—auto, boat, home, umbrella, and so on—are weighted by difficulty, with the result that umbrella transactions count for five times as much as auto transactions in FOM reports.

These two measures, quality and quantity, are then weighted for the particular unit (policy service weights quality at 60%, quantity at 40%). Individual quantity standards vary by grade level and experience. USAA expects both quality and quantity to improve over time. The company gives special recognition to employees whose performance shows significant improvement and provides coaching and additional training for those who show little or none.

Service timeliness, resource utilization, and customer satisfaction are all monitored and analyzed for the group as a whole. The current measure for timeliness is the percent of calls answered within 20 seconds. Resource utilization measures the ratio of hours worked to hours paid. Customer satisfaction is culled from questionnaires mailed to a random sample of customers after they've dealt with a policy service representative.

—Tom Ehrenfeld

And by that time, I suppose, the poorest performers had quit.

Most of them, yes. But there was more to it than that. We weren't making changes just to weed out poor performers. We were also improving management. Another new system we introduced at that time was a thing I call "painting the bridge."

When I was 12 years old, my father took me to visit West Point, and on the way we drove across Bear Mountain Bridge. Part of it was a bluish gray, and part of it was orange, and of course I wanted to know why. My father explained to me how bridges are painted—from one end to the other and then back to the start, which, by then, needs repainting. It's an endless cycle to keep the bridge in working order.

Painting the bridge is the same kind of exercise. An independent team of 14 organizational experts starts at one end of the company and goes through it one division at a time, with an eye to organizational health and organizational development. They look at structures, job content, duplications of effort, inefficiencies, and more. They do a desk-by-desk audit, working from the trenches up.

Most important, they question everything. Does this job need to exist? Does this department need to exist, or could it be merged with another function? Is this work being done the best possible way? Is this piece of infrastructure essential? The team does away with unnecessary work, titles, and fiefdoms. They hold managers' feet to the fire and remember the promises those same managers made the last time the team came through, two years earlier.

It's not a new concept. The air force does the same thing, which is where we got the idea. But we do it better. We're more sensitive to the impact on individual employees. Significant changes have to be discussed with personnel, and if there's no agreement, I have to arbitrate. They're not popular, those 14 people, but they're respected because they keep the company healthy. They keep cutting out the fat. The bridge keeps getting painted. We keep making better managers, and we keep enriching the jobs.

And greater efficiency makes jobs more rewarding?

People don't want to spend their lives doing effortless, pointless work. In that sense, painting the bridge is another way of making sure that jobs have meaning, along with giving people opportunities to educate themselves, to broaden their experience by changing jobs, to become decision makers.

But all those programs aside, the biggest piece of job enrichment was and still is service. Fulfilling the mandate to "love thy neighbor as thyself"—or however you choose to express the golden rule—enriches the job and enriches life.

No matter where we start, you always come back to service. Why is it so important to your work force?

In a military organization, the first thing you worry about is the morale of your troops, and the key to morale is the quality of work life. At USAA, that includes the fitness centers and the softball diamonds and the cafeterias as well as good salaries and benefits, a clean, cheerful place to work, and 52 four-day workweeks every year. It also includes the dress code and high expectations. We give a lot, and we demand a lot. But most of all, the quality of work life here is a matter of our service orientation.

In the military, we found that perhaps the most important factor in esprit de corps is being needed by the other guys in your unit. That's a fairly simple concept in a platoon or on a ship, but it's a little harder in a large corporation. In our case, it's a matter of feeling needed by the membership. I think you'll find that most of the service representatives who answer the 90,000 phone calls we get every day are anxious to help the people on the other end of the line. We know they've got a problem—that's why they're calling. They're reporting an accident, or the body shop didn't fix their car right, or maybe the body shop can't even *find* the car to tow it in. Something's wrong, and they live complicated, busy lives and want to get this thing wrapped up and want our help. Members trust us to help them, and our people know that. I think that makes them feel good. I think they like being needed.

You talk about serving your members as if that were the most important and satisfying assignment in the world. Let me ask an obvious question. What makes them so special?

Well, they're well-educated, affluent, and honest. Today 42% have graduate degrees, largely because of the military policy of sending officers to professional schools in addition to an academy or officer training school. The median family income is almost twice the national median.

Moreover, the overwhelming majority are thoroughly honorable people, and of course that's important to an insurance company. When newly commissioned officers tell us they've had this many speeding tickets and this many accidents, we take their word for it. Some companies check every single application, but the money we'd spend would be way out of proportion to the number of misrepresentations we'd find.

The same goes for claims. If one of our members calls us and says, "Somebody stole four hubcaps off my car while I was in a meeting," our operator will punch that into a computer and say, "Okay, that's a 1989 Buick. They run $80 apiece. We'll send you a check for $320." And the check would go out that same day—written, addressed, stuffed, stamped, and sorted by computer. Most companies would go out and look at the car. That costs a lot of money.

So the niche market you have is a good one.

Yes. Exceptionally good.

But when you came to USAA, that niche was not very happy with the company. What was your strategy? Or was it simply better service?

My initial goal was simply to improve service. We had to start taking care of the people we were already supposed to be serving but weren't serving well.

Remember that because of our bylaws, we can't compete with other companies for their customers. But they can compete with us for ours. Any company can take my business away from me—or try to. But we can sell only to our niche. And I don't want to expand those bylaws. I don't want to take on the world. I want us to serve a niche and serve all its personal financial needs as best we can.

At the same time, I did want to penetrate our market better. In the old days, we'd insured only active-duty and retired officers. Those who separated at the end of a tour of duty or left before the end of their 20-year hitch, they were out. USAA changed its bylaws in 1962 to allow separated officers to keep their memberships, but the company had done nothing to bring back the ex-officers who'd left. In 1968, we had 75% of active-duty officers and only a fraction of all those former officers. So we set out to get them back and then hold onto them. Today 95% of all active-duty officers and warrant officers are members, and we've managed to capture several hundred thousand of those separated and retired officers as well.

If I wanted to expand our world further, my next obligation might be to take on enlisted personnel, which would be nine times what we're doing now. But how far do we want to go? Aren't we better off serving the needs of our members and customers and making sure that service, not growth, is the objective?

But many of your employee policies depend on growth. You can't go on promoting 45% of your employees every year unless the company is growing. What if military budgets get cut, there are very few new officers, and your customer base shrinks?

We've taken care of that in two ways. First, it's only our property and casualty insurance—auto and homeowners—that we sell to members only. Anyone at all can use our bank and credit cards or buy our life insurance and mutual funds. Second, we have added one group to our auto and homeowners market. In 1971, we began offering associate membership to the children and grandchildren of members. As associate members, they can buy the insurance, but they have no ownership. Most of our growth today comes from that segment.

Can you do that and maintain the quality of your membership? In terms of education, affluence, self-discipline?

They tend to be chips off the old block. Take education. Something like 42% of their parents did graduate work. Now we see the children getting educations at the same level. We are a little tighter on underwriting on those children, since the culture they've grown up in is not quite the duty-honor-country culture their parents knew. But there's plenty of growth potential there; so far we've penetrated only 40% of that market.

But why don't *you broaden your membership? There must be other professional groups that would meet your standards for education, income—even integrity. Why not doctors or architects or airline pilots?*

But where do we stop? And do we give them ownership? Our present members get special treatment, and they need special treatment.

If we bring in architects and engineers and doctors, and if the nonmilitary professionals come to outnumber the officers, what happens when the country goes to war? I'm afraid they'd be apt to say, "Let's put in a war clause. I don't want to insure the lives of people when someone's actually trying their best to kill them!"

No, I want to stick to our members. You know, it takes a certain kind of courage to stick to a niche, and I've thought a lot about niche marketing. Instead of skimming the market with a series of gimmicky products that will always attract *someone*, it means forming a bond with your customers, and it means providing for their needs in depth.

I wanted USAA to think about the events in the life of a career officer and then work out ways of helping him get through them. Or "her," though in those days it was pretty much only "him."

Anyway, he gets married, he buys a house, he has children, they learn to drive, they go to college, he retires. All of it on a fairly small, flat income.

So one of the first things I did at USAA was to send our members questionnaires asking if they were interested in life insurance, banking, a car-buying service, car leasing, home mortgages, mutual funds, a whole smorgasbord of offerings. And the answer was yes, they were interested in all of it. On the basis of those replies, I managed to persuade the board to change the bylaws and offer those products.

You wanted to offer them broader services. But didn't that put you into direct competition with financial institutions other than insurance companies?

Right, and we couldn't compete on bonding alone. We would also have to outperform others on price, quality, convenience, and efficiency. We were going to have to offer mutual funds as good as the best. From here in San Antonio, we were going to have to offer banking services to people all over the country and the world. We were going to have to do marketing and servicing by telephone, which was still a fairly innovative concept in 1968.

What it all pointed to was technology. Computers, automation, telecommunications. And that was a new idea—it was certainly new to USAA.

We had two pieces of electronic hardware back then, and we chose people to operate it on the basis of their high-school math grades. It was like buying a piano and then assigning concert duty to anyone who knew what notes looked like. It was a case of the deaf leading the blind. We had no training program and no systems-development people.

The systems were archaic. In auto insurance, every application and letter that came in went through 55 steps. The first person would open the envelope, remove the paper clips, and pass it to the second person, who would check addresses on big Rolodexes and write in corrections with a pen, then pass it to the third person, and the fourth person, and so on—55 steps. There were people who did nothing but staple and people who did nothing but stuff envelopes and people who did nothing but punch their time cards in and out.

And, incidentally, the ones who weren't doing much work weren't having much fun. The average employee stayed with the company for 11 months. We were giving terrible service and boring our employees—and that is a question of cause and effect. No one's happy in a slack, easy job. Working harder makes people happier. Or at least working better makes people happier. Technology was going to be our way of doing better work.

How did you go about it?

The first thing I did was to bring in an automated policy-writing system. We didn't have the resources to develop our own, so we bought one from another insurance company and had them come in and train our people. It worked with code sheets and punch cards that were run through in batches at night, very primitive stuff, but we thought it was wonderful.

From there we gradually moved on to a quasi-on-line system for claims that tracked and more or less integrated the entire claims process. It would look pretty old-fashioned today, but at the time—the mid-1970s—it was the Cadillac of the industry. And it was a danger for us.

In what way?

Information technology has to be a strategic competitive weapon—not just a cost center. We'd spent a lot of money and acquired the best automated claims system in the country, probably in the world—so the danger was complacency. We were in danger of resting on our laurels, of using that new system as if it were merely a better machine rather than a new way of doing business.

We had no cause for complacency, because we were still basically reactive. Someone would ask for the automation of some task, some state would pass a new law or regulation, and we would adapt with the latest technology we could find. It was short-term thinking. And I was beginning to see that we needed a broad systems strategy that looked ahead.

The result was a five-year plan. It consisted of 81 projects and had a projected price tag of $100 million. In the end, it took us six years and $130 million. But that wasn't bad, considering that along the way we enlarged the scope of the plan, made a lot of changes, dropped some projects, added others, and incorporated new technology as it came along. More important, we achieved our basic goal, to create an AIE—an automated insurance environment—that includes policy writing, service, claims, billing, customer accounting, everything.

More important yet, it changed the way we think. Now when you want to buy a new car, get it insured, add a driver, and change your coverage and address, you can make one phone call—average time, five minutes—and nothing else is necessary. One-stop, on-line, the policy goes out the door the next morning about 4 A.M. In one five-minute phone call, you and our service representative have done all the work that used to take 55 steps, umpteen people, two weeks, and a lot of money.

That's faster and more efficient, all right, but how does it represent a change in the way you think?

It changes everybody's definition of what's possible, of what we can do, of what they themselves can do. First, it's a radical change in the status of the service representative. Thirty years ago, this was a little bit of a sweatshop. For example, employees were issued pencils one at a time. When you thought you'd used it up, you took it to the pencil lady, and she measured it, and if it was short enough, she gave you a new one. Compare that with the situation today, where technology gives people the direct power and authority to make things happen, to create change. Our employees aren't just agents for the company, they *are* the company.

Second, it's a revolution in the relationship between the company and the customers, who now have instantaneous access to and control over their own financial transactions, no matter whom they're talking to. We've got 14,000 employees, but every time you call, you're talking to someone who's got your file in front of them. Someday, we won't even mail the policies out. You'll trust us to make the changes and keep the policy here.

Third, it means an end to paper—almost. We get about 150,000 pieces of mail every morning, of which 60% to 65% are checks. Of the remainder, less than half ever leaves the mailroom. All of our policy-service correspondence is imaged, indexed, prioritized, and it's then instantly available anywhere in the company. Work management is hugely simplified and leveraged. We can change priorities on the fly, for example. Someone gets sick and her work can be sent to someone else. A supervisor can check a backlog, find out why it's there, change the order and logic of the priorities, and clear it away.

We've only just started building an image system for claims, where there's quite a bit of paper—affidavits, powers of attorney, photographs—but the future there is even greater.

You mean a step beyond paperlessness?

In claims, the next step is the integrated workstation. We're working with IBM to develop a multimedia system that will include imaging, pictures, voice, and video. Say you're discussing a court case with a doctor and a lawyer in Florida. You'll be able to go through the file together—color photographs of injuries, a recording of the original telephoned claim, a video of the damage to the car—all of that on a telephone-integrated desktop workstation.

We're also going to build in knowledge-based systems—expert systems—that will leverage the knowledge of our experts down to a level below them. People will be able to underwrite and approve loans, for example, at a level much higher than their education and experience would otherwise allow.

We ran a little experiment with an expert system to detect fraud, and it worked so well—90% accuracy—that we've kept it.

Don't expert systems lead to de-skilling? How do you get people to internalize an electronic decision tree?

Right now, we have service people who do automobile, homeowners, and renters, including pretty difficult and unusual problems. But there are limitations on how many areas they can cover efficiently. Where we're headed, we hope, is to integrated expert systems that will allow those same people to do mutual funds, life insurance, credit cards, banking services, and other things as well, including some fairly complicated transactions. It's the next challenge, and I think it means an increase in skills, comprehension, and job satisfaction, not a decrease.

The systems we're developing are transparent. You can ask them why, and they'll explain the rules and show you why they did what they did. What's more, if you find a new rule, you can add it to the sequence. So both the operator and the system can learn.

How did you get your people to accept such challenges? How did you get them to accept technology in the first place? A lot of knowledge workers have found it threatening.

We're not interested in technology for its own sake, only if we can turn it into better service and more satisfying jobs. To begin with, we've never laid off a single soul because of technology, and we hope we never have to. We also spend an inordinate amount of time keeping users involved from the moment we begin developing any new program. Consequently, when we finally get the product, it's what they need, want, and like. They can sit down and say, "Yes, this feels right."

We use what we call living laboratories, users who test it and kick it and break it during development. When the product is ready, they become the nucleus that goes out and sells it to the first group that's going to use it. They can say, "You're going to love it, and here's why."

Then, by and by, that first group sells it to the next group, and so on. It takes a lot of planning to make sure it's not threatening, to make sure it will lead to better service and better jobs. We try very hard to think of everything—the productivity effects, the sociological effects, the comfort effects, as well as the bottom-line effects. For us, customers and employees are both precious resources.

So far, the employees have loved it. They can't wait to get the newer applications. So it's worked for the company. Over the last ten years, we've had 35% growth in policies in force, but the growth in service personnel has been zero. And people love these jobs. How did we do that? We did it with technology.

So the ultimate result of a really tenacious dedication to service, job enrichment, and niche marketing turns out to be an exceptional flowering of technology.

The big companies love developing new systems with us because we put a strain on everything they make. If a system can be broken, we'll break it. We're the largest single electronic business site in the country. We do eight million transactions a day, counting one transaction every time somebody hits "enter" on a keyboard.

There's no computer built that can handle our volume alone. We have six IBM 3090s, the biggest thing they build, all lashed together. We also have elaborate backups. Everything we do is written somewhere else on another tape or another disk almost simultaneously.

If we lost our entire center—if an airplane flew right into the building—it would take us from 2 to 11 days to get back in operation, depending on the day of the week. All we'd lose would be the conversations taking place at the moment of the disaster.

And the cost? I know you spent $130 million developing some of these systems, which have come to constitute a virtual core competence of this corporation. But how much does technology cost you annually? And how much do you continue to spend on development?

We don't think of technology as a cost center. It's a strategic weapon. It contributes to service, so cost is not the only or even the primary consideration.

But isn't there a strategic line somewhere between customer service and financial irresponsibility? Isn't there ever a conflict between altruism and profits?

What you need to understand is that what you call core competence and strategy and altruism and mission are all the same thing for USAA. They're all a matter of community. This company has formed a bond with its members, and the members have a natural bond with one another. We're a family, if you like. And our part of the family, the company, provides financial services for the rest of the family, the members. That's the knitting we stick to, that's our strategy, that's our goal. Not the narrow slots of property insurance or life insurance or banking or credit cards or technological leadership or whatever, but the financial security and peace of mind that our family needs and wants.

3
The Power of Predictability

Howard H. Stevenson and Mihnea C. Moldoveanu

In the beginning, life was uncertain, brutish, and short. Was the creature behind the bush the hunter's lunch, or was it looking for lunch? A moment's hesitation, and the hunter went hungry or satisfied another hunter's appetite. Over time, the hunter was able to predict, just by watching the creature's shadow, whether it was suitable prey. Bands of hunters put their individual experiences to collective use: If some people flushed and chased prey, and then others ambushed, the probability that everyone would eat increased. Being part of a group offered physical protection, which the solitary hunter didn't have, and gave the hunters confidence in their ability to predict the outcome of their expeditions. Without such confidence, the members of the first organizations might well have starved.

As people turned from hunting to farming, then to manufacturing, the link between organizations and the need for predictability became more complex. People joined organizations to make their lives more predictable, and those organizations depended on other organizations to perform certain activities in a predictable manner. Consider Adam Smith's pin maker. He went to work with other pin makers because trying to earn a living by making and selling pins on his own would have been even riskier than hunting on his own.

Membership in an organization gave the pin maker economic security, but think about the degree of predictability that his activities

Howard H. Stevenson is the Sarofim-Rock Professor of Business Administration at the Harvard Business School in Boston, Massachusetts. Mihnea C. Moldoveanu is a research associate and doctoral candidate, also at the Harvard Business School.

required: Coal and iron had to be mined, the iron had to be turned into steel, and the steel had to be delivered to his workplace. The pin maker's ability to get his job done depended on a complex sequence of events over which he had little control, but the events were predictable enough that he needed to concentrate only on creating a sharp point on a steel wire and cutting it as many times as possible during the hours allotted to work. In turn, milliners, who needed pins to fashion hats, were able to concentrate on their work without having to worry about what went on in the pin makers' workplace or in the steelworks.

Fast-forward to the 1960s, when global organizations—many the size of small countries—promised their employees not only economic security but also personal fulfillment and respect from fellow employees and the community, in return for performing a handful of clearly delineated activities. Like the pin maker, each individual depended on the predictability of other employees with whom he or she had little contact. And most members of such organizations could work with the same assurance that the pin maker had: Other people understood what they were supposed to do, would do it, and all would be rewarded for a job well done.

Leaders of global organizations—indeed, leaders of all organizations—have focused on increasing predictability for their subordinates and thus for the organization as a whole. Recall Frederick W. Taylor's turn-of-the-century theory of scientific management, according to which the manager's job was to set clear standards of performance. Later generations of gurus urged managers to develop a strong, clearly defined corporate culture and involve employees in managerial decision making. As a result, managers learned to help employees calculate the consequences of their actions and gauge which activities would improve their standing in the company. Predictability in the workplace led employees to make sacrifices today, confident that they would be rewarded tomorrow. It led managers to invest in training, secure in the knowledge that their employees would remain with the company long enough to pay back some of that investment. In sum, predictability built the trust that allowed people to synchronize their actions in mutually productive ways.

What is happening to predictability in an intensely competitive, rapidly changing global economy? It is being destroyed. The practices that leaders are adopting to make their organizations more competitive are ignoring the human need for predictability. Consider the effects of the tonics now being taken in the name of competitive well-being: Reengineering throws out all the old procedures and rules of thumb by which an organization has operated. Continuous-improvement programs promise only that an organization's rules will continue to change. Matrix management requires that two (or more) managers, who need not agree with each other, judge employees' work and determine their future in the company. "Rightsizing" sheds people, often regardless of their individual skills or performance.

Nowhere is the notion of predictability more threatened than in the virtual organization, in which individuals are left to fend for themselves, much like the solo hunter. In fact, judged by the standard of predictability, the virtual organization is not much of an organization at all. Instead of producing and selling something, knowing what the exact reward for performing that work will be, members of virtual organizations spend most of their time negotiating their share of the value produced and their relationships with other players—both customers and suppliers—who are constantly moving in and out of their virtual world. The pin maker, who enjoyed predictability up and down the value chain, was able to spend his time making pins. The individual in the virtual organization, however, must *create* a value chain before anything of value can be produced.

The need for predictability is not a need for guarantees. In fact, many people seek out games of chance in the spirit of nothing ventured, nothing gained. But such games have rules and calculable probabilities of achieving one of a set of known outcomes. The participants can weigh the odds and act accordingly, like restaurateurs who buy supplies and staff their kitchens based on the probability that a certain number of people will dine at their restaurants on a given day of the week in a given season. Even if people can't know the odds of achieving a certain outcome, they are willing to accept uncertainty if they believe that their experience gives them an advantage. Commercial fishermen can't know the exact odds of whether a storm will blow up on a given day, but they keep their boats and their gear maintained and trust that their experience will enable them to navigate rough seas. Similarly, R&D managers can't know whether their teams will develop a winning product, but they enlist the best people and develop the best processes to improve the odds of a breakthrough.

In many organizations today, however, people can't control the outcomes of their actions or even tip the odds in their favor, no matter how much experience they have. Moreover, even if they do achieve a desired outcome, they can't always predict the consequences. Imagine trying to interest someone in playing a competitive sport in which the determination of whether the high score or the low score wins is not made until after the final whistle. No one of sound mind would participate. Similarly, imagine asking division managers to cut costs without letting them know whether their divisions will be rewarded or put up for sale if they achieve that outcome. People will go mad if punishment and reward are doled out randomly and if they cannot know in advance whether a given outcome will be a win or a loss.

The discontinuities that so many current management practices introduce into people's lives may not drive them mad, but they do encourage them to keep their résumés up to date and their commitments to their employers minimal. Employees' concerns are not What can I do to create value? but What do they really want me to do? How will I be evaluated and by whom? Is my division part of the company's core business? If the restructuring succeeds, what will it mean for me? Reengineering, restructuring, rightsizing, matrix management, and the creation of virtual organizations may yield short-term efficiencies, but the cost is a lot of time and energy spent reading tea leaves.

Many managers explain the erosion of predictability inside their organizations by pointing to the difficulty of surviving in an unpredictable world. Despite their efforts to do the right thing with respect to quality, business processes, environmental compliance, skills development, technology, and labor relations, many companies may suddenly find themselves in the wrong business and, soon thereafter, out of business. Customers are fickle. Every decision has to be backed up by a flood of information. The government continually changes its tax and regulatory requirements. Political change often makes planning impossible, and savings evaporate, skills are devalued, and human interactions take sudden, unanticipated turns. Fortunes rise and fall with the performance of the stock market rather than of the company. All that unpredictability is real, but too often, managers think first about making their own lives more predictable. Golden parachutes, strategic restructuring, downsizing, and an emphasis on earnings per share all improve predictability for those at the top at the expense of those below them.

People will do whatever they can to find a world in which they can predict the outcomes of their actions and the consequences of those outcomes. Some flock to employers that offer their faithful a clearly defined mission and a role in achieving it. By laying down a few rules by which people can succeed, companies such as Microsoft, Amway, and McKinsey simplify a complicated world.

Other people give their first loyalty to professions or industries—accounting, finance, investment banking, or marketing—rather than to a company. For those people, professional titles offer the same kind of predictability as a well-known brand. Still others become lone wolves, who take without giving, unencumbered by the imperative to build trust. They often can be found acting as CEOs and advisers for hire, taking millions of dollars for a couple of years' work and leaving others to clean up after them.

Are the leaders of today's organizations supposed to think first and foremost about providing a safe haven in an unpredictable world? No. The manager's primary responsibility, of course, is to ensure that the organization does what it sets out to do as efficiently as possible. But meeting that challenge means enlisting other people, who won't be able to work efficiently if they feel that there is no order around them and if they can't determine where their actions will lead them. That is not to say that managers should reject the various programs that promise organizational improvement. Such programs are some of the only tools for survival in an intensely competitive and uncertain world. But managers must recognize the paradox that many of those tools are in fact destroying what holds organizations together.

The best way to approach organizational change is with the realization that dire predictions are probably better than no predictions at all or positive predictions that no one believes. When Winston Churchill became prime minister of Great Britain in 1940, he told the House of Commons, "I have nothing to offer but blood, toil, tears, and sweat." The leaders of today's organizations must start with the same kind of honest assessment of the organization's situation, the possible outcomes of any action the organization may take, and what each outcome will mean. If, for example, managers try to fool their employees, and perhaps even themselves, by downsizing a little at times, promising after each round of layoffs that, at last, the organization is healthy, they destroy predictability—and morale—for those who have been kept on. Better to make one cut than to amputate two inches at a time.

In addition to making few promises and keeping the ones they do make, managers can help maintain predictability during a time of change by establishing the rules by which people can succeed and then playing by those rules themselves. People who perform well according to the rules will not find their lives disrupted by abrupt and arbitrary changes. They will understand the consequences of a given action and what those consequences will mean for them. If, on the other hand, managers seem to decide arbitrarily whom to let go when they have to downsize, without considering employees' performance, they make life highly unpredictable for everyone. Moreover, they fail to improve the quality of the organization.

Creating an environment in which people can predict the consequences of their actions goes hand in hand with ensuring predictability in an organization's relations with both customers and suppliers. Good marketing and consistently high quality help customers know what to expect from a company. If customers come to trust a company, they are likely to turn to it often to solve their problems and to learn about new products and services.

A similar logic applies to suppliers. Managers might be tempted to spend a lot of time searching for the cheapest supplier, but what will the company get out of such arrangements? Unpredictable service, most likely. Cultivating relationships with a stable set of suppliers helps each side know what to expect from the other. When a company takes the time and effort to share its strategy with suppliers, it motivates them to do whatever they can to help the company produce the best products, now and in the future. Moreover, solid relations with suppliers also make life more predictable for the company's employees, who can then focus on delivering the best products and services to their customers.

Human beings have finite energy and finite time in which to expend it. The more that managers make clear to employees and other stakeholders which courses of action will improve their lives, the more that employees can focus on creating value. What our ancestors discovered holds true today: Survival still depends on the ability to respond quickly to change, and organizations can still help people predict the outcomes of their actions and thus act swiftly and predictably. Without predictability, people will be too scared not only to take risks but to take any actions at all. Life within an organization will become what it was for the solitary hunter: uncertain, brutish, and short.

PART

III

Investor Loyalty

3
Capital Disadvantage: America's Failing Capital Investment System

Michael E. Porter

To compete effectively in international markets, a nation's businesses must continuously innovate and upgrade their competitive advantages. Innovation and upgrading come from sustained investment in physical as well as intangible assets—things like employee skills and supplier relationships. Today the changing nature of competition and the increasing pressure of globalization make investment the most critical determinant of competitive advantage.

Yet the U.S. system of allocating investment capital both within and across companies is failing. This puts American companies in a range of industries at a serious disadvantage in global competition and ultimately threatens the long-term growth of the U.S. economy.

These are the principal findings of a two-year research project sponsored by the Harvard Business School and the Council on Competitiveness, a project that included 18 research papers by 25 academic experts. This article draws on those papers and my research to offer a

Author's note: This article draws heavily on the research and commentary of my colleagues on the project on Capital Choices, cosponsored by the Harvard Business School and the Council on Competitiveness. Rebecca Wayland's research assistance and insights have contributed importantly to this study.

The issues discussed in this article are the subject of a large body of literature, which is extensively referenced in the project papers. Among the more broadly based studies is Michael T. Jacobs, *Short-Term America* (Harvard Business School Press, 1991). Other valuable contributions include the report of the Institutional Investor Project at the Columbia University Center for Law and Economic Studies, *Institutional Investors and Capital Markets: 1991 Update*, and the Symposium on the Structure and Governance of Enterprise, *Journal of Financial Economics*, September 1990.

comprehensive analysis of the causes and recommended cures for the U.S. investment problem.

Critics of U.S. business frequently blame recent competitive short-comings on various issues: a short time horizon, ineffective corporate governance, or a high cost of capital. In fact, these issues are symptoms of a larger problem: the operation of the entire capital investment system. The system includes shareholders, lenders, investment managers, corporate directors, managers, and employees, all of whom make investment choices in a context determined by government regulations and prevailing management practices. The American system creates a divergence of interests among shareholders, corporations, and their managers that impedes the flow of capital to those corporate investments that offer the greatest payoffs. Just as significant, it fails to align the interests of individual investors and corporations with those of the economy and the nation as a whole.

The U.S. system for allocating investment capital has many strengths: efficiency, flexibility, responsiveness, and high rates of corporate profitability. It does not, however, direct capital effectively within the economy to those companies that can deploy it most productively and within companies to the most productive investment projects. As a result, many American companies invest too little, particularly in those intangible assets and capabilities required for competitiveness—R&D, employee training and skills development, information systems, organizational development, and supplier relations. At the same time, many other companies waste capital on investments that have limited financial or social rewards—for example unrelated acquisitions.

The problems in the U.S. system are largely self-created. Through a long series of regulatory and other choices with unintended consequences, changes have occurred in areas such as the pattern of corporate ownership, the way investment choices are made, and the nature of internal capital allocation processes within companies. At the same time, the nature of competition has changed, placing a premium on investment in increasingly complex and intangible forms—the kinds of investment most penalized by the U.S. system.

Finally, the American economy has become far more exposed to global competition, making investment even more important and bringing a cross-section of U.S. companies into contact with companies based in nations with significantly different capital allocation systems. It is this comparison between the U.S. system and other nations' systems that points up the real danger of continuing current practices.

The U.S. system first and foremost advances the goals of shareholders interested in near-term appreciation of their shares—even at the expense of the long-term performance of American companies. It is flexible, capable of rapidly shifting resources among sectors—even if this is not the path to innovation, dynamism, and improved productivity. It helps the United States prosper in some industries because of the high rewards it offers—even as it pressures others toward under- or overinvestment in differing ways.

The systemic nature of the problem also suggests the need to question much of what constitutes the American system of management: its emphasis on autonomy and decentralization, its process of financial control and investment decision making, its heavy use of incentive compensation systems. Failure to change the system will simply ensure the continued competitive decline of key sectors in the U.S. economy.

Yet our analysis of the U.S. investment capital allocation system also reveals how much potential for competitive strength exists in the United States. The United States possesses an enormous pool of investment capital. The problem lies in how this capital is allocated—at what rates and into what kinds of investments. One consideration is whether there is over- or underinvestment. A second is whether an investment is complemented by associated investments—that is, whether there are linkages among different forms of investments. For example, a physical asset such as a new factory may not reach its potential level of productivity unless the company makes parallel investments in intangible assets such as employee training and product redesign. A third consideration is whether private investments also create benefits for society through spillovers or externalities. For example, a company that invests in upgrading its employees and suppliers not only enhances its own competitiveness but also creates better trained workers and stronger suppliers that may allow it to pursue entirely new strategies in the future. Nations that encourage appropriate investment across a wide variety of forms and create these social benefits can leverage their pool of capital to build a strong and competitive national economy.

Meaningful change will be difficult because the American investment problem is far more complex than the conventional wisdom suggests. Many proposals to solve America's investment problem focus on only one aspect of the system, and they ignore the critical connections that tie the system together. To work, reform must address all aspects of the American system, and address them all at once. Policy-makers, institutional investors, and corporate managers must all play a role in creating systemwide change.

Evidence of an American Investment Problem

For more than a decade, anecdotal evidence from managers and academics has suggested that American companies have invested at a lower rate and with a shorter time horizon than German or Japanese competitors. There are a variety of measures of the comparative rates, patterns, and outcomes of U.S. investments and the behavior of U.S. investors that support and expand that earlier view. Among them are the following:

The competitive position of important U.S. industries has declined relative to those of other nations, notably Japan and Germany.

Aggregate investment in property, plant and equipment, and intangible assets, such as civilian R&D and corporate training, is lower in the United States than in Japan and Germany.

Leading American companies in many manufacturing industries such as construction equipment, computers, and tires are outinvested by their Japanese counterparts.

American companies appear to invest at a lower rate than both Japanese and German companies in nontraditional forms such as human resource development, relationships with suppliers, and start-up losses to enter foreign markets.

R&D portfolios of American companies include a smaller share of long-term projects than those of European and Japanese companies.

Hurdle rates used by U.S. companies to evaluate investment projects appear to be higher than estimates of the cost of capital.

U.S. CEOs believe their companies have shorter investment horizons than their international competitors and that market pressures have reduced long-term investment. Foreign CEOs agree.

The average holding period of stocks has declined from more than seven years in 1960 to about two years today.

Long-term growth has declined as an influence on U.S. stock prices.

Many recent U.S. policy proposals such as government funding of specific industries, R&D consortia, and joint production ventures implicitly reflect a private investment problem.

These findings present a broadly consistent picture of lagging American investment. But interestingly, the research has turned up some important complexities that derail simplistic explanations of America's reduced investment levels and shorter time horizon. For example:

The American investment problem varies by industry and even by company. A convincing explanation—and worthwhile remedies—must address these differences.

The United States does well in funding emerging industries and high-risk startup companies that require investments of five years or more. How does a low-investing, short-horizon nation achieve such a performance?

The average profitability of U.S. industry is higher than that in Japan and Germany, yet American shareholders have consistently achieved no better or lower returns than Japanese (and recently German) shareholders. There is thus no simple connection between average corporate returns on investment and long-term shareholder returns, as much conventional wisdom about shareholder value seems to suggest.

U.S. industry has overinvested in some forms, such as acquisitions. How does this overinvestment square with lower average rates of investment and underinvestment in crucial forms such as intangible assets?

There is persuasive evidence that some American companies systematically overinvest—this is documented by studies of the gains achieved from takeovers. Why is it that some companies underinvest while other companies apparently invest too much?

The United States has the most efficient capital markets of any nation and highly sophisticated investors. How can such efficient capital markets be guilty of producing apparently suboptimal investment behavior?

The investment problem seems to be more significant today than it was several decades ago. What accounts for this worsening situation?

Explaining these paradoxes and the differences in investment behavior across industries, companies, and forms of investment is essential to gaining a complete understanding of the American investment problem.

The Determinants of Investment

The determinants of investment can be grouped into three broad categories: the macroeconomic environment; the allocation mecha-

Exhibit I.

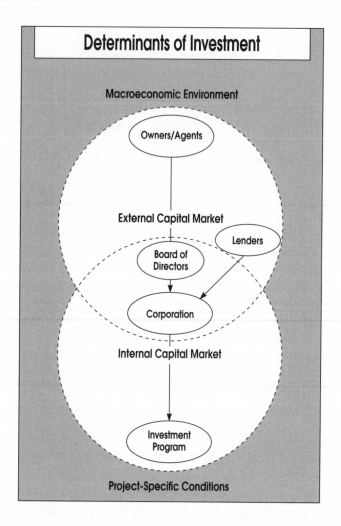

nisms by which capital moves from its holders to investment projects; and the conditions surrounding specific investment projects themselves (see Exhibit I).

The macroeconomic environment establishes the context in which investment by all companies in a nation takes place. A stable and growing economy tends to encourage investment, reassuring investors that returns will persist over the long term. In the United States, high federal budget deficits, low national savings rates, sporadic and unpredictable changes in tax policy, and a consumption-oriented tax code have dampened public and private investment over the past two decades.

Capital allocation mechanisms determine how the available pool of capital in a nation is distributed among industries, companies, and forms of investment. They operate through two distinct but related markets: the external capital market through which holders of equity and debt provide capital to particular companies; and the internal capital market in which companies allocate the internally and externally generated funds at their disposal to particular investment programs. The Harvard Business School Council on Competitiveness research has focused on the operation and linkages between these dual markets and their effects on investment behavior.

Finally, some projects will yield greater payoffs than others, depending on the nature of the industry, the competitive position of the company, and the nation or region in which the investment is made. As my previous research in *The Competitive Advantage of Nations* has indicated, the capacity to invest and innovate depends on the presence of specialized skills, technology, and infrastructure; sophisticated and demanding local customers; capable local suppliers; competitive local companies in closely related industries; and a local environment that encourages vigorous competition.

The External Capital Market

Investment behavior in the external capital market is shaped by four attributes (see Exhibit II). First is the pattern of share ownership and agency relationships—the identity of the owners, the extent of their representation by agents such as pension funds and money managers, and the size of the stakes they hold in companies. Second are owners' and agents' goals, which define the outcomes they seek to achieve through their investment choices. Goals are affected by a number of factors, including whether owners can hold debt and equity jointly and whether there is a principal-agent relationship. Third are the approaches and types of information used by owners and agents to measure and value companies. Fourth are the ways in which owners and agents can influence management behavior in the companies whose shares they own. These four attributes of the external capital market are all interrelated, and over time they will become mutually consistent.

Although exceptions may exist, each nation is characterized by a

Exhibit II.

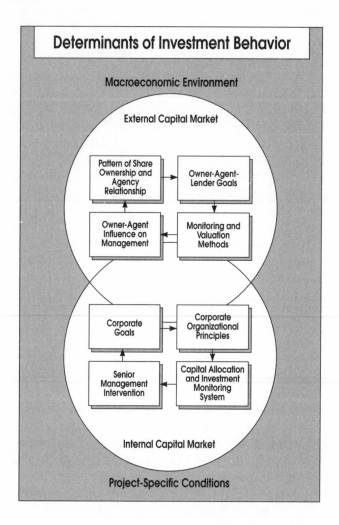

consistent system of influences that affect the majority of investors and corporations. The predominant configuration of the external capital market in the United States is strikingly different from that in Japan and Germany.

In the case of the United States, the attributes combine to create a system distinguished by fluid capital: funds supplied by external capital providers move rapidly from company to company, usually based on perceptions of opportunities for near-term appreciation. In the United

States, publicly traded companies increasingly rely on a transient ownership base comprised of institutional investors, such as pension funds, mutual funds, or other money managers, who act as agents for individual investors. In 1950, such owners accounted for 8% of total equity; by 1990, the figure had reached 60%.

These institutional agents hold highly diversified portfolios with small stakes in many—perhaps hundreds—of companies. For example, in 1990 the California Public Employees Retirement System (CalPERS) reportedly held stock in more than 2,000 U.S. companies; its single largest holding was 0.71% of a company's equity. This fragmented pattern of share ownership is due in part to legal constraints on concentrated ownership, fiduciary requirements that encourage extensive diversification, and investors' strong desire for liquidity.

The goals of American institutional investors are purely financial and are focused on quarterly or annual appreciation of their investment portfolio compared with stock indices. Because managers are measured on their short-term performance, their investment goals understandably focus on the near-term appreciation of shares. Mutual funds and actively managed pension funds—which represent 80% of pension assets—hold their shares, on average, for only 1.9 years.

Because of their fragmented stakes in so many companies, short holding periods, and lack of access to proprietary information through disclosure or board membership, institutional investors tend to base their investment choices on limited information that is oriented toward predicting near-term stock price movements. The system drives them to focus on easily measurable company attributes, such as current earnings or patent approvals, as proxies of a company's value on which to base market timing choices. The value proxies used vary among different classes of companies and can lead to underinvestment in some industries or forms of investment while allowing overinvestment in others. Given the difficulty of outperforming the market with this approach, some institutions have moved to invest as much as 70% to 80% of their equity holdings in index funds. This method of investing capital involves no company-specific information at all.

Finally, in the American system, institutional agents do not sit on corporate boards, despite their large aggregate holdings. As a consequence, they have virtually no direct influence on management behavior. Indeed, with small stakes in the company and an average holding period of two years or less, institutional agents are not viewed by management as having a legitimate right to serious attention.

The Japanese and German systems are markedly different (see Ex-

Exhibit III.

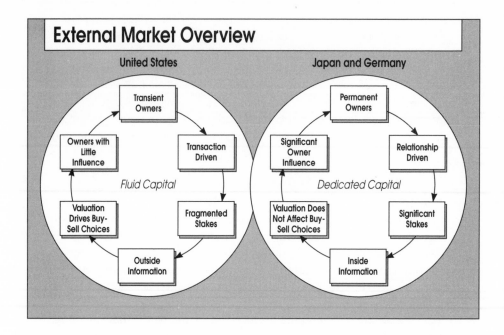

hibit III). Overall, Japan and Germany have systems defined by dedicated capital. The dominant owners are principals rather than agents; they hold significant stakes, rather than small, fragmented positions. These owners are virtually permanent; they seek long-term appreciation of their shares, which they hold in perpetuity. Unlike the U.S. system, in which the goals are driven solely by the financial transaction, the goals in these systems are driven by relationships. Suppliers and customers own stakes in each other, not to profit from the share ownership itself but to cement their business relationship.

The pattern of ownership and the goals of owners directly affect monitoring and valuation approaches. Since owners hold significant shares for long periods of time, they have both the incentive and the ability to engage in extensive and ongoing information gathering about the companies they own. And unlike the American system, principal Japanese and German owners are driven not by the need to make quick decisions on buying or selling stock for profit-taking but by the desire to assess the ongoing prospects of the company. They therefore command the respect of management, have access to inside information concerning the company, and, particularly in Germany, can exert considerable influence on management behavior.

Interestingly, while the permanent Japanese and German owners hold their company shares for long periods of time, the nonpermanent owners in these countries are prone to high-velocity stock churning, turning their shares over more frequently than owners do in the United States, and basing their investment decisions on even less information. While roughly 70% of Japanese stock is held for the long term, the remaining 30% is traded at such a rapid frequency that the average rate of trading in Japan is similar to the rate of trading in the United States. Yet in both Japan and Germany, share prices and pressure from nonpermanent owners and agents have virtually no direct or indirect influence on management decisions.

The Internal Capital Market

The internal capital market, the system by which corporations allocate available capital from both internal and external sources to investment projects within and across business units, mirrors the external capital market. The four attributes that shape investment behavior in the internal capital market parallel those that shape the external market (see Exhibit II). These four attributes are the particular goals that corporations set; the organizational principles that govern the relationship between senior management and units; the information and methods used to value and monitor internal investment options; and the nature of interventions by senior managers into investment projects.

An important aspect is highly imperfect information about future prospects and information asymmetries between capital holders—top managers—and those overseeing specific investment opportunities—business unit or functional managers. How a company organizes and manages its operations will affect the information that is available and the investments made by the company.

The U.S. internal market system is structured to maximize measurable investment returns. It is organized to stress financial returns, to motivate managers to achieve financial targets, to raise accountability for unit financial, and to base decision making and investment allocation heavily on financial criteria.

In the U.S. system, corporate goals center on earning high returns on investment and maximizing current stock prices. Management exercises the dominant influence on corporate goals, interpreting signals about desired behavior from the external capital market, influenced by compensation based on current accounting profits or unrestricted stock options that heighten stock price sensitivity.

Boards, which have come to be dominated by outside directors with no other links to the company, exert only limited influence on corporate goals. The presence of knowledgeable major owners, bankers, customers, and suppliers on corporate boards has diminished. An estimated 74% of the directors of the largest U.S. corporations are now outsiders, and 80% are CEOs of other companies. The move to outside directors arose out of calls for greater board objectivity. But the cost of objectivity has been directors who lack ties to the company and whose own companies are in unrelated businesses. As a consequence, they often lack the time or ability to absorb the vast amounts of information required to understand a company's internal operations. Moreover, most directors have limited stakes in the companies they oversee. While the median aggregate holdings of the board account for an estimated 3.6% of equity, many directors have no shares at all or only nominal holdings.

In terms of the organizational principles, the structure of American companies has undergone a significant change over the past two decades, with a profound impact on the internal capital market. Many American companies have embraced a form of decentralization that involves highly autonomous business units and limited information flows both vertically and horizontally. As a consequence, top management has become more distanced from the details of the business. Senior managers have little knowledge or experience in many of the company's businesses and often lack the technical background and experience to understand the substance of products or processes—partly because such knowledge is unnecessary in the typical decision-making process. Understandably, decision making in this system involves comparatively limited dialogue among functions or business units. Extensive diversification by American companies into unrelated areas has accentuated these tendencies and has further impeded the flow of information throughout the organization.

Both as a cause and an effect, capital budgeting in the U.S. system takes place largely through "by the numbers" exercises that require unit or functional managers to justify investment projects quantitatively. The system rarely treats investments such as R&D, advertising, or market entry as investments; rather they are negotiated as part of the annual budgeting process, which is primarily driven by a concern

Exhibit IV.

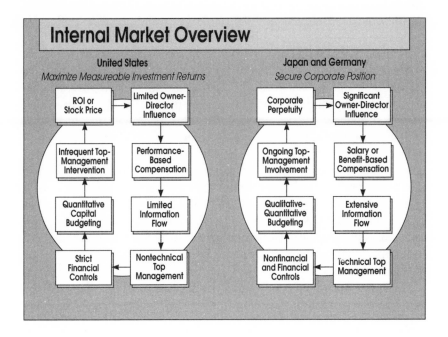

for current profitability. Intangible investments such as cross-functional training for workers may not even be tracked in the financial system—and thus may be sacrificed in the name of profitability.

Senior managers intervene infrequently, exerting central control through strict financial budgeting and control systems that focus on the unit's performance. Investment projects are placed on accelerated schedules under tight budgets, and senior managers step in only when financial measures indicate that a project is failing.

Both the Japanese and German systems are profoundly different from the American system (see Exhibit IV). For both, the predominant aim is to secure the position of the corporation and ensure the company's continuity. Information flow is far more extensive, and financial criteria play less of a determining role in investment decisions than in the United States.

In both systems, the perpetuation of the enterprise is the dominant goal. In Japan, this goal is reinforced by the fact that most directors are members of management; moreover, lifetime or permanent employment is the norm in significant-sized companies. In Germany, the supervisory board consists of representatives of banks and other significant owners, and in large companies, 50% of the board comprises representatives of employees. All major constituencies thus influence corporate goals. As far as top managers' performance incentives are concerned, in both Germany and Japan, current earnings or share prices play only a modest role in promotion or compensation.

Companies practice a form of decentralization that involves much greater information flow among multiple units in the company as well as with suppliers and customers. Japanese and German managers tend to have engineering or technical backgrounds, spend their careers with one company, advance through tenure in one or a few units, and possess a deep knowledge of the company's important businesses. Top managers get involved in all important decisions, which are usually made after extensive face-to-face consultation and discussions aimed at building consensus. This is both an effect and a cause of the fact that companies in Japan and Germany tend to be less diversified than U.S. companies; where diversification occurs, it tends to be into closely related businesses.

Financial control and capital budgeting are part of the management process—but technical considerations and a company's desire to ensure its long-term position in the industry drive investments. German companies are particularly oriented to attaining technical leadership; Japanese companies especially value market share, new product development, technological position, and participation in businesses and technologies that will be critical in the next decade.

In comparing the U.S., Japanese, and German systems, important differences in management practices emerge. For example, American managerial innovations have resulted in less face-to-face consultation, information flow, and direct management involvement in investment choices—all in the name of responsiveness and efficiency. Many of these innovations were the American solution to the problems of size and diversity that arose in the diversification boom of the 1960s and preceded the major changes that have occurred in the external capital market.

In contrast, Japanese innovations in management, such as just-in-time manufacturing, total quality management, and greater cross-functional coordination, have resulted in more vertical and horizontal information flow and involvement by management in decisions. This comes at the expense of efficiency in the short run—but often results in greater effectiveness and efficiency over time, as knowledge and capabilities accumulate.

The extensive flow of information is perhaps the most potent strength of the Japanese and German systems. Ironically, the U.S. system, designed to boost management responsiveness to the marketplace, actually limits and constrains managers in responding effectively by limiting the information used in decisions, working against crucial forms of investment, and all but blocking the achievement of cross-unit synergies.

Comparative Systems of Capital Allocation

The external and internal capital allocation markets are linked; together they combine to form a self-reinforcing national system for allocating investment capital. The way companies allocate capital internally is influenced by their perceptions of how equity holders and lenders value companies. Conversely, the perceptions of owners and agents about how companies are managed and how they allocate their funds internally will influence the way in which investors value companies and the way in which they attempt to affect management behavior. The use of stock options in management compensation creates a direct link between stock market valuation and management behavior.

Overall, the nature of the American system of capital allocation creates tendencies and biases in investment behavior that differ greatly from those in Japan and Germany (see Exhibit V). The American system:

> Is less supportive of investment overall because of its sensitivity to current returns for many established companies combined with corporate goals that stress current stock price over long-term corporate value. This explains why the average level of investment in American industry lags that in both Japan and Germany.

> Favors those forms of investment for which returns are most readily measurable—reflecting the importance of financial returns and the valuation methods used by investors and managers. This explains why the United States underinvests, on average, in intangible assets, where returns are more difficult to measure.

> Is prone to underinvest in some forms and, simultaneously, to overinvest in others. The U.S. system favors acquisitions, which involve assets that can be easily valued, over internal development projects that are more difficult to value and constitute a drag on current earnings. The greater overall rate of acquisitions in the United States is consistent with these differences.

Exhibit V.

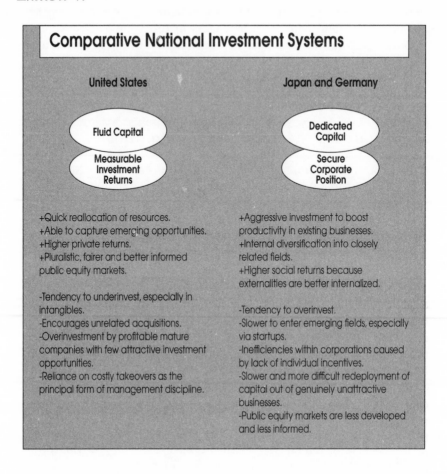

Encourages investment in some sectors while limiting it in others. It is at its best with companies in obviously high-technology or emerging industries, especially those with rapid growth and high perceived upside potential. The American system also supports investment in turn-arounds or other situations of clear discontinuity. In these cases, investors recognize that current earnings are irrelevant and seek other value proxies such as patents, new product announcements, research pipelines, and growth of new service locations that are more supportive of investment. This explains why the United States invests more than its competitors in some industries but less in others, why it performs well in funding emerging companies, and why it often awards high stock prices to turnarounds with current losses.

Allows some types of companies to overinvest. For example, case studies of takeovers demonstrate a tendency by managers to continue investing (and to continue accumulating cash) as long as current earnings are satisfactory or until the company's situation so clearly deteriorates that it changes hands. This explains why some companies waste resources while American industry as a whole lags in investment.

It is important to note that there are companies and owners in the United States who operate differently from the predominant national system—who have overcome the disadvantages of the American system and achieve superior results. Examples of these are companies that have permanent and active family ownership, such as Cargill, Hallmark, Hewlett-Packard, Motorola, and others, which seem to enjoy competitive advantages in investing.

For example, two of Motorola's most important businesses, semiconductors and cellular telephones, were almost canceled in their early stages because they did not generate clearly measurable financial returns. Robert Galvin, a member of the founding family of Motorola and the company's chief executive officer, intervened in both cases and continued the investments. In the semiconductor situation, Galvin overrode the decision of his board of directors. Today semiconductors and cellular telephones form the foundation for a large part of Motorola's business, generating substantial financial returns for its shareholders.

Investors such as Warren Buffett's Berkshire Hathaway have succeeded by, in effect, becoming permanent owners of acquired companies, supporting capable managements and concentrating on building the company. Overall, however, the U.S. system as it applies to the great majority of American owners, investors, managers, directors, and employees works at cross-purposes to investment decisions that will produce competitive companies and a strong national economy.

Trade-Offs Among Systems

While the U.S. system has significant disadvantages, it would be incorrect to conclude that it lacks any advantages or that the systems of Japan and Germany are ideal. Each national system necessarily involves trade-offs; thus while the U.S. system needs reform, it also embodies important strengths that should be preserved.

The U.S. system, for example, is good at reallocating capital among sectors, funding emerging fields, and achieving high private returns each period. These benefits, of course, come at a price. The responsiveness and flexibility of the system are achieved at the expense of failing to invest enough to secure competitive positions in existing businesses, investing in the wrong forms, and overinvesting in some circumstances.

The Japanese and German systems also have strengths and weaknesses. These systems encourage continued, aggressive investment to upgrade capabilities and increase productivity in existing businesses. They also encourage internal diversification into related fields, building upon and extending corporate capabilities. These qualities, however, also exact a cost in Japan and Germany. For example, these systems create their own tendency to overinvest in capacity, to proliferate products, and to maintain unprofitable businesses indefinitely in the name of corporate perpetuity. They also exhibit a slower tendency to redeploy capital out of genuinely weak businesses and an inability to enter emerging fields rapidly, particularly through start-ups. Managers generally have fewer performance incentives, and companies have a harder time dismissing poor performers.

In general, the U.S. system is geared to optimize short-term private returns; the Japanese and German systems optimize long-term private and social returns. By focusing on long-term corporate position and creating an ownership structure and governance process that incorporate the interests of employees, suppliers, customers, and the local community, the Japanese and German systems better capture the social benefits that private investment can create.

There is some evidence that the national systems are converging—that Japan and Germany are moving toward a more American-like system. Japanese banks may be forced to liquidate some of their equity holdings to maintain adequate cash balances; in Germany, there are proposals to limit bank ownership of equity. Yet these changes are modest—if Japanese or German owners are forced to sell some of their equity holdings, they will first sell their nonpermanent shares that are actively traded and have little influence on corporate behavior. Any major change in Japan and Germany would represent a substantial threat to those nations' economies due to their relatively uninformed traded capital markets.

Changes are also occurring in the United States, as institutional investors have discussions with management and some boards take a more active role in corporations. As in Japan and Germany, these changes appear isolated and sporadic, and the underlying causes of the U.S. investment problem remain the same. Neither small improvements in the United States nor hopes that Japan and Germany will change are substitutes for meaningful reform of the U.S. system.

The Case of Cummins Engine: Increasing Private Ownership in a Publicly Traded Company

Cummins Engine Company, a $3.4 billion industrial corporation, illustrates how a creative management team can structure a "privately owned, publicly traded" American company, approximating some of the advantages in the Japanese and German systems. In 1990, Cummins chairman and chief executive officer, Henry Schacht, concluded a deal that resulted in 40% of the company's stock being in the hands of patient investors, including three of its important business partners, company employees, and the founding Miller family. While it is still too early to evaluate the arrangement definitively, recent results indicate that Cummins' strategy may be paying off.

The Cummins story begins in 1919, when the company was founded in Columbus, Indiana. After World War II, Cummins enjoyed rapid growth into the 1970s. By 1979, Cummins Engine was the world leader in large, heavy diesel engines, with a 46% share of the market for over-the-road trucks. Following a succession of financings, the family stake in the company diminished; by 1980, 75% of the company's shares on the New York Stock Exchange were held by fragmented public investors.

In the 1980s, three factors combined to change the diesel engine market. First, the market's overall growth slowed significantly. Second, the emergence of energy efficiency and clean air as important policy issues put increased pressure on Cummins to invest in R&D—an expenditure that had already mushroomed from $22 million in 1971 to $68 million in 1980. Third, foreign competition intensified as Japanese producers prepared to enter the U.S. market armed with an estimated 30% cost advantage.

To respond to these challenges, Cummins embarked on a three-part strategy supported by an ambitious investment program. Cummins broadened its traditional product line within the heavy-duty markets and expanded into smaller diesel engines; entered the non-truck engine markets and developed its international operations; and initiated a full-scale restructuring program designed to reduce its costs by 30%, with prices scheduled to come down with costs. Cummins estimated the three measures would cost $1 billion; the company's total market value was $250 million.

By 1985, Cummins' strategy had yielded a new product line and a 5% reduction in costs. That year, however, Japanese producers entered the U.S. diesel market with products priced 30% below Cummins'. Faced with this challenge, Cummins chose to cut its prices to match the Japanese competitors, even though its costs had not yet fallen to that level— thereby sacrificing profits rather than market share. As a consequence, Cummins suffered losses for the next three years, while reaching cost parity with the Japanese by the late 1980s.

In 1989, Cummins faced a different kind of challenge. After Hanson PLC, known for buying companies and dramatically cutting costs and investment, acquired a 9.8% stake in the company, Cummins' customers became alarmed at the threat of future cuts in Cummins' investment program. In July 1989, the Miller family took the unprecedented step of buying back the Hanson shares, ending the uncertainty. However, almost immediately, Hong Kong investor Industrial Equity Pacific began acquiring a large position in Cummins and demanded a seat on the board. Cummins initiated a lawsuit against IEP, which ultimately sold its stake at a loss in 1991.

These two threats convinced Schacht and other top Cummins managers that the interests of the current shareholders and the interests of customers, employees, the community, and managers were in danger of diverging—and that Cummins' strategy was potentially in jeopardy. To address this issue, Schacht sought to revise Cummins' ownership structure.

In 1990, Schacht concluded a deal with three important business partners. Ford, which bought a 10% stake, Tenneco-J.I. Case, a 10% stake, and Kubota, a 5% stake. In addition, Ford took an option for an additional 10% of Cummins' shares. Each owner paid a 25% premium above Cummins' then-current stock price of $52 per share and agreed not to sell the stock for six years. The two largest shareholders, Ford and Tenneco, each received a seat on the Cummins board of directors. Financially, the deal targeted a 15% return on equity over a seven-year business cycle.

The Miller family retained a 4% stake in the company; employees held 10%. Together, these stable, long-term shareholders held 40% of the company's equity. Interestingly, other Cummins' customers applauded the move, even though it involved their competitors, citing the advantages of stable ownership and better products for all customers.

Under the new ownership structure, representatives of Ford and Tenneco participated on the board and actively supported the investment program. Senior managers worked without employment contracts, preventing management entrenchment and allowing strong board intervention. Accompanying the shift in ownership at Cummins were several reorganizations designed to streamline operations.

In 1990, Cummins continued to suffer reversals, this time a result of the recession and the onset of competition from a revitalized Detroit Diesel Corporation. In January 1991, Cummins stock hit a low of $32.50 per share.

Recent indications, however, suggest that Cummins' nine-year effort is beginning to pay off. New product introductions have been successful; in the traditional heavy duty truck market, Cummins' market share appears to have stabilized and begun a recovery. The company's international off-highway business has continued to grow. The Japanese challengers have exited the major U.S. markets. During 1991, Cummins reached breakeven and showed a profit for the first quarter of 1992. Finally, Cummins' stock rose to $76 per share in June 1992, a 100% increase over its $32.50 price of January 1991.

—Rebecca Wayland

Proposals for Reform

Overall, the American system for capital allocation is not serving the American economy well. None of the participants in the system is satisfied, and each one blames the other for the problem. American managers complain that owners and agents do not have the company's long-term interests at heart and are seeking only high, short-term profits. Institutional investors see managers as self-serving, overpaid, and underperforming when it comes to shareholder value. Owners are dismayed that many institutional investors underperform market averages. Small shareholders feel vulnerable and powerless. Employees fear a system that may cost them their jobs. Communities and their elected representatives worry about takeovers that threaten people's jobs, income, and the stability of the whole community.

Each group is behaving rationally—given the current circumstances. All are trapped in a system that ultimately serves the interests of no one. Each is pursuing its own narrow goals within the system—but the goals operate at cross-purposes.

Not surprisingly, there are calls for reform and regulation from all sides. Also, not surprisingly, many of the current proposals for reform would actually prove counterproductive, treating either symptoms or only a fragment of the problem and, in the process, further skewing the operation of the larger system.

One set of proposals, for example, seeks to slow down securities trading by taxing securities transactions or increasing margin requirements. These proposals, however, merely increase the inefficiency of the equity markets without addressing the underlying problem—the lack of alignment between investors' and managers' goals. Another set of proposals seeks to reduce the rate of trading by limiting corporate disclosures—for example, doing away with quarterly financial reports. The most likely result of this reform, however, would probably be to make investors even less informed.

A third group of proposals seeks to rebalance the relative power of owners and managers, for instance, by strengthening the proxy system or increasing the number of outside directors. These proposals also fail to address the systemic nature of the problem. "Objective" outside directors, for example, are closely aligned with management, they are not as expert in the business, and they lack the detailed knowledge of the company needed for a truly objective evaluation of a business's prospects. Moreover, if the goals of owners, managers, and shareholders remain unaligned, strengthening one player at the expense of another will only tip the system in one particular direction.

A fourth set of proposals would increase the use of stock options in management compensation. Yet unless restrictions were placed on managers' ability to exercise those options, this step would only heighten current pressures toward maximizing current stock price.

Finally, there are proposals that address the investment problem indirectly while seeking to improve overall U.S. competitiveness; for example, calls for providing government subsidies to particular sectors, creating joint production ventures, and relaxing U.S. antitrust laws. These measures may allow companies to economize on investment—but they run the risk of blunting innovation and undermining competitiveness. They do not address the reasons why companies seem unable to make the investments needed for competitiveness. The only real solution to the failure of the U.S. capital allocation system is to address the system as a "system."

Directions For Systemic Reform

The aim of reform should be to create a system in which managers will make investments that maximize the long-term value of their companies. The interests of capital providers must be aligned with those of the corporation so that investors seek out high-quality information that fosters more appropriate investment choices. CEOs and top managers must organize and manage their companies in ways that encourage investment in the forms that build competitiveness. And public policymakers must craft laws and regulations designed to align private returns and the public good. Policymakers should not create protective measures to shield companies from these pressures but can exert constructive pressures on companies and managers, provided they have appropriate goals and information.

In all of this, it is essential to remember that the United States is an internally consistent system with many component parts. Reform should therefore come through a series of changes, ideally all at once. In addition, appropriate reform will require that each important constituency in the system give up some of its perceived benefits. For example, institutions should not expect to gain greater influence over management without giving up some of their current trading flexibility; management should not expect informed and committed owners without giving them a real voice in decisions.

Reform is needed in five broad areas:

1. Improve the macroeconomic environment; enlarging the pool of capital and increasing the stability of the environment will reduce risk premiums and lower the cost of capital. Public and private sector saving should be increased and a more stable macroeconomic environment created to encourage a stronger foundation for investment.

2. Expand true ownership throughout the system; the current concept of ownership in the U.S. system is too limited, involving just capital, and ownership is largely restricted to outside shareholders. Outside owners should be encouraged to hold larger stakes and to take a more active and constructive role in companies. Directors, managers, employees, and even customers and suppliers should all hold positions as important corporate owners.

3. Align the goals of capital providers, corporations, directors, managers, employees, customers, suppliers, and society. It is possible to create a system of incentives and to alter the rules in a way that helps align the goals of all these constituencies, which share an inherent long-term commonality of interest.

4. Improve the information used in decision making; even if goals are better aligned, the quality of information used to allocate capital throughout the system will affect investment choices. This means greater access to information that better reflects true corporate performance and more use of qualitative assessments of a company's performance and capabilities.

5. Foster more productive modes of interaction and influence among capital providers, corporations, and business units.

Accomplishing these reforms will require changes on the part of government, institutional investors, directors, and managers.

Implications for Public Policy

Government, through policies, laws, and regulations, plays a decisive role in creating a nation's system for allocating investment capital. The current U.S. system reflects explicit regulatory choices, most of which emerged in the 1930s to deal with abuses in the financial markets at that time. Yet the cumulative effects of regulation have had unintended consequences for U.S. corporations; these consequences have never been carefully examined.

The following reforms rest on principles that differ markedly from those that have defined the regulatory framework of the traditional U.S. system. It is possible to modify incentives and eliminate unneeded regulatory guidelines to encourage more competitive investment behavior and, at the same time, avoid abuses. For example, current regulations limit the size of ownership stakes to prevent abuses by large owners. A better approach would be to broaden corporate ownership and align the goals of capital providers, corporations, managers, employees, and society. Through this approach, capital providers would become knowledgeable and constructive participants rather than adversaries.

Remove restrictions on investor share ownership; encourage long-term employee ownership; lower tax barriers to holding significant private ownership stakes. It is essential to modify the structure of corporate ownership. The regulations and tax policies that artificially restrict the ability of investors to hold significant corporate stakes should be reexamined. Ownership by employees is desirable, provided that employee owners are long term rather than transient. Under this provision, the market would continue to have the strength of a wide investor base, while gaining the benefit of owners with larger stakes in particular companies. The large number of substantial U.S. institutional investors will prevent any undue concentration of economic power.

Create a long-term equity investment incentive. The single most powerful tool for modifying the goals of owners and agents is a significant incentive for making long-term investments in corporate equity. This proposal aims to change the concept of ownership and the approach to valuing companies and, at the same time, to encourage the broad form of investment where the social benefits are the greatest.

Such an incentive would be carefully designed and narrowly drawn. It would apply only to investments in corporate equity of operating companies, and it would not apply to capital gains from investments in nonoperating companies holding real estate or other financial assets. Capital gains from bond appreciation, real estate appreciation, collectibles, and other sources would also be excluded. The incentive would require a minimum five-year holding period, with greater incentives provided for even longer holdings. It would be applied prospectively, limited to new investments and new gains.

The enactment of such an incentive would lead to changes throughout the entire system by changing the goals of owners and agents. Owners would begin to favor agents who deliver a greater proportion of income in the form of long-term equity gains and to penalize those who realize only short-term gains from rapid trading. Institutional investors, in turn, would modify their monitoring and valuation approaches, seeking out companies with attractive prospects five or more years in the future. A further consequence would be the development and distribution of better information, detailing the investment programs of companies and their long-term prospects, including physical and intangible assets.

If the long-term equity incentive is to have its full impact, it should be extended to currently untaxed investors, such as pension funds that account for a substantial fraction of equity capital and trading. The most practical way to do this is to pass through an equity investment incentive to pension or annuity beneficiaries. Beneficiaries would pay a rate of tax that varied depending on the source of their pension income. The effect of instituting such an incentive would be to create pressures from pension beneficiaries and trustees on their investment managers to deliver a higher and higher proportion of income from long-term equity gains. It should also be noted that extending the long-term equity incentive to pension beneficiaries extends the tax benefit to the U.S. work force, not just to Americans with high incomes.

Eliminate restrictions on joint ownership of debt and equity. Financial institutions should be allowed to hold equity for investment purposes in companies to which they have provided debt financing. Debt holders who also hold equity have greater incentive to invest in information and monitoring and to provide new debt financing for worthy projects.

Reduce the extent of subsidies for investment in real estate. U.S. tax policy has led to a disproportionate investment in real estate compared with other forms of investment that create greater social returns. Future investment incentives should redress this imbalance, favoring R&D, corporate equity, and training, rather than real estate.

Modify accounting rules so that earnings better reflect corporate performance. Because many of the most important forms of investment must be expensed under current accounting standards, accounting earnings are a flawed measure of true earnings. The accounting profession should create new standards for accounting for intangible assets such as R&D.

Expand public disclosure to reduce the cost of assessing true corporate value. Disclosure should be extended to include areas such as a company's expenditures on training, its stock of patents, or the share of sales contributed by new products, information that provides important measures of long-term corporate value.

Allow disclosure of "insider" information to significant long-term owners, under rules that bar trading on it. A small group of institutions and other owners who have held a significant ownership stake for a qualifying period—1% or more for one year or more—should have access to more complete information about company prospects than is required to be disclosed publicly, provided they do not disclose the information to third parties. Greater disclosure would open up an avenue for significant long-term owners to have a more informed dialogue with management, and it would support more informed valuation based on long-term prospects.

Loosen restrictions on institutional board membership. A direct role for significant owners on boards of directors will make boards more representative of long-term owner interest—provided, that is, that the goals of owners and managers have been realigned.

Encourage board representation by significant customers, suppliers, financial advisers, employees, and community representatives. The current trend in board membership has created boards populated by busy, underinformed CEOs. A far better approach would be to create a role on boards of directors for significant customers, suppliers, investment bankers, employees, and others linked closely to the company and with a direct interest in its long-term prosperity.

Codify long-term shareholder value rather than current stock price as the appropriate corporate goal. Existing corporate law identifies long-term shareholder value as the appropriate corporate goal. In practice, however, short-term stock price may take precedence as managers or directors who clearly compromise short-term shareholder returns are often subject to lawsuits. To remedy this situation, long-term shareholder value should be identified as the explicit corporate goal. The burden of proof should shift so that managers must explain any decision that is not consistent with long-term shareholder value.

Extend tax preferences only to those stock options and stock purchase plans with restrictions on selling. The use of unrestricted stock options and employee stock purchase plans fails to make managers and employees true owners because managers are prone to sell shares based on short-term stock price movements. To qualify for tax benefits, such plans should be restricted in terms of holding period and percentage of shares sold at any one time.

Provide investment incentives for R&D and training. Making the existing R&D tax credit permanent and creating a parallel tax credit for training investments would help stimulate private investments that become valuable national assets.

Implications for Institutional Investors

The American system of capital allocation creates perverse outcomes for institutional investors, especially for pension funds. These institutions should be the ideal long-term investors. Instead, the American system produces the paradoxical situation in which many institutions are entrusted with funds for extremely long periods, yet they trade actively. Transaction costs mean that many institutions underperform the market. Institutions are at odds with management, whom they see as misapplying corporate resources, yet they feel powerless to do anything about it. And worst of all, institutions are trapped as crucial actors in a system that undermines the long-term earning power of the American companies on which they have ultimately to depend.

Even without public policy changes, action by institutions can change this system. First and foremost, institutions must understand why managements view them as adversaries. They must understand the subtle consequences of their monitoring and valuation practices on corporate investment behavior. And they must recognize that greater influence over management will require less flexibility, slower trading, and greater knowledge of and concern for company fundamentals. Here are some specific changes institutional investors can pursue:

Increase the size of stakes. Increasing the size of stakes will help align the goals of investors and companies, improve the ability of investors to conduct in-depth research on the companies whose shares they hold, and send signals that institutions are serious owners who are interested in the long-term performance of the company.

Reduce turnover and transaction costs. Institutional investors underperform the market largely because of the transaction costs associated with the high turnover of investments. Reducing stock turnover will improve the return that institutions provide to their clients.

Select companies more carefully based on fundamental earning power. Companies with sustained growth potential and earning power will ultimately be rewarded with higher stock prices, even in the current system. The focus of valuation models should shift in this direction. To address information costs, institutions might also form syndicates in which one institution acts as the lead owner in the relationship.

Encourage changes in agent measurement and evaluation systems to reflect long-term investment performance. A new bargain between owners and institutional agents should shift the measurement and reward system toward fees tied to annual or multiyear results and ongoing reporting of fully loaded transaction costs from trading.

Transform interactions with management to productive, advisory discussions. Current interactions between institutional investors and managements are too often cat-and-mouse games played around guessing next period's earnings. What is needed instead are substantive discussions about the long-run competitive position of the company.

Create special funds to test these new approaches. Institutions should create special funds earmarked for long-term investing in significant corporate stakes in exchange for greater influence over management. If necessary, new agreements with owners would be drafted, modifying the funds' fiduciary responsibilities.

Support systemic public policy changes. By supporting the public policy reforms outlined above, institutional investors can help balance and integrate the American system.

Some institutions will resist these changes; they involve new skills, a new definition of investment success, and reductions in liquidity and flexibility. But institutional investors will realize big direct benefits— and benefit further by the creation of stronger, more competitive U.S. companies, on which their portfolios ultimately depend.

The Case of Thermo Electron Corporation

Thermo Electron Corporation, a $676 million company with products in a variety of high-technology fields, illustrates how a large company can structure itself within the U.S. capital allocation system to overcome the market's pressure toward underinvestment and to create opportunities for smaller, riskier, high-growth divisions.

Since its founding by George Hatsopoulos in 1959, Thermo Electron has grown from a startup focusing on high-technology capital equipment to a *Fortune* "500" company with products and research operations in the environmental, energy, metals processing, and biomedical fields. As Thermo Electron increased its portfolio of high-technology activities, its image in the capital markets became that of a large, mature company rather than an entrepreneurial venture. The startup losses required to develop and commercialize new technologies drained corporate earnings while the growth of emerging divisions was often lost in the company's consolidated financial results. Hatsopoulos, deeply concerned about the high effective cost of equity capital in the United States, set out to devise a way to finance the expansion of Thermo Electron that minimized the cost of funds and motivated employees. In 1983, he began the practice of issuing minority stakes in promising high-technology divisions to the public.

One example of how the practice works—and why it is important—is the spin-off Thermo Cardiosystems, Inc. (TCI), which is currently commercializing its research on HeartMate, implantable cardiac-assist devices (called "ventricular assist devices" or VADs) that could ultimately offer an alternative to heart transplants. The initial research on HeartMate lasted 22 years and cost a total of $50 million, with grants from the National Institutes of Health providing the funding. The research was conducted at Thermo Electron and later at Thermedics, a division that was one of Hatsopoulos's early partial spin-offs. When the product reached the commercialization stage in 1988, the grant began to diminish substantially. Initial product tests for HeartMate had been promising. However, it would take at least another seven years of investment to complete the regulatory process, build manufacturing facilities, and develop the market. This need for continued investment threatened to drag down the earnings of the parent.

In 1988, the company created Thermo Cardiosystems, Inc. and sold a 40% stake on the American Stock Exchange. The partial spin-off shifted TCI's ownership structure from a fragmented group of Thermo Electron and Thermedics investors to a structure in which Thermedics-Thermo Electron owned 60%, and a number of other investors, who were specifically interested in the long-term development of the heart technology, owned the balance. The partial spin-off also allowed TCI to raise $14.5 million in new equity at a far lower cost than its parent. TCI managers and employees received options in TCI stock, undiluted by the performance of the larger corporation.

As the controlling investor in TCI, Thermo Electron remained actively involved in its operations. Thermo Electron top managers were active members of TCI's board of directors (7 of whom were insiders), reviewed its five-year plan and quarterly financial results (often benchmarking them against other divisions), met with managers each month, and engaged in frequent brainstorming sessions to resolve divisional problems. Employees from the parent corporation's research department and from other divisions shared specialized expertise in medical-related areas, and in the process of making the transition from research to manufacturing and sales. Top managers' compensation plans included options in the stock of other Thermo Electron companies to encourage this cooperation. The parent also provided cost-effective and sophisticated administrative services that TCI could not support independently.

Since 1989, TCI has continued its investment in HeartMate, receiving Food and Drug Administration approval for clinical trials, implanting the VAD in over 80 patients worldwide, and establishing 16 FDA-approved test centers in the United States and four sites overseas. In the marketplace, TCI has benefited from the credibility with hospitals and customers in the medical field established by other Thermo Electron products. Although the commercialization process is still underway, TCI managers believe that the partial sale strategy created by George Hatsopoulos has already been instrumental in supporting the investment and other activities needed to bring HeartMate to the medical market.

—Rebecca Wayland

Implications for Corporations

Managers are not simply victims of the American system; they have helped create it. Managers have not only shaped the internal market through organizational and managerial practices, but they have also defined their relationship with the external market through such things as board composition, disclosure practices, and the nature of discussions with investors. American managers can play the leadership role in redefining the U.S. capital allocation system; they are the group best positioned to make changes in the current system and to benefit most from reform.

They also may have the most to change. Stated boldly, our research suggests the need to reexamine much of what constitutes the U.S. system of management, with its extreme approach to managing decentralization, its limited flow of information, its heavy use of certain types of incentive compensation systems, and its reliance on financial control and quantitative capital budgeting processes. This system, a post-World War II innovation, carries subtle costs for investment behavior, particularly investments in intangible and nontraditional forms. Some of the most significant changes that management can initiate are the following:

Seek long-term owners and give them a direct voice in governance. The most basic weakness in the American system is transient ownership. However, managers seem to underestimate their ability to do anything about this fundamental problem. As a remedy, managers should seek to have a smaller number of long-term or nearly permanent owners, thus creating a hybrid structure of a "privately held" and publicly traded company. Having fewer long-term owners would alter virtually every facet of the owner-management relationship—including governance, information sharing, measurement, and valuation.

Refrain from erecting artificial antitakeover defenses that insulate management. In the absence of pressure from owners and directors on managers for long-term performance, takeovers are a necessary form of oversight. There have been, however, some inappropriate takeovers, and most takeovers occur only after a prolonged period of corporate decline. The solution is not to erect antitakeover provisions. Rather, it is to reshape the American system so that takeovers are limited to those situations where they are an appropriate response to management's failure to build a long-term competitive position for the company.

See management buyouts as a second-best solution. Management buyouts are only a second-best solution to the problems of the American system. Invariably, the controlling owner in management buyouts is a transaction-driven, financial owner who seeks to realize returns on the investment over a short period of time in order to distribute them to investors.

Nominate significant owners, customers, suppliers, employees, and community representatives to the board of directors. Directors from these categories are likely to have the company's long-term interests at heart and to encourage management to make investments that will improve long-term competitive position.

Link incentive compensation to competitive position. The incentive compensation systems now used in much of American business are counterproductive. The incentives are simply based on the wrong things. Bonuses based on current profits obviously undermine investment, and stock options increase managers' attention to short-term share prices, particularly if there are no restrictions on selling shares. Compensation systems need to move in the direction of linking pay more closely to long-term company prosperity and to actions that improve the company's competitive position.

Move away from unrelated diversification. Unrelated or loosely related diversification only wastes capital and exacerbates the current management biases against long-term investment. The only way to build competitive companies is to concentrate on a few core fields and invest heavily in them to achieve a unique position.

Shift from fragmented to integrated organizational structures. The decentralized, profit center-based management structure in many American companies must be overhauled. What is needed is a system that recognizes strategically distinct businesses as the proper unit of management but manages them differently. Senior managers at the corporate level must have a substantive understanding of the core technology and the industry. Top management must be involved directly and personally in all significant decisions, particularly investment decisions. There must be extensive consultation and coordination among related business units, with opportunities for the units to share functions and expertise. Such a system would shift measurement and control away from solely financial results, raise senior management confidence in understanding complex investment choices, and better capture complementarities among discrete investment options.

Transform financial control systems into position-based control systems. A new philosophy of management control must be instituted, based as much on the company's extended balance sheet as on its income statement. A company's extended balance sheet measures the assets that constitute its competitive position. Included in such a measurement would be: a broader definition of assets, such as market share, customer satisfaction, and technological capabilities; a measurement of asset quality and productivity in addition to asset quantity; and relative instead of absolute measures, tracking the company performance against significant competitors.

Move to universal investment budgeting. Conventional approaches to capital budgeting were never ideal for evaluating investment choices; they fail to deal with the changing nature of investment. A new system is needed to evaluate investment programs instead of just discrete projects; to treat all forms of investment in a unified manner; and to evaluate investments in two stages—first, determining the asset positions needed for competitiveness and second, evaluating exactly how to achieve those positions.

Toward a Superior American System

The recommendations outlined above are designed to attack the weaknesses of the American system systematically, while preserving the system's considerable strengths. These changes will align the goals of American shareholders, their agents, and American corporations; improve the information used in investment decisions; better capture the externalities in investment choices; evaluate management decisions on criteria more suitable for competitive performance; and make internal management processes more consistent with the true sources of competitive advantage.

If America can make progress on these fronts, it will not only reduce the disadvantages of the U.S. system but also produce a system that is superior to Japan's or Germany's. A reformed U.S. system would be characterized by long-term rather than permanent owners, well-informed rather than speculative traders, and flexible rather than lifetime employees. A reformed U.S. system would produce more careful monitoring of management and more pressure on poor performers than what exists in Japan or Germany. The result would be less wasted investment and less internal inefficiency. Finally, a reformed U.S. system, with its higher levels of disclosure and transparency, promises to be fairer to all shareholders than the Japanese or German systems.

But altering the American system will not be easy. There is a natural tendency to limit change to tinkering at the margins, yet systemic change will be necessary to make a real difference. All of the major constituencies will have to sacrifice some of their narrow self-interests in pursuit of a system that is better overall.

Nevertheless, today there is widespread dissatisfaction with the system as it exists and concern over the direction and performance of American companies in global competition. This suggests that systemic change may be possible. If real change were to occur, the benefits would certainly accrue to investors and companies. But what is more important, the benefits would yield improved long-term productivity growth in the United States, and thus greater prosperity for the entire American economy.

2
Reckoning with the Pension Fund Revolution

Peter F. Drucker

Fifteen years after it was first chronicled, the "unseen revolution" transforming corporate ownership in the United States is now visible to all. The 20 largest pension funds (13 of them funds of state, municipal, or nonprofit employees) hold around one-tenth of the equity capital of America's publicly owned companies. All told, institutional investors—that is, primarily pension funds—control close to 40% of the common stock of the country's large (and many midsize) businesses. The largest and fastest growing funds, those of public employees, are no longer content to be passive investors. Increasingly, they demand a voice in the companies in which they invest—for instance, a veto over board appointments, executive compensation, and critical corporate charter provisions.

Equally important, and still largely overlooked, pension funds also hold 40% or so of the medium-term and long-term debt of the country's bigger companies. Thus these institutions have become corporate America's largest lenders as well as its largest owners. As the finance texts have stressed for years, the power of the lender is as great as the power of the owner—sometimes greater.

The rise of pension funds as dominant owners and lenders represents one of the most startling power shifts in economic history. The first modern pension fund was established in 1950 by General Motors. Four decades later, pension funds control total assets of $2.5 trillion, divided about equally between common stocks and fixed-income securities. Demographics guarantee that these assets will grow aggressively for at least another ten years. Barring a prolonged depression, pension funds will have to invest $100 billion to $200 billion in new resources every year throughout the 1990s.

America's failure, until quite recently, to recognize (let alone address) this power shift accounts in large measure for much of the financial turbulence of the 1980s—the hostile takeovers, the leveraged buyouts, and the general restructuring frenzy. Two problems in particular demand attention: For what should America's new owners, the pension funds, hold corporate management accountable? And what is the appropriate institutional structure through which to exercise accountability?

Actually, the United States is quite late among developed countries in concentrating ownership of large companies in a small number of institutions. In Germany, the country's three major banks have long controlled around 60% of the share capital of the larger companies, partly through direct holdings, partly through the holdings of their customers that, under German law, the banks manage and vote on. In Japan, the majority of large companies are members of a small number (ten at most) of industrial groups, the now-familiar *keiretsu*. In a keiretsu, 20% to 30% of the share capital of each member company is held by the other members and by the group's bank and trading company, and practically all credit to the member companies is provided by the group's bank. In Italy, half of the country's large businesses have been owned or controlled by the state since the 1930s. (IRI, the biggest state holding company, is the second-largest company in all of Europe.) The rest of Italy's big businesses are under the control of five or six huge conglomerates such as the Fiat Group.

Ownership in the United States is quite different. It is indeed unique. In Europe and Japan, stock ownership is a means to non-financial ends. A German bank's income from the companies to which it is the *hausbank* comes through commercial relationships rather than through its ownership stake. Deutsche Bank, Germany's largest financial institution, gets many times as much in fees from client companies for mundane services such as letters of credit as it receives from them in stock dividends. The keiretsu's first concern is power—power in the market, power over suppliers and subcontractors, power and influence with ministries and civil servants. As for tangible benefits, a keiretsu company profits far more from the business it gets from the other members than from their dividends. The government holdings in Italy constitute the largest concentration of economic power in any market economy. They serve primarily political objectives. The companies are run to provide jobs in politically important regions, to create lucrative executive positions for the party faithful, and to supply campaign funds for the parties in power.

Neither the German banks nor the Japanese keiretsu nor Italy's government nor its conglomerates has much interest in share prices or capital gains. They do not intend to sell. The American pension fund, by contrast, has no commercial ties to the companies in which it invests or to which it lends. It is not a "business" at all but an "asset manager." There are, as we shall see, important lessons to be learned from developments in Europe and in Japan, both as to what to do and what not to do. But in the United States, the rapid shift of ownership and credit power to these new and quite different owners poses totally new and very different problems.

Pension funds first emerged as the premier owners of the country's share capital in the early 1970s. But for 15 or 20 years thereafter, the realities of pension fund ownership were ignored. In part this was because the pension funds themselves did not want to be "owners." They wanted to be passive "investors" and short-term investors at that. "We do not buy a company," they asserted. "We buy shares that we sell as soon as they no longer offer good prospects for capital gains over a fairly short time." Moreover, the development was totally at variance with American tradition and with what everybody took for granted—and many still take for granted—as the structure of the U.S. economy. Long after pension funds had become the largest holders of equity capital, the United States was still referred to as the country of "people's capitalism" in which millions of individuals each owned small pieces of the country's large companies. To be sure, employees have become the owners of America's means of production. But their ownership is exercised through a fairly small number of very large "trustees."

Finally, though, the fog has begun to lift. The trustees of pension funds, especially those representing public employees, are waking up to the fact that they are no longer investors in shares. An investor, by definition, can *sell* holdings. A small pension fund may still be able to do so. There are thousands of such small funds, but their total holdings represent no more than a quarter or so of all pension fund assets. The share holdings of even a midsize pension fund are already so large that they are not easily sold. Or more precisely, these holdings can, as a rule, be sold only if another pension fund buys them. They are much too large to be easily absorbed by the retail market and are thus permanently part of the circular trading among institutions.

Ownership in the United States is far less concentrated than in Germany, Japan, or Italy—and will remain far less concentrated. Hence the U.S. pension fund still has more elbow room than the big bank in Germany, the keiretsu in Japan, or the industrial conglomerate in Italy. But some large U.S. pension funds each own as much as 1% or even 2% of a big company's total capital. All pension funds together may own 35% of the company's total capital. (For example, pension funds own 75% of the equity of the Chase Manhattan Bank.) The 1% holder cannot sell easily. And the 40% holder, that is, the pension fund community at large, cannot sell at all. It is almost as committed as the German hausbank to a client company or the Japanese keiretsu to a member company. Thus the large funds are beginning to learn what Georg Siemens, founder of Deutsche Bank and inventor of the hausbank system, said a hundred years ago when he was criticized for spending so much of his and the bank's time on a troubled client company: "If one can't sell, one must care."

Pension funds cannot be managers as were so many nineteenth-century owners. Yet a business, even a small one, needs strong, autonomous management with the authority, continuity, and competence to build and run the organization. Thus pension funds, as America's new owners, will increasingly have to make sure that a company has the management it needs. As we have learned over the last 40 years, this means that management must be clearly accountable to somebody and that accountability must be institutionally anchored. It means that management must be accountable for *performance* and *results* rather than for good intentions, however beautifully quantified. It means that accountability must involve financial accountability, even though everyone knows that performance and results go way beyond the financial "bottom line."

Surely, most people will say, we know what performance and results mean for business enterprise. We should, of course, because clearly defining these terms is a prerequisite both for effective management and for successful and profitable ownership. In fact, there have been two definitions offered in the 40 years since World War II. Neither has stood the test of time.

The first definition was formulated around 1950, at about the same time at which the modern pension fund was invented. The most prominent of the period's "professional managers," Ralph Cordiner,

CEO of the General Electric Company, asserted that top management in the large, publicly owned corporation was a "trustee." Cordiner argued that senior executives were responsible for managing the enterprise "in the best-balanced interest of shareholders, customers, employees, suppliers, and plant community cities." That is, what we now call "stakeholders."

Cordiner's answer, as some of us pointed out right away, still required a clear definition of results and of the meaning of "best" with respect to "balance." It also required a clear structure of accountability, with an independent and powerful organ of supervision and control to hold management accountable for performance and results. Otherwise, professional management becomes an enlightened despot—and enlightened despots, whether platonic philosopher kings or CEOs, neither perform nor last.

But Cordiner's generation and its executive successors did not define what performance and results produce the best balance, nor did they develop any kind of accountability. As a result, professional management, 1950s-style, has neither performed nor lasted.

The single most powerful blow to Cordiner-style management was the rise of the hostile takeover in the late 1970s. One after the other of such managers has been toppled. The survivors have been forced to change drastically how they manage or at least to change their rhetoric. No top management I know now claims to run its business as a "trustee" for the "best-balanced interests" of "stakeholders."

Pension funds have been the driving force behind this change. Without the concentration of voting power in a few pension funds and the funds' willingness to endorse hostile transactions, most of the raiders' attacks would never have been launched. A raider who has to get support from millions of dispersed individual stockholders soon runs out of time and money.

To be sure, pension fund managers had serious doubts about many buyouts and takeovers, about their impact on the companies in play, and about their value to the economy. Pension fund managers—especially the moderately paid civil servants running the funds of public employees—also had serious aesthetic and moral misgivings about such things as "greenmail" and the huge fortunes earned by corporate raiders, lawyers, and investment bankers. Yet they felt they had no choice but to provide money for takeovers and buyouts and to tender their shares into them. They did so in droves. (See "The Culture of Capital.")

The Culture of Capital

Anthropologists work primarily by watching and listening—living with the natives, learning their language, observing their customs, and talking with them at great length. In years of field work, we have studied Tanzanian coffee farmers, Caribbean monkeys, American lawyers, and now, most recently, the managers of U.S. pension funds.

We chose seven large funds—three public and four private—because they seemed to typify the growing power of institutional capital and were said to differ on significant variables such as investment philosophy, use of outside money managers, and approaches to proxy voting and over-all corporate governance. The actual differences greatly exceeded our expectations. Indeed, the differences were so great we began to wonder if it makes any sense to generalize about "institutional investors" or "pension funds" when discussing economic policy or arguing for changes in the law.

We interviewed managers and staff at each fund, asking first for a description of the fund's investment approach. We expected people to account for structure and strategy in economic terms. Instead, they spoke of political battles, personal disputes, and quirks of history. Our most striking finding is, in fact, the extent to which pension fund insiders do *not* offer economic explanations for the ways they manage money. The explanations they do offer often have some of the mythic quality that anthropologists have found in cultures from New Guinea to the South American rain forest. We can summarize our findings under five headings.

Creation Myths. The creation myths collected by anthropologists in more than 800 societies typically have two characteristics relevant to the folklore about the origins of pension fund investment strategies. First, they are self-evident to those who hold them and thus not open to question or analysis. Second, because they are self-evident, their adherents rarely think to look for alternatives.

Pension fund managers are aware of symbolic events and people of heroic proportions who preceded them, but the details are lost. At one public fund, we heard how the present trusteeship arrangement, with an unusually large lay board, had evolved in response to turf battles among prominent state politicians. For reasons lost in oral history, one private fund began life as a legally independent corporation, then, for equally obscure reasons, it stayed behind when the company moved its head-quarters to another city. Employees attributed the fund's remarkable independence to the physical separation of sponsor and fund offices, then used this independence to explain the fund's steadfast policy of highly selective, long-term investment. In other words, though they believed in the policy as such, they ascribed it to evolution rather than to planning.

We were struck repeatedly by their willingness to accept inherited structures and strategies without question. Again and again, we heard that practices were "instinctive" or "part of the corporate culture." To judge only by what we were told, the role of rigorous financial analysis seems to be secondary at best.

The Civil Service Culture. Anthropology's bread-and-butter concept is culture—the beliefs and practices that define a society's (or an organization's) way of life. The civil service culture of public pension funds exerts a powerful influence over the way these funds invest their resources. Staffs, for example, are small and modestly paid, and one executive echoed many others in pointing out that this environment attracts people who care more about security than achievement.

Many executives believe the principal authority public funds must answer to is the press and that the press is interested more in disaster than success. Not surprisingly, therefore, many public funds favor indexing—the practice of tying one's own portfolio to the performance of the market as a whole, either by investing in index funds or by buying and holding a collection of shares as diverse as, say, the Standard & Poor's "500." Indexing may keep a fund from outperforming the market, but it is also a guarantee against underperforming. If an indexed fund goes down, executives can blame its poor performance on the market as a whole, an explanation that even the press can understand.

Personal Responsibility and Blame. Indexing is a good example of fund management's preoccupation with responsibility. The most prominent feature of some fund structures is their ability to shift responsibility for decision making away from identifiable individuals. At one fund with complex, flexible investments, the CEO spent almost an hour trying to explain the decision chain. The larger the sums of money, the more people were involved. Truly substantial decisions were made by multiple committees, often with interlocking memberships. The complexity was such that it would be virtually impossible for anyone to assign credit for a major success or affix blame for a major failure.

In sharp contrast, there was no doubt about the responsibility for decisions at one private fund with a fairly stable portfolio. Each of a very few investment analysts was responsible for two or three industries, and their recommendations were virtually final. While it would be hard to say which was the chicken and which the egg, there was a clear correlation in the minds of these analysts between individual responsibility and the fund's buy-and-hold investment strategy.

Two other private funds we studied did not manage any of their money in-house but delegated virtually all investment decisions to outside managers. At one, fund and sponsor together decided on a buy-and-hold strategy and hired outsiders to implement it, their performance closely monitored by identifiable fund executives. At the other, the objective was diversity for its own sake. The fund had 21 external managers implementing 21 different strategies that fund executives did not always understand. The fund's CEO insisted that the purpose of this diversity was to reduce the overall volatility of the portfolio, but one highly successful external manager remarked that the true purpose of diversity is to ensure mediocrity and avoid criticism.

Such thinking is widespread at public funds, which is one reason they index. Another reason is cultural. Employees of private funds point out that good performance reduces their sponsor's contribution and hence the cost of its goods and services. But public funds are apt to be more defensive. For some public fund managers, indexing is an admission of helplessness in the face of market forces and a rejection of the pursuit of superior performance as illusory or irrelevant. Whether or not indexing is economically efficient, no one could espouse this position in a corporate environment.

Authority and the Employee Retirement Income Security Act. In many cultures, people can displace responsibility for their actions onto such external forces as nature and the supernatural. Private fund executives often invoke ERISA as an external force absolving them of responsibility for critical decisions. Public funds generally operate under the old common-law standard of the "prudent person," although some states have explicitly adopted the ERISA standard. (Many legal scholars view the two standards as materially the same.)

Despite the lack of rules governing specific situations under either standard, fund executives repeatedly place the responsibility for particular decisions on the law. For instance, executives at several funds say that both standards absolutely rule out so-called social investing—supporting projects that will provide jobs and infrastructure, say, or ruling out investments in companies with poor environmental records. But some public fund officers take just the opposite view. One told us he could see no reason not to invest in roads, for example, if roads paid a decent return on capital and were essential to the state's economy. "I don't think you have to wear blinders to be a fiduciary," he said.

What emerged was a picture of fund executives continually recreating the law to support their own judgments on contentious issues. Although the actual language of the legal standards is often ambiguous, fund executives commonly describe themselves as following explicit prescriptions, what one called ERISA's "clear-cut rules." Questions of blame are preempted by fixing responsibility on an unyielding external force.

Language and Thought. Anthropologists have long recognized that how people talk about something reflects how they think about it. Eskimos, for example, have many words for what we call simply "snow." Language may also limit thinking. Some argue that one reason for the slow pace of economic reform in the Soviet Union is that Soviet policymakers have no tradition of speaking and writing in units of less than five years. A similar relationship between language and thought may limit the ability of U.S. pension executives to invest for the long term.

Executives themselves deny the charge of short-term myopia. In almost every case, their response to our question was some variant of "Not us!"

We have two reasons for believing that these executives delude themselves. To begin with, the everyday discourse of the investment world focuses on the short term. We can cite examples almost endlessly: companies issue quarterly reports, the SEC requires quarterly filings, fund managers make quarterly or semiannual reports to their sponsors. What's more, the advent of the computer has now brought about continuous scrutiny of equity performance and the daily measurement of investor effectiveness.

Of course, short-term evaluation is often necessary. The problem is that short-term rhetoric has crowded out alternatives. The papers on an analyst's desk do not include many five-year financial reports or ten-year business plans. One manager at a fund with a buy-quality-and-hold strategy complained that conventional financial reporting simply didn't help him. He then told us how he had developed his own painstaking system to monitor long-term positive and negative trends in the companies he followed. The investment world is so constrained by its professional rhetoric that a serious commitment to the long term is an act of intellectual originality as well as a burdensome undertaking.

The second reason is our discovery of what we call the composite villain. At five of the seven funds, the portion of fund assets allocated to relatively high-turnover strategies made up only a small fraction of total assets, typically 5% to 10%. But 5% to 10% of hundreds of billions of dollars is a great deal of money, even by macroeconomic standards. So it may be that pension funds contribute to short-term pressures in a subtle, cumulative way that is all but imperceptible to pension fund managers themselves.

—John M. Conley and William M. O'Barr[1]

One reason for their support was that these transactions kept alive the illusion that pension funds could in fact sell their shares—that is, that they were "investors" still. Takeovers and LBOs also offered immediate capital gains. And since pension fund portfolios have by and large done quite poorly, such gains were most welcome—though, as will be discussed shortly, they too were more illusion than reality.

What made takeovers and buyouts inevitable (or at least created the opportunity for them) was the mediocre performance of enlightened-despot management, the management without clear definitions of performance and results and with no clear accountability to somebody. It may be argued that the mediocre performance of so many of America's large corporations in the last 30 years was not management's fault, that it resulted instead from wrong-headed public policies that have kept American savings rates low and capital costs high. But captains are responsible for what happens on their watches. And whatever the reasons or excuses, the large U.S. company has not done particularly well on professional management's watch—whether measured by competitiveness, market standing, or innovative performance. As for financial performance, it has, by and large, not even earned the minimum-acceptable result, a return on equity equal to its cost of capital.

The raiders thus performed a needed function. As an old proverb has it, "If there are no grave diggers, one needs vultures." But takeovers and buyouts are very radical surgery. And even if radical surgery is not life-threatening, it inflicts profound shock. Takeovers and buyouts deeply disturb and indeed alienate middle managers and professionals, the very people on whose motivation, effort, and loyalty a business depends. For these people, the takeover or dismantling of a company to which they have given years of service is nothing short of betrayal. It is a denial of all they must believe in to work productively and with devotion. As a result, few of the companies that were taken over or sold in a buyout performed any better a few years later than they had performed under the old dispensation.

But weren't takeovers and buyouts at least good for shareholders? Perhaps not. In a typical transaction, shareholders (and this means primarily the pension funds) received, say, $60 for a share that had been quoted on the stock exchange for an average of $40 in the year before the deal. This 50% premium is proving to have been an illusion in many cases. Perhaps $25 of the $60 was not solid cash but the value put by the raider or the raider's investment banker on convertible warrants, unsecured loans, or junk bonds. These noncash nonsecurities, which were bought by many of the same institutions that sold shares, are rapidly losing value. Many pension funds immediately did sell these now-depreciating pieces of paper. But they sold them to other pension funds or institutional investors—there are no other buyers. Thus the net financial value of these transactions to the pension fund community at large remains suspect indeed.

Today nearly all CEOs of large U.S. companies proclaim that they run their enterprises "in the interest of the shareholders" and "to maximize shareholder value." This is the second definition of performance and results developed over the past 40 years. It sounds much less noble than Cordiner's assertion of the "best-balanced interest," but it also sounds much more realistic. Yet its life span will be even shorter than yesterday's professional management. For most people, "maximizing shareholder value" means a higher share price within six months or a year—certainly not much longer. Such short-term capital gains are the wrong objective for both the enterprise and its dominant shareholders. As a theory of corporate performance, then, "maximizing shareholder value" has little staying power.

Regarding the enterprise, the cost of short-term thinking hardly needs to be argued. But short-term capital gains are also of no benefit to holders who cannot sell. The interest of a large pension fund is in the value of a holding at the time at which a beneficiary turns from being an employee who pays into the fund into a pensioner who gets paid by the fund. Concretely, this means that the time over which a fund invests—the time until its future beneficiaries will retire—is on average 15 years rather than 3 months or 6 months. This is the appropriate re-turn horizon for these owners.

There is, however, one group that does—or at least thinks it does—have an interest in short-term gains. These are the employers with "defined benefit" pension plans. Until now, in a classic case of the tail wagging the dog, the interests of these employers have dominated how the pension fund community approaches its role as owner. In a defined-benefit plan, retiring employees receive fixed annual payments, usually a percentage of their wages during the last three or five years on the job. The employer's annual contribution fluctuates with the value of the fund's assets. If in any given year that value is high (compared with the amount needed on an actuarial basis to cover the fund's future pension obligations) the employer's contribution is cut. If the fund's asset value is low, the contribution goes up.

We owe the defined-benefit trust to mere accident. When General Motors management proposed the pension fund in 1950, several powerful board members resisted it as a giveaway to the union. The directors relented only when promised that, under a defined-benefit plan, the company would have to pay little or nothing. An ever-rising stock market, so the argument went, would create the assets needed to pay future pensions. Most private employers followed the GM model, if only because they too deluded themselves into believing that the stock market rather than the company would take care of the pension obligation.

Needless to say, this was wishful thinking. Most defined-benefit plans have done poorly, precisely because they have been chasing inappropriate short-term gains. The other kind of plan, the "defined contribution" plan under which the employer contributes each year a defined percentage of the employee's annual salary or wages, has done better in a good many cases. Indeed, defined-benefit plans are rapidly losing their allure. Because they have not delivered the promised capital gains, a great many are seriously underfunded. From now on, as a result of new accounting standards, such underfunding has to be shown as a liability on the employing company's balance sheet. This means that even in a mild recession (in which both a company's earnings and the stock market are down), a good many companies will actually be pushed to, if not over, the brink of insolvency. And what many of them have done in good years—that is, to siphon off the actuarial surplus in the pension fund and show it as "net income" in their income statement—is unlikely to be permitted much longer.

Company after company is therefore going out of defined-benefit plans. By the end of the decade, they will have become marginal. As a result, short-term gains as an objective for the major owners of American business will no longer dominate. They are already playing second fiddle. Public-employee funds are defined-contribution plans, and they constitute the majority of the biggest funds. Being independent of corporate management, they, rather than the pension funds of private businesses, are taking the lead and writing the new script.

We no longer need to theorize about how to define performance and results in the large enterprise. We have successful examples. Both the Germans and the Japanese have highly concentrated institutional ownership. In neither country can the owners actually manage. In both countries industry has done extremely well in the 40 years since its near destruction in World War II. It has done well in terms of the overall economy of its country. It has also done exceedingly well for its shareholders. Whether invested in 1950, 1960, 1970, or 1980, $100,000 put into something like an index fund in the stock exchanges of Tokyo or Frankfurt would today be worth a good deal more than a similar investment in a New York Stock Exchange index fund.

How, then, do the institutional owners of German or Japanese industry define performance and results? Though they manage quite differently, they define them in the same way. Unlike Cordiner, they do not "balance" anything. They maximize. But they do not attempt to maximize shareholder value or the short-term interest of any one of the enterprise's "stakeholders." Rather, they *maximize the wealth-producing capacity of the enterprise.*[2] It is this objective that integrates short-term and long-term results and that ties the operational dimensions of business performance—market standing, innovation, productivity, and people and their development—with financial needs and financial results. It is also this objective on which all constituencies depend for the satisfaction of their expectations and objectives, whether shareholders, customers, or employees.

To define performance and results as "maximizing the wealth-producing capacity of the enterprise" may be criticized as vague. To be sure, one doesn't get the answers by filling out forms. Decisions need to be made, and economic decisions that commit scarce resources to an uncertain future are always risky and controversial. When Ralph Cordiner first attempted to define performance and results—no one had tried to do so earlier—maximizing the wealth-producing capacity of the enterprise would indeed have been pretty fuzzy. By now, after four decades of work by many people, it has become crisp. All the elements that go into the process can be quantified with considerable rigor and are indeed quantified by those archquantifiers, by the planning departments of large Japanese companies and by many of the German companies as well.

The first step toward a clear definition of the concept was probably taken in my 1954 book, *The Practice of Management,* which outlined eight key objective areas for a business. These areas (or some variations thereof) are still the starting point for business planning in the large Japanese company. Since then, management analysts have done an enormous amount of work on the strategy needed to convert objectives into performance, including the pioneering work of Harvard Business School's Michael Porter and important new concepts such as "core competence" developed in *HBR* by C.K. Prahalad and Gary Hamel.[3]

Financial objectives are needed to tie all this together. Indeed, financial accountability is the key to the performance of management and enterprise. Without financial accountability, there is no accountability at all. And without financial accountability, there will also be no results in any other area. It is commonly believed in the United States that the Japanese are not profit conscious. This is simply not true. In fact, their profitability goals as measured against the cost of capital tend to be a good deal higher than those of most American companies. Only the Japanese do not start with profitability; they end with it.

Finally, maximizing the wealth-producing capacity of the enterprise also helps define the roles of institutional owners and their relationship to the enterprise. German and Japanese management structure and style differ greatly. But institutional owners in both countries support a management regardless of short-term results as long as the company performs according to a business plan that is designed to maximize the enterprise's wealth-producing capacity—and that is agreed upon between management and whatever organ represents the owners. This makes both sides focus on results. It makes management accountable. But it gives a performing company's management the needed continuity and security.

What we have is not the "final answer." Still, it is no longer theory but proven practice. And its results, to judge by German and Japanese business performance, are clearly superior to running the enterprise as a "trustee" for stakeholders or to maximize short-term gains for shareholders.

The one thing that we in the United States have yet to work out— and we have to work out ourselves—is how to build the new definition of management accountability into an institutional structure. We need what a political scientist would call a constitution—provisions that spell out, as does the German company law, the duties and responsibilities of management and that clarify the respective rights of other groups, especially the shareholders. *What* we have to do the Germans and the Japanese can show us. *How* we do it will have to be quite different to fit U.S. conditions.

In both Germany and Japan, managements are supervised closely and judged carefully. In Germany, a senior executive of the hausbank sits on the board of each company in which the bank has substantial holdings, usually as chairperson of the supervisory board. The bank's representative is expected to move fast whenever management fails to perform to exacting standards. In Japan, the chief executives of the major companies in a keiretsu—headed either by the CEO of the group's bank or by the CEO of the group's trading company—function as the executive committee of the whole group. They meet regularly. The top executives of the Mitsubishi group, for instance, meet every other Friday for three or four hours. They carefully review the business plans of each group's companies and evaluate the performance of each group's managements. Again and again, though usually without fanfare, chief executives who are found wanting are moved out, kicked upstairs, or shifted to the sidelines.

The analysis and scrutiny of management's performance is organized as systematic work in both countries. In Germany, it is done by the *sekretariat* of the big banks—invented in the 1870s by Deutsche Bank, which modeled it on the Prussian general staff. The sekretariat works constantly on the companies for which its bank is the hausbank and on the board of which one of the bank's executives sits. Since the bank also handles the commercial banking business of these companies, the sekretariat has access to both their financial and business data. There is no sekretariat in Japan. But the same function is discharged by the large and powerful planning departments of the keiretsu's main bank and of the keiretsu's trading company. They too have access to commercial and business data in addition to financial information.

Even the largest U.S. pension fund holds much too small a fraction of any one company's capital to control it. Law wisely limits a corporate pension fund to a maximum holding of 5% of any one company's stock, and very few funds go anywhere near that high. Not being businesses, the funds have no access to commercial or business information. They are not business-focused, nor could they be. They are asset managers. Yet they need the in-depth business analysis of the companies they collectively control. And they need an institutional structure in which management accountability is embedded.

In an American context, the business analysis—call it the business audit—will have to be done by some kind of independent professional agency. Certain management consulting firms already do such work, though only on an ad hoc basis and usually after a company has gotten into trouble, which is rather late in the process. The consulting divisions of some of the large accounting firms also perform business analysis assignments. One of them, KPMG Peat Marwick, actually offers a systematic business audit to nonprofit organizations, which it calls a resource-development system. And several firms have recently come into being to advise pension funds—mostly public funds—on the industries and companies in which they invest.

I suspect that in the end we shall develop a formal business-audit practice, analogous perhaps to the financial-audit practice of independent professional accounting firms. For while the business audit need not be conducted every year —every three years may be enough in most cases—it needs to be based on predetermined standards and go through a systematic evaluation of business performance: starting with mission and strategy, through marketing, innovation, productivity, people development, community relations, all the way to profitability. The elements for such a business audit are known and available. But they need to be pulled together into systematic procedures. And that is best done, in all likelihood, by an organization that specializes in audits, whether an independent firm or a new and separate division of an accounting practice.

Thus it may not be too fanciful to expect that in ten years a major pension fund will not invest in a company's shares or fixed-income securities unless that company submits itself to a business audit by an outside professional firm. Managements will resist, of course. But only 60 years ago, managements equally resisted—in fact, resented— demands that they submit themselves to a financial audit by outside public accountants and even more to publication of the audit's findings.

Still, the question remains: Who is going to use this tool? In the American context, there is only one possible answer: a revitalized board of directors.

The need for an effective board has been stressed by every student of the publicly owned corporation in the last 40 years. To run a business enterprise, especially a large and complex enterprise, management needs considerable power. But power without accountability always becomes flabby or tyrannical and usually both. Surely, we know how to make boards effective as an organ of corporate governance. Having better people is not the key; ordinary people will do. Making a board effective requires spelling out its work, setting specific objectives for its performance and contribution, and regularly appraising the board's performance against these objectives.[4]

We have known this for a long time. But American boards have on the whole become less, rather than more, effective. Boards are not effective if they represent good intentions. Boards are not effective if they represent "investors." Boards of business enterprises are effective if they represent strong owners, committed to the enterprise.

Almost 60 years ago, in 1933, Adolph A. Berle, Jr. and Gardner C. Means published *The Modern Corporation and Private Property,* arguably the most influential book in U.S. business history. They showed that the traditional "owners," the nineteenth-century capitalists, had disappeared, with the title of ownership shifting rapidly to faceless multitudes of investors without interest in or commitment to the company and concerned with only short-term gains. As a result, they argued, ownership was becoming divorced from control and a mere legal fiction, with management becoming accountable to no one and for nothing. Then, 20 years later, Ralph Cordiner's *Professional Management* accepted this divorce of ownership from control and tried to make a virtue out of it.

By now, the wheel has come full circle. The pension funds are very different owners from nineteenth-century tycoons. They are not owners because they want to be owners but because they have no choice. They cannot sell. They also cannot become owner-managers. But they are owners nonetheless. As such, they have more than mere power. They have the responsibility to ensure performance and results in America's largest and most important companies.

Notes

1. John M. Conley is a professor of law at the University of North Carolina at Chapel Hill. William M. O'Barr is a professor of cultural anthropology and sociology at Duke University in Durham, North Carolina.

2. This concept has long historical roots. The great English economist Alfred Marshall (1842–1924) first wrote of the "going concern" as the wealth-producing entity in a modern economy of a hundred years ago. And the idea underlies the protection of the going concern (Chapter 11 bankruptcy) put forth during the New Deal into U.S. bankruptcy law. But as an operational guide to managing a business, maximizing the wealth-producing capacity of the enterprise has emerged only in the last 40 years.

3. C.K. Prahalad and Gary Hamel, "The Core Competence of the Corporation," *Harvard Business Review,* May–June 1990.

4. The most thorough and persuasive analysis of what makes an effective board is a book by Harvard Business School Professor Myles L. Mace, *Directors: Myth and Reality* (Boston: Harvard Business School Press, 1986).

PART

IV

Customer Loyalty

1
Zero Defections: Quality Comes to Services

Frederick F. Reichheld and W. Earl Sasser, Jr.

The *real* quality revolution is just now coming to services. In recent years, despite their good intentions, few service company executives have been able to follow through on their commitment to satisfy customers. But service companies are beginning to understand what their manufacturing counterparts learned in the 1980s—that quality doesn't improve unless you measure it. When manufacturers began to unravel the costs and implications of scrap heaps, rework, and jammed machinery, they realized that "quality" was not just an invigorating slogan but the most profitable way to run a business. They made "zero defects" their guiding light, and the quality movement took off.

Service companies have their own kind of scrap heap: customers who will not come back. That scrap heap too has a cost. As service businesses start to measure it, they will see the urgent need to reduce it. They will strive for "zero defections"—keeping every customer the company can profitably serve—and they will mobilize the organization to achieve it.

Customer defections have a surprisingly powerful impact on the bottom line. They can have more to do with a service company's profits than scale, market share, unit costs, and many other factors usually associated with competitive advantage. As a customer's relationship with the company lengthens, profits rise. And not just a little. Companies can boost profits by almost 100% by retaining just 5% more of their customers.

While defection rates are an accurate leading indicator of profit swings, they do more than passively indicate where profits are headed. They also direct managers' attention to the specific things that are causing customers to leave. Since companies do not hold customers captive, the only way they can prevent defections is to outperform the competition continually. By soliciting feedback from defecting customers, companies can ferret out the weaknesses that really matter and strengthen them before profits start to dwindle. Defection analysis is therefore a guide that helps companies manage continuous improvement.

Charles Cawley, president of MBNA America, a Delaware-based credit card company, knows well how customer defections can focus a company's attention on exactly the things customers value. One morning in 1982, frustrated by letters from unhappy customers, he assembled all 300 MBNA employees and announced his determination that the company satisfy and keep each and every customer. The company started gathering feedback from defecting customers. And it acted on the information, adjusting products and processes regularly.

As quality improved, fewer customers had reason to leave. Eight years later, MBNA's defection rate is one of the lowest in its industry. Some 5% of its customers leave each year—half the average rate for the rest of the industry. That may seem like a small difference, but it translates into huge earnings. Without making any acquisitions, MBNA's industry ranking went from 38 to 4, and profits have increased sixteenfold.

The Cost of Losing a Customer

If companies knew how much it really costs to lose a customer, they would be able to make accurate evaluations of investments designed to retain customers. Unfortunately, today's accounting systems do not capture the value of a loyal customer. Most systems focus on current period costs and revenues and ignore expected cash flows over a customer's lifetime. Served correctly, customers generate increasingly more profits each year they stay with a company. Across a wide range of businesses, the pattern is the same: the longer a company keeps a customer, the more money it stands to make. (See Exhibit I.) For one auto-service company, the expected profit from a fourth-year customer is more than triple the profit that same customer generates in the first year. When customers defect, they take all that profit-making potential with them.

It may be obvious that acquiring a new customer entails certain one-time costs for advertising, promotions, and the like. In credit

Exhibit I.

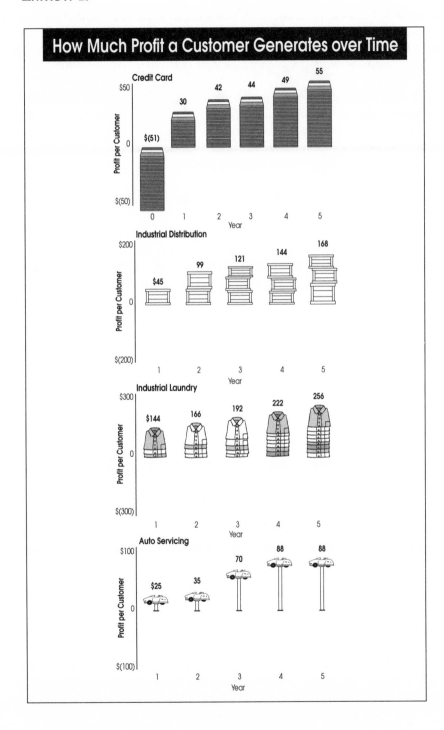

How Much Profit a Customer Generates over Time

cards, for example, companies spend an average of $51 to recruit a customer and set up the new account. But there are many more pieces to the profitability puzzle.

To continue with the credit card example, the newly acquired customers use the card slowly at first and generate a base profit. But if the customers stay a second year, the economics greatly improve. As they become accustomed to using the credit card and are satisfied with the service it provides, customers use it more and balances grow. In the second year—and the years thereafter—they purchase even more, which turns profits up sharply. We found this trend in each of the more than 100 companies in two dozen industries we have analyzed. For one industrial distributor, net sales per account continue to rise into the nineteenth year of the relationship.

As purchases rise, operating costs decline. Checking customers' credit histories and adding them to the corporate database is expensive, but those things need be done only once. Also, as the company gains experience with its customers, it can serve them more efficiently. One small financial consulting business that depends on personal relationships with clients has found that costs drop by two-thirds from the first year to the second because customers know what to expect from the consultant and have fewer questions or problems. In addition, the consultants are more efficient because they are familiar with the customer's financial situation and investment preferences.

Also, companies with long-time customers can often charge more for their products or services. Many people will pay more to stay in a hotel they know or to go to a doctor they trust than to take a chance on a less expensive competitor. The company that has developed such a loyal following can charge a premium for the customer's confidence in the business.

Yet another economic boon from long-time customers is the free advertising they provide. Loyal customers do a lot of talking over the years and drum up a lot of business. One of the leading home builders in the United States, for example, has found that more than 60% of its sales are the result of referrals.

These cost savings and additional revenues combine to produce a steadily increasing stream of profits over the course of the customer's relationship with the company. (See Exhibit II.) While the relative importance of these effects varies from industry to industry, the end result is that longer term customers generate increasing profits.

To calculate a customer's real worth, a company must take all of these projected profit streams into account. If, for instance, the credit

Exhibit II.

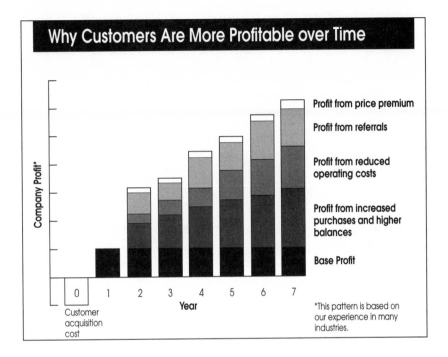

Why Customers Are More Profitable over Time

Profit from price premium

Profit from referrals

Profit from reduced operating costs

Profit from increased purchases and higher balances

Base Profit

Company Profit*

Year

0 1 2 3 4 5 6 7

Customer acquisition cost

*This pattern is based on our experience in many industries.

card customer leaves after the first year, the company takes a $21 loss. If the company can keep the customer for four more years, his or her value to the company rises sharply. It is equal to the net present value of the profit streams in the first five years, or about $100.

When a company lowers its defection rate, the average customer relationship lasts longer and profits climb steeply. One way to appreciate just how responsive profits are to changes in defection rates is to draw a defection curve. (See Exhibit III.) This shows clearly how small movements in a company's defection rate can produce very large swings in profits.

The curve shows, for example, that as the credit card company cuts its defection rate from 20% to 10%, the average life span of its relationship with a customer doubles from five years to ten and the value of that customer more than doubles—jumping from $134 to $300. As the defection rate drops another 5%, the average life span of a customer relationship doubles again and profits rise 75%—from $300 to $525.

Exhibit III.

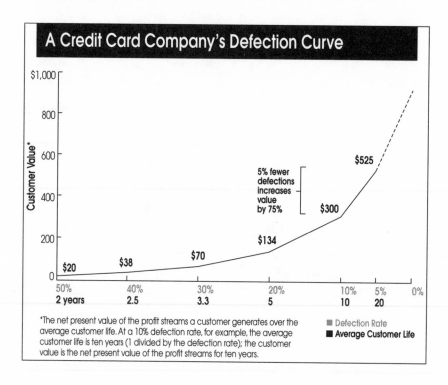

A Credit Card Company's Defection Curve

*The net present value of the profit streams a customer generates over the average customer life. At a 10% defection rate, for example, the average customer life is ten years (1 divided by the defection rate); the customer value is the net present value of the profit streams for ten years.

■ Defection Rate
■ Average Customer Life

The credit card business is not unique. Although the shape of defection curves vary across industries, in general, profits rise as defection rates fall. Reducing defections by just 5% generated 85% more profits in one bank's branch system, 50% more in an insurance brokerage, and 30% more in an auto-service chain. (See Exhibit IV.) MBNA America has found that a 5% improvement in defection rates increases its average customer value by more than 125%.

Understanding the economics of defections is useful to managers in several ways. For one thing, it shows that continuous improvement in service quality is not a cost but an investment in a customer who generates more profit than the margin on a one-time sale. Executives can therefore justify giving priority to investments in service quality versus things like cost reduction, for which the objectives have been more tangible.

Knowing that defections are closely linked to profits also helps explain why some companies that have relatively high unit costs

Exhibit IV.

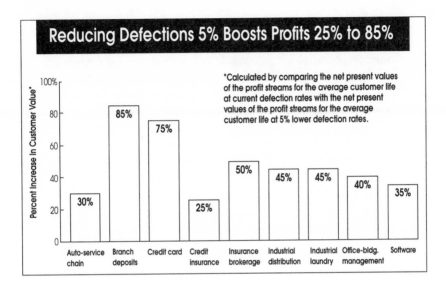

Reducing Defections 5% Boosts Profits 25% to 85%

*Calculated by comparing the net present values of the profit streams for the average customer life at current defection rates with the net present values of the profit streams for the average customer life at 5% lower defection rates.

Percent Increase In Customer Value*

Auto-service chain	Branch deposits	Credit card	Credit insurance	Insurance brokerage	Industrial distribution	Industrial laundry	Office-bldg. management	Software
30%	85%	75%	25%	50%	45%	45%	40%	35%

can still be quite profitable. Companies with loyal, long-time customers can financially outperform competitors with lower unit costs and high market share but high customer churn. For instance, in the credit card business, a 10% reduction in unit costs is financially equivalent to a 2% decrease in defection rate. Low-defection strategies can overwhelm low-cost strategies.

And understanding the link between defections and profits provides a guide to lucrative growth. It is common for a business to lose 15% to 20% of its customers each year. Simply cutting defections in half will more than double the average company's growth rate. Companies with high retention rates that want to expand through acquisition can create value by acquiring low retention competitors and reducing their defections.

Defections Management

Although service companies probably can't—and shouldn't try to—eliminate all defections, they can and must reduce them. But even to approach zero defections, companies must pursue that goal in a coordinated way. The organization should be prepared to spot customers who leave and then to analyze and act on the information they provide.

Watch the door. Managing for zero defections requires mechanisms to find customers who have ended their relationship with the company—or are about to end it. While compiling this kind of customer data almost always involves the use of information technology of some kind, major investments in new systems are unnecessary.

The more critical issue is whether the business regularly gathers information about customers. Some companies already do. Credit card companies, magazine publishers, direct mailers, life insurers, cellular phone companies, and banks, for example, all collect reams of data as a matter of course. They have at their disposal the names and addresses, purchasing histories, and telephone numbers of all their customers. For these businesses, exposing defections is relatively easy. It's just a matter of organizing the data.

Sometimes, defining a "defection" takes some work. In the railroad business, for instance, few customers stop using your service completely, but a customer that shifts 80% of its shipments to trucks should not be considered "retained." The key is to identify the customer behaviors that both drive your economics and gauge customer loyalty.

For some businesses, the task of spotting defectors is challenging even if they are well defined, because customers tend to be faceless and nameless to management. Businesses like retailing will have to find creative ways to "know" their customers. Consider the example of Staples, the Boston-based office products discounter. It has done a superb job of gathering information usually lost at the cashier or sales clerk. From its opening, it had a database to store and analyze customer information. Whenever a customer goes through the checkout line, the cashier offers him or her a membership card. The card entitles the holder to special promotions and certain discounts. The only requirement for the card is that the person fill out an application form, which asks for things like name, job title, and address. All subsequent purchases are automatically logged against the card number. This way, Staples can accumulate detailed information about buying habits, frequency of visits, average dollar value spent, and particular items purchased.

Even restaurants can collect data. A crab house in Maryland, for instance, started entering into its PC information from the reservation list. Managers can now find out how often particular customers return and can contact those who seem to be losing interest in the restaurant.

What are defectors telling you? One reason to find customers who are leaving is to try to win them back. MBNA America has a customer-defection "swat" team staffed by some of the company's best telemarketers. When customers cancel their credit cards, the swat team tries to convince them to stay. It is successful half of the time.

But the more important motive for finding defectors is for the insight they provide. Customers who leave can provide a view of the business that is unavailable to those on the inside. And whatever caused one individual to defect may cause many others to follow. The idea is to use defections as an early warning signal—to learn from defectors why they left the company and to use that information to improve the business.

Unlike conventional market research, feedback from defecting customers tends to be concrete and specific. It doesn't attempt to measure things like attitudes or satisfaction, which are changeable and subjective, and it doesn't raise hypothetical questions, which may be irrelevant to the respondents. Defections analysis involves specific, relevant questions about why a customer has defected. Customers are usually able to articulate their reasons, and some skillful probing can get at the root cause.

This information is useful in a variety of ways, as the Staples example shows. Staples constantly tracks defections, so when customers stop doing business there or don't buy certain products, the store notices it immediately and calls to get feedback. It may be a clue that the competition is underpricing Staples on certain goods—a competitive factor management can explore further. If it finds sufficient evidence, Staples may cut prices on those items. This information is highly valued because it pinpoints the uncompetitive products and saves the chain from launching expensive broad-brush promotions pitching everything to everybody.

Staples's telemarketers try to discern which merchandise its customers want and don't want and why. The company uses that information to change its buying stock and to target its catalogs and coupons more precisely. Instead of running coupons in the newspaper, for instance, it can insert them in the catalogs it sends to particular customers or industries that have proved responsive to coupons.

Defections analysis can also help companies decide which service-quality investments will be profitable. Should you invest in computerized cash registers or a new phone system? Which of the two will address the most frequent causes of defection? One bank made a large investment to improve the accuracy of monthly account statements. But when the bank began to study defectors, it learned that less than 1% of its customers were leaving because of inaccurate statements.

A company that is losing customers because of long lines can estimate what percentage of defectors it would save by buying new cash registers, and it can use its defection curve to find the dollar value of saving them. Then, using standard investment-analysis techniques, it can compare the cost of the new equipment with the benefit of keeping customers.

Achieving service quality doesn't mean slavishly keeping all customers at any cost. There are some customers the company should not try to serve. If particular types of customers don't stay and become profitable, companies should not invest in attracting them. When a health insurance company realized that certain companies purchase only on the basis of price and switch health insurers every year, for example, it decided not to waste its efforts seeking their business. It told its brokers not to write policies for companies that have switched carriers more than twice in the past five years.

Conversely, much of the information used to find defectors can point to common traits among customers who stay longer. The company can use defection rates to clarify the characteristics of the market it wants to pursue and target its advertising and promotions accordingly.

The Zero Defections Culture

Many business leaders have been frustrated by their inability to follow through on their public commitment to service quality. Since defection rates are measurable, they are manageable. Managers can establish meaningful targets and monitor progress. But like any important change, managing for zero defections must have supporters at all organizational levels. Management must develop that support by training the work force and using defections as a primary performance measure.

Everyone in the organization must understand that zero defections is the goal. Mastercare, the auto-service subsidiary of Bridgestone/ Firestone, emphasizes the importance of keeping customers by stating it clearly in its mission statement. The statement says, in part, that the company's goal is "to provide the service-buying public with a superior buying experience that will encourage them to return willingly and to share their experience with others." MBNA America sends its paychecks in envelopes labeled "Brought to you by the customer." It also has a customer advocate who sits in on all major decision-making sessions to make sure customers' interests are represented.

It is important to make all employees understand the lifetime value of a customer. Phil Bressler, the co-owner of five Domino's Pizza stores in Montgomery County, Maryland, calculated that regular customers were worth more than $5,000 over the life of a ten-year franchise contract. He made sure that every order taker, delivery person, and store manager knew that number. For him, telling workers that customers were valuable was not nearly as potent as stating the dollar amount: "It's so much more than they think that it really hits home."

Mastercare has redesigned its employee training to emphasize the importance of keeping customers. For example, many customers who stopped doing business with Mastercare mentioned that they didn't like being pressured into repairs they had not planned on. So Mastercare now trains store managers to identify and solve the customer's problem rather than to maximize sales. Videos and role-playing dramatize these different definitions of good service.

Mastercare's message to employees includes a candid admission that previous, well-intentioned incentives had inadvertently caused employees to run the business the wrong way; now it is asking them to change. And it builds credibility among employees by sharing its strategic goals and customer outreach plans. In the two target markets where this approach has been used, results are good. Employees have responded enthusiastically, and 25% more customers say they intend to return.

Senior executives at MBNA America learn from defecting customers. Each one spends four hours a month in a special "listening room" monitoring routine customer service calls as well as calls from customers who are canceling their credit cards.

Beyond conveying a sense of urgency, training should teach employees the specifics of defections analysis, like how to gather the information, whom to pass it on to, and what actions to take in response. In one company's branch banking system, retention data is sent monthly to the regional vice presidents and branch managers for review. It allows the regional vice presidents to identify and focus on branches that most need to improve service quality, and it gives branch managers quick feedback on performance.

Employees will be more motivated if incentives are tied to defection rates. MBNA, for example, has determined for each department the one or two things that have the biggest impact on keeping customers. Each department is measured daily on how well performance targets are met. Every morning, the previous day's performance is posted in several places throughout the building. Each day that the company hits 95% of these performance targets, MBNA contributes money to a bonus pool. Managers use the pool to pay yearly bonuses of up to 20% of a person's salary. The president visits departments that fall short of their targets to find out where the problem lies.

Great-West Life Assurance Company of Englewood, Colorado also uses incentives effectively. It pays a 50% premium to group-health-insurance brokers that hit customer-retention targets. This system gives brokers the incentive to look for customers who will stay with the company for a long time.

Having everyone in the company work toward keeping customers and basing rewards on how well they do creates a positive company atmosphere. Encouraging employees to solve customer problems and eliminate the source of complaints allows them to be "nice," and customers treat them better in return. The overall exchange is more rewarding, and people enjoy their work more. Not just customers but also employees will want to continue their relationship with the business. MBNA is besieged by applicants for job openings, while a competitor a few miles away is moving some of its operations out of the state because it can't find enough employees.

The success of MBNA shows that it is possible to achieve big improvements in both service quality and profits in a reasonably short time. But it also shows that focusing on keeping customers instead of simply having lots of them takes effort. A company can leverage business performance and profits through customer defections only when the notion permeates corporate life and when all organizational levels understand the concept of zero defections and know how to act on it.

Trying to retain all of your profitable customers is elementary. Managing toward zero defections is revolutionary. It requires careful definition of defection, information systems that can measure results over time in comparison with competitors, and a clear understanding of the microeconomics of defection.

Ultimately, defections should be a key performance measure for senior management and a fundamental component of incentive systems. Managers should know the company's defection rate, what happens to profits when the rate moves up or down, and why defections occur. They should make sure the entire organization understands the importance of keeping customers and encourage employees to pursue zero defections by tying incentives, planning, and budgeting to defection targets. Most important, managers should use defections as a vehicle for continuously improving the quality and value of the services they provide to customers.

Just as the quality revolution in manufacturing had a profound impact on the competitiveness of companies, the quality revolution in services will create a new set of winners and losers. The winners will be those who lead the way in managing toward zero defections.

2
Why Satisfied Customers Defect

Thomas O. Jones and W. Earl Sasser, Jr.

The scene is familiar: the monthly management meeting attended by a company's senior officers and the general managers of its operating divisions. The company's eight divisions operate in diverse markets, including light manufacturing, wholesale distribution, and consumer services. All are feeling pressure from strong competitors, and the corporation has created a customer-satisfaction survey as one method of measuring the impact of its quality-improvement process.

After dispensing with several items on the agenda, the group turns to the third-quarter customer-satisfaction indices, and a transparency is placed on the overhead projector. (See Exhibit I.) The CEO proudly points out that 82% of the customers surveyed responded with an overall satisfaction rating of either 4 (satisfied) or 5 (completely satisfied). Everyone in the meeting agrees that the company must be doing pretty well because only 18% of its customers were less than satisfied.

There are three divisions with average ratings of 4.5 or higher. There is general consensus that they have reached the point of diminishing returns and that further investing to increase customer satisfaction will not make good financial sense.

The group next examines the results of the division with the lowest average rating, a 2.7. This business unit manufactures bulk lubricants and sells to companies that repackage the product for sale to the retail channel. It is a highly competitive, commodity-type business and operates with very tight margins. The group concludes that the lubricant division's market is difficult and that its price-sensitive customers will never be satisfied. Moreover, the division's rating is equal to or above those of most competitors. There is a general consensus that its cus-

Exhibit I.

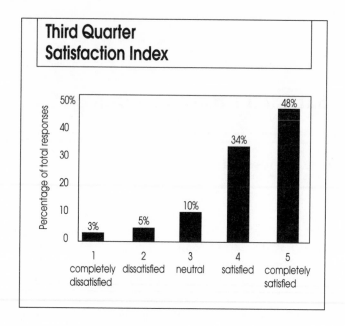

Third Quarter Satisfaction Index

Percentage of total responses

1 completely dissatisfied	3%
2 dissatisfied	5%
3 neutral	10%
4 satisfied	34%
5 completely satisfied	48%

tomers are a lost cause and that it does not pay to make additional investments to try to satisfy them.

Finally, the discussion turns to four business units whose customers generally are neutral or pleased but certainly not delighted. Two divisions manufacture large industrial machinery. Two other divisions provide after-market service for the products of both the company and its competitors. Each division has an average rating between 3.5 and 4.5, meaning that, although the majority of their customers are not dissatisfied or neutral, a significant number are. "Our battle plan is to find out what's making the least-satisfied customers mad and fix it!" the head of one industrial-machinery division says. The others nod in agreement.

Implicit in this discussion are a number of beliefs widely held by managers of the dozens of manufacturing and service companies we have studied. First, it is sufficient merely to satisfy a customer; as long as a customer responds with at least a satisfied rating (a 4), the company-customer relationship is strong. In other words, a level of satisfaction below complete or total satisfaction is acceptable. After all, this is the real world, where products and services are rarely perfect and people are hard to please. Second, the investment required to change customers from satisfied to completely satisfied will not provide an attractive financial return and therefore probably is not a wise use of resources. Indeed, there may even be instances—most notably, when competing in a cutthroat commodity market—where it doesn't pay to try to satisfy any customers. Finally, each division with a relatively high average rating (3.5 to 4.5) should focus on the customers in its lowest-satisfaction categories (1 to 2). Striving to understand the causes of their dissatisfaction and concentrating efforts on addressing them is the best use of resources.

The extensive research that we conducted on the relationship between customer satisfaction and customer loyalty, however, shows that these assumptions are deeply flawed. They either ignore or do not accord enough importance to the following aspects of the relationship: *Except in a few rare instances, complete customer satisfaction is the key to securing customer loyalty and generating superior long-term financial performance.* Most managers realize that the more competitive the market, the more important the level of customer satisfaction. What most do not realize, however, is just how important the level of customer satisfaction is in markets where competition is intense, such as hard and soft durables, business equipment, financial services, and retailing. In markets like these, there is a tremendous difference between the loyalty of merely satisfied and completely satisfied customers. (See Exhibit II.) As the steep curve for the automobile industry shows, completely satisfied customers are—to a surprising degree—much more loyal than satisfied customers. To put it another way, any drop from total satisfaction results in a major drop in loyalty. The same applies to commodity businesses with thin profit margins; the potential returns on initiatives to increase satisfaction in such businesses can be as high as the return on initiatives in more profitable businesses. In fact, attempts to create complete customer satisfaction in commodity industries will often raise the product or service out of the commodity category. In most instances, totally satisfying the members of the targeted customer group should be a top priority.

Even in markets with relatively little competition, providing customers with outstanding value may be the only reliable way to achieve sustained customer satisfaction and loyalty. There are two types of loyalty: true long-term loyalty and what we call false loyalty. A variety of factors can generate false loyalty or make customers seem deeply loyal when they are not. They include: government regulations that limit competition; high

Exhibit II.

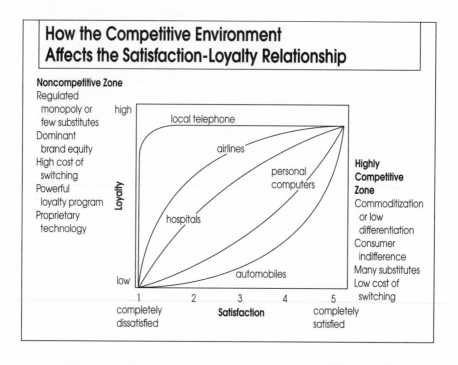

How the Competitive Environment Affects the Satisfaction-Loyalty Relationship

Noncompetitive Zone
Regulated
  monopoly or
  few substitutes
Dominant
  brand equity
High cost of
  switching
Powerful
  loyalty program
Proprietary
  technology

high

local telephone

airlines

personal
computers

hospitals

automobiles

Loyalty

low

**Highly
Competitive
Zone**
Commoditization
  or low
  differentiation
Consumer
  indifference
Many substitutes
Low cost of
  switching

1   2   3   4   5
completely   completely
dissatisfied   **Satisfaction**   satisfied

switching costs such as the cost of changing hospitals in the middle of treatment; proprietary technology that limits alternatives; and strong loyalty-promotion programs such as frequent-flier plans. But we made a startling discovery about customers in such markets. Whenever these customers have choices and feel free to make a choice, they act like customers in markets with intense competition: They will only remain rock-solid loyal if they are completely satisfied. That is why seemingly loyal customers defect when they exhaust their frequent-flier miles, when they complete a course of treatment at a hospital, when a regulated market is deregulated, and when alternative technologies are offered. In such markets, it is the companies, rather than their customers, who ultimately have no choice. They must strive to provide their prized customers—those they can serve most profitably—with outstanding value. The message is clear: It is absolutely critical for a company to excel in both defining its target customers and delivering a product or service that completely meets their needs.

Very poor service or products are not the only cause—and may not even be the main cause—of high dissatisfaction. Often the company has attracted the wrong customers or has an inadequate process for turning around the right customers when they have a bad experience. Customers typically fall into one of two categories: the right customers, or target group, whom the company should be able to serve well and profitably, and the wrong customers, whose needs it cannot profitably serve. Having the wrong customers is the result of a flawed process for attracting or obtaining customers. The company that retains difficult-to-serve, chronically unhappy customers is making an expensive long-term mistake. Such customers will continually utilize a disproportionate amount of the company's resources, will hurt the morale of frontline employees, and will disparage the company to other potential customers. Managers should actively discourage such people or organizations from remaining customers and should do their best not to attract others like them. On the other hand, managers of companies that are generally delivering high-quality services or products obviously want to keep their targeted customers and should strive to make amends when, inevitably, something goes wrong. Marked unhappiness among targeted customers often means a problem was not resolved to their satisfaction.

Different satisfaction levels reflect different issues and, therefore, require different actions. The levels of satisfaction among targeted customers are a good indicator of the level of quality of the products or services that they are receiving. But the way to raise the level of customer satisfaction from neutral to satisfied or from satisfied to completely satisfied is not just a matter of doing a better job of delivering the same value or experience that the company is currently delivering. There are four elements that affect customer satisfaction: the basic elements of the product or service that customers expect all competitors to deliver; basic support services such as customer assistance or order tracking that make the product or service incrementally more effective and easier to use; a recovery process for counteracting bad experiences; and extraordinary services that so excel in meeting customers' personal preferences, in appealing to their values, or in solving their particular problems that they make the product or service seem customized. As we will discuss later, the satisfaction or dissatisfaction level of the majority of a company's customers helps determine which of these elements the company should focus on delivering.

Even though the results of customer-satisfaction surveys are an important indicator of the health of the business, relying solely on them can be fatal. Customer-satisfaction surveys can generate valuable information that enables a company to compare the performance of one business unit or several business units in different time periods and locations. They can provide leading indicators of market shifts and can provide a clear sense of the product or service attributes that individual customers most desire. However, customer-satisfaction surveys cannot supply the breadth and depth of information about customers needed to guide the company's strategy and product-innovation process. Satisfaction surveys alone will not enable a company to fend off new competitors or to keep products and services attuned to customers' changing needs. For this reason, companies must also utilize a variety of other methods to listen to existing, potential, and former customers. (See "How to Listen to Customers.")

How to Listen to Customers

At the heart of any successful strategy to manage satisfaction is the ability to listen to the customer. There are five major categories of approaches that companies can use to listen to their customers. Most highly successful companies employ several, if not all. Many average or poor performers either use very few or, if they use many, do a poor job of incorporating the results into their strategies. The five categories are:

Customer-Satisfaction Indices. Surveying customers about their level of satisfaction and plotting the results can help managers understand just how satisfied or dissatisfied customers are with both their dealings with the company in general and with various elements of the company's product or service in particular. The fact that such indices are quantitative makes them a useful tool for comparing results from different time periods, locations, and business units.

Feedback. Customers' comments, complaints, and questions fall into this category. A company cannot implement a recovery strategy—a plan for making amends when something has gone wrong— if it does not know who has had a problem. Therefore, it is important to review the company's approach to soliciting feedback—especially complaints—on product and service quality.

Market Research. Although companies traditionally invest significantly in this area, they often overlook two critical listening points. Customers should be interviewed both at the time of arrival (when they become customers) and at the time of departure (when they defect) about the reasons for their behavior. New customers should not only be asked, "How did you hear about us?" but also, "What major experiences influenced your decision to try our product or service?" The answers to the first question will provide data about the effectiveness of the company's awareness advertising, and the answers to the second will supply information about specific factors that actually sparked the decision to try the product or service. It also is absolutely critical to understand why a customer defected. Gleaning that information requires a high degree of sensitivity and skill because most customers will blame the price or some other relatively basic product attribute in order to avoid discussing the real issue. Carefully questioning departing customers is important for two reasons: to isolate those attributes of the company's product or service that are causing customers to leave and to make a last-ditch attempt to keep the customer. One company we studied found that it recaptured a full 35% of its defectors just by contacting them and listening to them earnestly.

Frontline Personnel. Employees who have direct contact with the customer provide a superb means of listening. To take full advantage of frontline employees' interactions with customers, however, a company must train them to listen effectively and to make the first attempts at amends when customers have bad experiences. They also must have processes in place to capture the information and pass it along to the rest of the company. Many companies that excel in satisfying customers have institutionalized one other practice: All employees—not just those with frontline jobs—spend a significant amount of time interacting in depth with customers.

Strategic Activities. Some companies go to extremes to involve the customer in every level of their business. MTV, the cable music channel geared to 18-to 24-year-olds, insists that most of its employees must belong to the demographic target group. Southwest Airlines actually invites frequent fliers to its first round of group interviews with prospective flight attendants and considers these customers' opinions in decisions to invite certain candidates back for individual interviews. Intuit, the financial-software company, regularly brings in customers to participate in product-development sessions.

The Satisfaction-Loyalty Link

Executives at Xerox Corporation, which had conducted in-depth satisfaction studies of its office-products customers, played a major role in helping us define our research project. Xerox's intense interest in measuring customer satisfaction sprang from a set of beliefs that we share. High-quality products and associated services designed to meet customer needs will create high levels of customer satisfaction. This high level of satisfaction will lead to greatly increased customer loyalty. And increased customer loyalty is the single most important driver of long-term financial performance. Separate research has validated these beliefs. (See the preceding chapter, "Zero Defections: Quality Comes to Services," by Frederick F. Reichheld and W. Earl Sasser, Jr.)

Although these assumptions might seem relatively simple, one discovery by Xerox shattered conventional wisdom: Its totally satisfied customers were six times more likely to repurchase Xerox products over the next 18 months than its satisfied customers. The implications were profound: Merely satisfying customers who have the freedom to make choices is not enough to keep them loyal. The only truly loyal customers are totally satisfied customers.

The Research. Xerox's discovery intrigued us. Was this relationship between satisfaction and loyalty unique to Xerox? To investigate, we scrutinized more than 30 individual companies and analyzed data from five markets with different competitive environments and different types of customer relationships. The five markets were automobiles, personal computers purchased by businesses, hospitals, airlines, and local telephone services. To measure customer loyalty, we decided to rely mostly on customers' stated intent to repurchase products or services. (See "Measures of Loyalty.") We selected the five markets for particular reasons.

Measures of Loyalty

Broadly speaking, customer loyalty is the feeling of attachment to or affection for a company's people, products, or services. These feelings manifest themselves in many forms of customer behavior. The ultimate measure of loyalty, of course, is share of purchases in the category. In the automobile business, it is share of garage. In the clothing industry, it is share of closet. And in the restaurant business, as Taco Bell president and CEO John Martin says, it is "share of stomach."

Unfortunately, such information is rarely available at the individual customer level. But there are alternative measurements, which we have grouped into three major categories.

Intent to Repurchase. At any time in the customer relationship, it is possible to ask customers about their future intentions to repurchase a given product or service. Although their responses are simply indications of future behavior and are not assurances, they have very important benefits. First, companies can capture this information when they measure satisfaction, making it relatively easy to link intentions and satisfaction for analytical purposes. The fact that intent to repurchase can be measured at any time in the customer relationship makes it especially valuable in industries with a long repurchase cycle. Finally, intent to repurchase actually is a very strong indicator of future behavior. Although this measure will generally overstate the probability of repurchase, the degree of exaggeration usually is fairly consistent, meaning that the future results can be predicted fairly accurately. For example, an average of 60% to 80% of automobile customers queried 90 days after buying a car say they intend to repurchase the same brand, and 35% to 40% actually do so three to four years later.

Primary Behavior. Depending on the industry, companies often have access to information on various transactions at the customer level and can measure five categories that show actual repurchasing behavior: recency, frequency, amount, retention, and longevity. Although they are important measures of actual behavior, they only provide a glimpse of overall share and are most useful as an indication of changes over time. Moreover, sometimes they can send the wrong message. For example, the credit-card industry traditionally measured the willingness of the consumer to pay the annual fee as its prime measure of retention. During the late 1980s and early 1990s, those same companies saw that willingness rise while actual "share of wallet"—the degree to which customers used their particular card for making purchases when they had the option of using a credit card—decreased. The consumer was willing to pay the fee to have the credit card available but often did not use it. Therefore, recency, frequency, and amount of purchase were significantly better measures of loyalty.

Secondary Behavior. Customer referrals, endorsements, and spreading the word are extremely important forms of consumer behavior for a company. In most product and service categories, word of mouth is one of the most important factors in acquiring new customers. Frequently, it is easier for a customer to respond honestly to a question about whether he or she would recommend the product or service to others than to a question about whether he or she intended to repurchase the product or service. Such indications of loyalty, obtained through customer surveys, are frequently ignored because they are *soft* measures of behavior that are difficult to link to eventual purchasing behavior. However, since secondary behavior significantly leverages the positive experiences of a single customer, it is very important to understand what types of experiences create such behavior.

Automobiles. We chose automobiles to test whether Xerox's discovery—that its completely satisfied customers were significantly more likely to repurchase its products than its simply satisfied customers—was a fluke or the norm in highly competitive markets. By highly competitive markets we mean those in which there are many alternative products or services offered, the cost of switching is low, or the product is not important to the buyer (that is, where a valid substitute is no purchase at all). Our data on the buyers of 32 automobile models were provided by Robert Lunn of J.D. Power and Associates, the market-research company based in Agoura Hills, California. J.D. Power surveyed these individuals one year after they had purchased their vehicles. The 32 nameplates included both foreign and domestic models with high, medium, and low prices.

Personal Computers for Businesses. We studied this industry to explore the satisfaction-loyalty relationship in a market where the user is not the actual purchaser. Although the personal-computer market is highly competitive, considerable barriers prevent individual business users from switching to another manufacturer's personal computer: for example, centralized purchasing and corporate standards. On the other hand, central purchasing departments do periodically reconsider their suppliers. And in the last ten years, corporate purchasing departments have placed a greater focus on pleasing their customers: the actual users of the equipment they buy. To test how satisfaction affected the loyalty of the end users, we analyzed data from J.D. Power's 1994 survey of more than 2,000 business users of personal computers.

Hospitals. We chose the hospital market because of two interesting characteristics: Although it is shifting from a market dominated by semi-monopolies to one characterized by intense competition, there still remain significant barriers that impede end users (patients) from switching. Several factors affect the choice of a particular hospital. The patient's physician, health maintenance organization, or insurer often determines where he or she goes for treatment; after beginning treatment in a hospital, a patient tends to complete treatment there; and finally, in many parts of the country, there is only one hospital within a convenient distance. Nonetheless, there are moments when the barriers drop and patients can and do switch. To test how these kinds of barriers affect the satisfaction-loyalty relationship, we relied on data taken from 10,000 surveys of patients treated at nearly 82 hospitals in a range of locations in the United States. David Furse, president of NCG Research—a company based in Nashville, Tennessee, that measures service quality and customer satisfaction in the health care industry—provided us with the data.

Airlines. This market interested us because it is one in which the varying level of competition on routes and strong loyalty-promotion programs affect purchasing decisions. Since airlines are relatively efficient in responding to competitors' price changes, most people flying on a particular route heavily base their purchasing decisions on two other factors: time of departure and frequent-flier programs. Although some routes are highly competitive, the fact of the matter is that people who have to go to a certain place at a certain time often have few if any alternatives: The route is a virtual monopoly. To explore the impact of all these factors on the satisfaction-loyalty relationship, we analyzed data from a survey that J.D. Power conducted in the first quarter of 1994. The survey questioned approximately 20,000 passengers who used the eight largest domestic airlines and flew on 72 routes.

Local Telephone Services. We analyzed data provided by a Bell operating company to explore the nature of the relationship in actual or virtual monopolies, in which satisfaction seems to have little impact on loyalty. More specifically, we wanted to understand better how the satisfaction-loyalty relationship might change if the competitive environment suddenly changed—a critical issue for monopolies facing deregulation, global competition, and technological change. By actual or virtual monopolies, we mean companies that operate in markets where, thanks to government regulations, proprietary technology, or very strong brand equity, there is little or no competition. Others in this category include: electrical utilities; cable television providers; transportation utilities with special rights of way; companies with brand identities that are so strong that the customers perceive there to be no other choice; and companies in competitive industries where the barriers that prevent customers from switching to another supplier are high (a restaurant at the top of a ski lift, for example).

The Indications. Of the five markets, local telephone service, with nearly complete control over customers, was the only one for which the relationship between satisfaction and loyalty turned out exactly as one would expect. Customers remained loyal no matter how dissatisfied they were. But our study of other actual or virtual monopolies did yield one vitally important discovery: When the source of a monopoly's hold on customers suddenly disappears—whether the cause is deregulation, the emergence of an alternative technology, or the arrival of new competitors—the curve can snap into the shape of a highly competitive market in an astonishingly short period of time.

According to conventional wisdom, the link between satisfaction and loyalty in markets where customers have choices is a simple, linear relationship: As satisfaction goes up, so does loyalty. But we discovered that the relationship was neither linear nor simple. To a much greater extent than most managers think, completely satisfied customers are more loyal than merely satisfied customers.

In markets where competition is intense, we found a tremendous difference between the loyalty of satisfied and completely satisfied customers. In the automobile industry, even a slight drop from complete satisfaction created an enormous drop in loyalty. This dramatic phenomenon is not limited to markets for manufactured products: It also occurs in services. In his study of the loyalty of retail-banking depositors, John Larson, a vice president of Opinion Research Corporation in Princeton, New Jersey, found that completely satisfied customers were nearly 42% more likely to be loyal than merely satisfied customers.

How about the curves for hospitals, airlines, and personal computers sold to businesses—industries whose holds on customers fall somewhere between automobiles and local telephone services? They also held surprises. We discovered that customer satisfaction in those industries, too, can affect customer loyalty much more than managers generally assume. Equally if not more important, we discovered that at certain times or under certain circumstances, satisfaction has a much bigger impact on loyalty. In these cases, the curve can snap into the shape of a curve of a more competitive—even a highly competitive—market.

Of the three midrange markets, the steepest drop in the loyalty of end users relative to satisfaction was in the business-PC market. Why should manufacturers of personal computers care? Why should manufacturers care? Because, when the time comes for IT or purchasing departments to replace the current generation of PCs, end-user satisfaction may suddenly have a big impact on customer loyalty. The curve snaps.

The next steepest drop in loyalty occurred in the hospital market—and it promises to become steeper as competition in the industry intensifies. Nonetheless, most hospitals are still operating as if they had little effective competition. They continue to place little emphasis on patient satisfaction. One can speculate about the reasons. Perhaps their managers think that the centralization of purchasing power makes health maintenance organizations and insurers, rather than individuals, the ones to please. Perhaps they think this centralization will only raise the barriers that block dissatisfied patients from switching. If so, they may be in for a shock. After all, many HMOs and insurers provide their subscribers with a menu of hospitals from which to choose. Moreover, individuals often can switch health plans if they don't like the hospitals on the menu—a fact not lost on HMOs. Although a patient may not be free to change hospitals at any time, there will be a time when the patient or HMO or insurer can. The curve snaps.

In mixed markets such as airlines, achieving a high level of customer satisfaction matters for several reasons. Although a combination of limited choice and artificial restraints such as frequent-flier programs often cause even completely dissatisfied airline customers to remain fairly loyal, the relationship between satisfaction and loyalty does resemble a competitive market on routes where several carriers offer flights at around the same time. This fact means that complete customer satisfaction is very important on both competitive routes and monopoly routes. Why is it important on monopoly routes? Because, as several larger airlines have learned, customers who have suffered years of mediocre or poor service on such routes can still take their revenge. When traveling on other routes where there is competition, they can choose another airline. And if a new, lower-priced competitor suddenly challenges the monopoly, even a frequent-flier program will not be enough to retain them.

Take heed. Although customers sometimes defect en masse, their departure may also occur in harder-to-spot dribs and drabs or spurts. Patients typically defect only after completing a course of treatment. An advertising agency client may defect only when it is time to undertake a new marketing campaign. A major corporate customer may defect from a bank only when an account executive with whom the customer had a personal relationship leaves. In these cases, the business is suddenly operating in a more competitive environment. The curve snaps. It is a time of maximum vulnerability for the company. And if it takes a while to lose such customers, it takes just as long to recapture them once they have moved to another supplier.

What is the overarching lesson? Customers are reasonable, but they want to be completely satisfied; if they are not and have a choice, they can be lured away easily. (See Table I.) In today's turbulent world, measuring customers' outward loyalty does not suffice. Nor does

Table I.

They Suffered the Consequences	
Industries or Companies That Experienced a Rapid Change in Customer Loyalty	**Reason for Shift in Customer Loyalty**
Telecommunications, airlines, electrical power, savings and loan associations	Deregulation
Xerox, Roche (Valium)	Loss of patent protection
Electronics, U.S. auto industry	Entrance of new competitors
American Express, IBM	Reduction in brand dominance
IBM, Digital Equipment Corporation	Advent of new technologies

knowing whether the satisfaction-loyalty relationship a company enjoys with the majority of its customers is the norm for its market. It is essential to understand what portion of customers' seeming loyalty is true loyalty based on a company's delivery of superior value and what part is artificial. Measuring customer satisfaction is one of the safest ways to obtain this information. If there is a solid likelihood that the level of competition in a market is going to increase, it is obviously better to seek to increase customer satisfaction before the curve snaps than after. The safest approach is to seek total customer satisfaction.

Consequently, most managers should be concerned rather than heartened if the majority of their customers fall into the satisfied category. Those customers have reasons for not being completely satisfied. Some element (or elements) of their experience with the company was not acceptable, and that shortfall in performance is sufficient for them to consider alternatives. Some might ask, Then why did these customers say they were satisfied in the first place? The answer is: Regardless of how they feel, customers of companies with reasonably good product or service quality tend to find it difficult to respond negatively to customer-satisfaction surveys. As a result, their satisfaction responses typically fall in the upper end of the scale—a 4 or 5 on

Table II.

Interpreting Levels of Satisfaction		
Response	**Description**	**Loyalty**
5	completely satisfied	very loyal
3–4	satisfied	easily switched to a competitor
1–2	dissatisfied	very disloyal

a scale of 1 to 5. Rather than thinking of customers as loyal or disloyal, managers would be better off treating them as three separate groups. (See Table II.)

Like the managers of the company described at the beginning of this article, most managers probably would be happy to learn that 82% of their customers fell into category 4 or 5. The more appropriate reaction would be, "We have a problem. Only 48% of our customers are completely satisfied, and 52% are up for grabs."

Using Customer-Satisfaction Information

Customer-satisfaction information can be a critical barometer of how well a company is serving its customers. This information also can show a company what it needs to do to increase its customer satisfaction level by level until the majority of its customers are totally satisfied. The key is understanding what customers are saying when they provide various responses.

The first step is to make the measurement of customer satisfaction and loyalty a priority and to ensure that the process is unbiased, consistent, broadly applied, and able to capture and store information on individual customers. The process should be unbiased because typically there are forces within the company that will attempt to distort it for their own purposes. It should be consistent so that period-to-period changes have meaning. It should be broadly applied so that products, locations, and business units can be compared in order to help managers decide how to use the company's limited resources

Table III.

How to Decide What Actions to Take		
	Bulk of Responses	**Strategic Response**
Stage 1	2–3 (dissatisfied)	Deliver the basic product or service elements as expected of anyone in the industry
Stage 2	3–4 (neutral)	Provide an appropriate range of supporting services Develop proactive service recovery to make amends when something goes wrong
Stage 3	4–5 (satisfied)	Understand and achieve results in customers' terms

most effectively. Last but not least, the measurement process should capture information on individual customers so that the company can tailor its satisfaction-improvement programs to its individual customers' situations.

The second step is to create a curve by plotting individual customer responses. In addition to assessing how satisfied or dissatisfied customers are, managers should compare their company's curve with those shown in the industries we surveyed and consider the factors that shaped their own company's curve. Is the company retaining its customers through false-loyalty mechanisms, or is their loyalty the result of the value that the company provides through its product or services?

The third step is to determine the most appropriate strategies for raising customer satisfaction. (See Table III.)

A dissatisfied customer is probably having problems with the core value of the company's product or service—the basic elements that customers expect everyone in the industry to be able to provide. Although it may seem obvious that the basic product desired by customers often shifts as competitors improve, new competitors arrive, and new technologies redefine the game, it is even more obvious from business history that keeping up with such shifts is one of management's most difficult challenges. The match between the basic product or service and the customers it is designed to serve must be reviewed continually to ensure that there is still a good fit.

A neutral customer is probably happy with the basic product or service but would like to be offered a consistent set of support services. And to ensure that neutral and satisfied customers do not slip back into the realm of the dissatisfied if bad luck happens to strike, companies also need highly responsive recovery processes. Well-designed support services—and they almost always are *services*—make the basic product or service easier to use or more effective. And recovery processes help the customer get back on track if problems occur.

The vast majority of companies that excel in satisfying customers rank the ability to react when something goes wrong as one of the most important factors in satisfying customers. That ability greatly influences whether customers heap scorn or praise on the company when talking to others. (See "Apostles and Terrorists: A Company's Best Friends and Worst Enemies.") Strong recovery processes are especially vital in industries such as airlines, automobiles, production equipment, and mail-order retailing—businesses in which the product or service is complex or some delivery and servicing processes lie outside the company's control.

Apostles and Terrorists: A Company's Best Friends and Worst Enemies

Although it is important and valuable to track and understand the satisfaction and loyalty of customers as a group, it is equally critical to understand the attitudes and behavior of individual customers. Depending on their unique behavioral attributes (prior individual biases), intensity of satisfaction or dissatisfaction (attitude), and ability to act on their satisfaction or dissatisfaction (competitive market dynamics), customers behave in one of four basic ways: as loyalists, as defectors, as mercenaries, or as hostages. Turning as many customers as possible into the most valuable type of loyalist, the apostle, and eliminating the most dangerous type of defector or hostage, the terrorist, should be every company's ultimate objective. (See Table IV.)

The Loyalist and the Apostle

In most cases, the loyalist is a customer who is completely satisfied and keeps returning to the company. The loyalist is a company's bedrock. This customer's needs and the company's product or service offerings fit

Table IV.

Individual Customer Satisfaction, Loyalty, and Behavior			
	Satisfaction	**Loyalty**	**Behavior**
Loyalist/Apostle	high	high	staying and supportive
Defector/Terrorist	low to medium	low to medium	leaving or having left and unhappy
Mercenary	high	low to medium	coming and going; low commitment
Hostage	low to medium	high	unable to switch; trapped

exceptionally well, which, not surprisingly, is why loyalists often are the easiest customers to serve. Occasionally, the match is so good that even a 5 on a 1-to-5 satisfaction scale doesn't fully capture the strength of the relationship.

Within the loyalist camp are individuals who are so satisfied, whose experience so far exceeds their expectations, that they share their strong feelings with others. They are apostles.

One company that excels in creating apostles is Intuit, maker of Quicken, the phenomenally successful financial-management software. Although Intuit has fewer than ten sales employees, it has hundreds of thousands of salespeople: its highly satisfied customers, who found the company's product and its customer-service staff so responsive to their unique needs that they had to tell someone else. "When you treat a customer so well that he or she goes out and tells five friends how great it is to own your product—that's when you're doing it right," says Scott Cook, Intuit's cofounder and chairman of the board.

Treating customers exceptionally well does not mean merely treating them well when everything basically is going right. It also means treating them exceptionally well when something goes terribly wrong. Highly dissatisfied customers typically include people who were highly satisfied until they purchased a single shoddy product or suffered a service failure or a sequence of unrelated failures. If a company excels in making amends—that is, in recovering—when such failures occur, customers' faith in the company is not just restored, it is deepened; and they become apostles, spreading the good word about the company to potential customers.

Of course, a company can only turn such customers into apostles if they come forward. For this reason alone, it more than pays to provide customers with numerous opportunities to express their dissatisfaction. Companies with world-class recovery organizations frequently ask customers if they are satisfied, provide toll-free customer comment numbers, fully involve frontline employees in the crusade to identify and help customers frustrated by service or product failures, and regularly review their approaches to dealing with customer problems.

The Defector and the Terrorist

Defectors' ranks include those who are more than dissatisfied, quite dissatisfied, and neutral. The merely satisfied—many more than most managers realize—defect, too. And as we've said, so do once highly satisfied customers who have encountered failures. Letting those customers defect is perhaps the biggest mistake managers can make. When a company has strong processes in place to understand such customers' needs better and to shower attention on them if isolated problems strike, most of them can be converted or turned once again into highly satisfied customers.

Not all defectors should be retained, however. The unreasonable demands of unhappy customers whose needs do not fit with the company's capabilities can devour excessive resources and wreak havoc on employee morale. For just this reason, such outstanding service organizations as Nordstrom department stores, Sewell Village Cadillac Company in Dallas, and Southwest Airlines regularly "fire" customers they cannot properly serve. They recognize counterproductive efforts when they see them.

The most dangerous defectors are the terrorists. These are the customers who have had a bad experience and can't wait to tell others about their anger and frustration. They are the airline passengers who because of bad weather were stranded at an alternate airport and were not given appropriate assistance. They are the retail customers who found that the product they just bought did not work and encountered an inept or uncaring service employee when they tried to get help or compensation. They are the new car owners who had to return countless times to try to get the same problem fixed. With each telling, their stories grow in intensity and the actual facts become increasingly distorted.

Unfortunately, terrorists generally are far more committed and hence more effective at telling their stories than apostles. Like many apostles, they had bad experiences. But in their case, no one listened, no one responded, no one corrected the problem.

The Mercenary

Another customer who can make a company's life miserable is the mercenary. This individual defies the satisfaction-loyalty rule: He may be completely satisfied but exhibit almost no loyalty. These customers are often expensive to acquire and quick to depart. They chase low prices, buy on impulse, pursue fashion trends, or seek change for the sake of change. Although it often takes as much effort to please them as to please long-term loyal customers, they do not remain long enough for the relationship to turn a profit.

The Hostage

Hostages are stuck. These individuals experience the worst the company has to offer and must accept it. Many companies operating in a monopolistic environment see little reason to respond to the plight of hostages. After all, these customers can't go anywhere. So why bother to correct the problems?

There are two important reasons why companies should bother. First, if the competitive environment suddenly shifts, these companies will then pay the price. Their customers will defect quickly and many will become terrorists. Second, hostages are very difficult and expensive to serve. They may be trapped, but they still take every opportunity to complain and to ask for special service. Hostages can devastate company morale, and their negative impact on per unit costs is astounding.

A completely satisfied customer typically believes that the company excels in understanding and addressing his or her personal preferences, values, needs, or problems. To figure out how to satisfy customers in this fashion, a company has to excel at listening to customers and interpreting what they are saying.[1]

Consider the experience of having a car repaired. A customer's basic goal is to have it fixed properly. To obtain a relatively neutral customer, a dealership or service station must repair the customer's vehicle competently. In the last decade, a large number of dealerships have expanded their services to include overnight and express drop-off, loaner vehicles, and free washing and waxing. Some also have instituted the practice of checking back with customers within 24 hours to make sure the problem was properly fixed, and a handful of really great dealerships check again after two weeks. If there is still a problem, fixing it becomes the top priority. These value-added support and recovery services are crucial for moving customers from neutral to satisfied. In recent years, dealerships that sell Japanese cars—most notably, Lexus dealerships—have reexamined the car-servicing experience from the customer's perspective. They found that what most customers want is to have their car repaired with minimum inconvenience and that *their* definition of the car-servicing experience includes taking the car to the dealership, arranging for transportation while it is in the shop, and picking it up once it is fixed. These dealers *completely satisfy* customers by picking up their cars at their homes or offices, leaving loaner vehicles, competently repairing, cleaning, and waxing the cars, returning them later in the day, picking up the loaners—and, of course, checking later to make sure that the cars were properly repaired.

An independent multiplex movie theater that we came across in the Southwest last year is another example of a business that excels in figuring out what its customers really want and giving it to them. Its managers discovered that customers' actual movie-going experience started about two blocks from the theater, where the typical customer, especially one who is running a bit late, enters the traffic approaching the parking lot and starts to become anxious about parking and purchasing a ticket. To address such concerns, the theater's managers placed attendants two blocks from the theater to sell tickets and help people enter the parking lot. The managers discovered that customers also resented having to leave the viewing area and then stand in line in the lobby to buy food. In response, the theater began to serve food throughout the facility; it even served seated customers until the main features began. Finally, the managers learned that customers detested dirty bathrooms. In response, the theater began cleaning its bathrooms four times an hour. The end result: a large number of highly satisfied, highly loyal customers.

The three-phase approach to increasing customer satisfaction has important implications. First, different actions are required to raise the satisfaction of customers of a family of products or services whose level of satisfaction differs. Second, it is absolutely critical to accomplish the three stages in order. It is possible to make a quantum leap—to move customers from neutral to completely satisfied, for instance—by completely redesigning the product or service, by introducing new technology, or by reengineering the underlying delivery process. But we have found that not many companies succeed at that. Such leaps often fall short because the company overlooked the support services that had evolved informally over the years and did not redesign them, too.

In the final analysis, the company that will survive and flourish over the long term is the one that continually works to understand the relationship between satisfaction and loyalty for each of its customers, for each of its business units, and for each of the industries in which it competes. Horst Schulze, president and COO of the Ritz-Carlton Hotel Company, the 1992 winner of the Malcolm Baldrige National Quality Award, put it the best. "Unless you have 100% customer satisfaction—and I don't mean that they are just satisfied, I mean that they are excited about what you are doing—you have to improve," he said. "And if you have 100% customer satisfaction, you have to make sure that you listen just in case they change . . . so you can change with them."

Note

1. Not all customers are saying the same thing. Opinion Research Corporation's John Larson has performed several studies comparing the satisfaction drivers for customers at different levels of satisfaction. In a study for a large information-services company, he found that dissatisfied customers were interested in core product attributes such as accuracy of data. Neutral customers were interested in account management issues such as the account manager's ability to relay account status quickly and accurately. And satisfied customers were interested in the degree to which the company's services supported the customer's strategic business objectives.

3
Competing on Customer Service: An Interview with British Airways' Sir Colin Marshall

Steven E. Prokesch

Few businesses are as brutally competitive as airlines. But just because the competition is tough, that's no reason to be tough on customers, says Sir Colin Marshall, the chairman of British Airways. Convinced that travelers care mainly about price, many airlines—most notably the major U. S. carriers—seem to have made cutting costs the top priority at the expense of their service quality. But Marshall doesn't think it has to be that way. Even in a cutthroat, mass-market business such as air travel, he argues, there are plenty of people who will pay a premium for good service—even among those who travel economy. It may sound crazy, but just look at British Airways' profits: While the world airline industry has racked up billions of dollars in losses in the last five years, British Airways has remained solidly profitable.

With his talk of building brand equity and commanding a premium by "orchestrating service to fill customers' value-driven needs," Marshall, who is 61 years old, is clearly an iconoclast in the airline industry. Then again, he is not a product of the industry. His first job was as a ship's purser. He then worked all over the world as a manager for Hertz and later Avis, where he became CEO in 1976. After the conglomerate Norton Simon acquired Avis in 1979, Marshall's responsibilities expanded to include Hunt-Wesson foods, which instilled in him an appreciation for the power of brands. Sears, the British retailer and shoe manufacturer, lured him back to London in 1981 by offering him the deputy CEO's job. Then in 1983, John King came calling. Appointed by Margaret Thatcher, the industrialist was in the midst of his struggle to turn loss-ridden, state-owned British Airways into a competitive airline that investors might want to own.

Together, King and Marshall transformed the airline, which they privatized in 1987. Marshall, who joined British Airways as CEO and succeeded King as chairman in 1993, has presided over British Airways' metamorphosis from a company that seemed to disdain customers to one that strives to please them. Although Marshall certainly isn't yet proclaiming victory on that front, a much larger challenge is now looming. In a bid to become the first truly global airline, British Airways has been forging alliances with other carriers around the world. It has taken sizable stakes in USAir, Australia's Qantas Airways, France's TAT European Airlines, and Deutsche BA. If delivering consistent, high-quality service in a complex people business is tremendously difficult for one company, think about trying to get a group of companies to do it. From his offices in London, Marshall talked with *Harvard Business Review* senior editor Steven E. Prokesch about competing in service industries.

HBR: *How can a large competitor such as British Airways differentiate itself in a commodity services business that is so cutthroat?*

Sir Colin Marshall: You're always going to be faced with the fact that the great majority of people will buy on price. But even for a seeming commodity such as air travel, an element of the traveling public is willing to pay a slight premium for superior service. They are the people we've been trying to attract and retain as customers. We don't just mean people who fly business class, first class, or the Concorde. Many service companies ignore the fact that there also are plenty of customers in the lower end of the market who are willing to pay a little more for superior service.

It all comes back in the end to value for money. If you can deliver something extra that others are not or cannot, some people will pay a slight premium for it. I want to stress that when I say "slight," I mean precisely that. In our case, we're talking about an average of 5%. On our revenues of £5 billion, however, that 5% translates into an extra £250 million, or $400 million, a year.

It's true that we can't command a premium everywhere, but we've succeeded in most of our international markets, including the majority of routes between Britain and the East Coast of the United States. That's why our profits from and share of that market have continued to climb in recent years despite the tough competition on routes such as the one between London's Heathrow airport and New York's John F. Kennedy airport, and despite growing competition from strong companies such as American, United, and Virgin Atlantic.

In industry after industry, companies seem to be competing mainly on cost and price. That certainly seems to be the case in the U.S. airline industry. What do you think of this approach?

I think it is flawed. Most of the major U.S. airlines have not been very innovative or creative. Compared with international flying anyway, the flying experience in the United States today is pretty ghastly. We've conducted extensive research with USAir and have very strong indications that many people in the United States are willing to pay a premium not to be treated like cattle. They want to be respected and rewarded for their business—and not just with frequent-flier miles, which have become a commodity, a price of entry into the market. We think we—through USAir—could revolutionize the U.S. airline industry and create an entirely new section of the industry. USAir is beginning to implement this strategy with its new Business Select service.

There are two sides to the business equation: costs and revenues. Any business that focuses on one at the expense of the other is going to pay very heavily. You can't walk away from the fact that if somebody can do the job better and cheaper, you have a problem and you have to do something about it. But you can do it without undermining the fabric of what you have built up. When business conditions got tough in recent years, we did not take meat cleavers to our product. We did not reduce costs indiscriminately. We did not reduce the quality of the wine. We did not stop investing in airport lounges and in training people. We continued making that investment despite the fact that it would have been very easy not to. Why is it that people prefer to fly business class with us? It's because our product is better.

There are different ways to think about how to compete in a mass-market service business such as ours. One is to think that a business is merely performing a function—in our case, transporting people from point A to point B on time and at the lowest possible price. That's the commodity mind-set, thinking of an airline as the bus of the skies. Another way to compete is to go beyond the function and compete on the basis of providing an experience. In our case, we want to make the process of flying from point A to point B as effortless and pleasant as possible. Anyone can fly airplanes, but few organizations can excel in serving people. Because it's a competence that's hard to build, it's also hard for competitors to copy or match.

To use a rather overdone term, we decided that our goal should be to make our service more seamless than our competitors'. By that I mean we aim to remove some of the common hassles that one encounters when traveling today, thereby making the customer's whole experience easier. For instance, we have worked with British government authorities to install fast-track channels at Heathrow and Gatwick airports to make it easier for our premium, or full-fare, passengers to speed through immigration and customs. And unlike many U.S. airlines, which charge people for access to their lounges, our lounges are part of our products. Access is included in our Concorde, First Class, Club World (intercontinental business class), and Club Europe (European business class) products and is a reward for our top frequent fliers. Everything in our lounges—from drinks to telephone service—is free.

There's another critical element of our approach to serving customers: Filling customers' value-driven needs. Every industry has a price of entry—the ante you have to pay to get into the game. In our industry, there are five basic services that everyone has to provide. We must: get passengers to where they want to go, do it safely, go when they want to go, provide some nourishment, and let them accrue frequent-flier miles. But our research shows that customers now take the basics for granted and increasingly want a company to desire to help them, to treat them in a personal, caring way. Fulfilling those desires is the centerpiece of how we wish to orchestrate our service.

What do you mean by orchestrating *service?*

I mean exactly that: arranging all the elements of our service so that they collectively generate a particular experience. We try to think about what kind of impression or feeling each interaction between the company and a customer will generate. For instance, we ask our crews not to load up passengers with food and drinks and then disappear— not for cost reasons but so we can create additional personal contacts with the customer. According to our research, just seeing crew members creates higher customer-satisfaction levels. Other airlines pile on the food and drinks so that their crew members don't have to go back.

I mentioned that we strive to make our customers' travel experience seamless, personal, and caring. We continually ask customers in focus groups to tell us what such an experience should look and feel like, and we have distilled their responses into service principles that are enshrined in two of our corporate goals. The goals are: "To provide overall superior service and good value for money in every market segment in which we compete" and "to excel in anticipating and quickly responding to customer needs and competitor activity." These corporate goals have, in turn, been incorporated into our customer service department's mission statement: "To ensure that British Airways is the customer's first choice through the delivery of an unbeatable travel experience."

We want to create an airline with a global scope but a homey feel. The phrase "nothing too small, nothing too big" captures what we're trying to achieve. The "nothing too big" or global image, our customers have told us, lets them know that we go where they're going and that we're professional. The "nothing too small" feeling lets them know that we have orchestrated our services to look after their individual needs. We want them to know that we carry millions but to feel that our individual interactions with them weren't mass produced. The theme of our latest worldwide advertising campaign is: "It's how we make you feel which makes us the world's favorite airline."

Could you provide a concrete illustration of a service you created in order to fill customers' value-driven needs?

When we found that many long-haul travelers felt poorly when they arrived at their destinations, we began our Well-Being in the Air program to help passengers combat fatigue and improve their circulation. It consists of healthful meal choices and a video demonstrating exercises that customers can perform in their seats. That's relatively small. But we also designed a whole new service—our Sleeper Service—for First Class customers flying long routes: They can eat a real dinner in the lounge before boarding and change into "sleeper suits" (pajamas) on the plane. Upon arriving in Britain, they can use our arrivals lounges, which are a major innovation. They're places where our First Class and Club World customers can get messages left overnight while they were in the air; have breakfast; read a newspaper; shower; get a manicure, haircut, or shave; have clothes pressed; and then catch a taxi or subway or train into town. We maintain full arrival-lounge facilities at Heathrow and Gatwick, our prime network-hub airports; and at Birmingham, Glasgow, and Manchester airports we offer similar complimentary comforts at hotels adjacent to the airport terminals.

Many passengers arriving on long overnight flights need a place to go when their flights get in very early—before public transport or offices are open. Our research revealed that they thought that airlines, including British Airways, took their money and dumped them without a care. In other words, we were not filling a value-driven need.

Our main arrivals lounges at the London airports are used by an average of around 200 customers each day. They unquestionably played a significant part in boosting our premium business by 9% during our last fiscal year, which ended March 31. The Sleeper Service has been similarly well received. Since its introduction in February 1995, First Class bookings between New York and London, for instance, have increased by as much as 25%. To varying extents, competitors are copying these initiatives, but British Airways enjoys the halo effect that comes from being first.

Not all potential customers will care about or value our approach to service. But even in a mass-market business, you don't want to attract and retain everyone. As far as we're concerned, the key is first to identify and attract those who will value your service and then to retain them as customers and win the largest possible share of their lifetime business. We know that 35% of our customers account for more than 60% of our sales. Using database-marketing techniques, we have focused more of our marketing effort on retaining those customers and increasing our share of their business. That's why our advertising spending is proportionately smaller than that of our competitors.

Although other companies employ similar marketing techniques, we think ours are pretty sophisticated. First, we extensively and continuously study the market to pinpoint the segments that offer the possibility of generating a higher profit margin—segments such as business women, unaccompanied minors, and consultants—and identify those people among our customers. Then we create extensive lifestyle profiles of each customer, which we use both to increase ticket purchases and to sell other products and services. In addition to tracking how recently and how frequently customers have flown with us for business and for leisure, we track their broader purchasing behavior, lifestyles, their ability to influence other people's purchasing decisions, and their value needs. But identifying such customers is only half the battle. Learning from them so you can design and improve services that they will highly value over time is the other half. That's where we think we especially excel.

Competing by delivering an experience, by filling customers' value-driven needs as you put it, must be extremely difficult in a service business. Presumably, it's much easier to achieve a consistent standard in consumer packaged goods because it's much easier to create a formula that gets a product to perform in a particular way and then to manufacture that product consistently.

You're absolutely right. With packaged goods, you can pull something off the line to test it periodically, and adjust it if there's something wrong. A packaged-goods business has the most incredible market data available to it. It knows how it's performing by store, even by positioning on the shelves in the store. That kind of reliable information is just not available in our industry or in service businesses generally because a service business is dealing with people's impressions and feelings. They don't actually buy an object; they buy an experience.

In addition, so many human interactions are involved in producing an experience in a service business that it is often difficult to measure which interaction or series of interactions caused a customer to feel satisfied or dissatisfied. On top of that, a customer may have a bad experience because of circumstances outside our control—a flight delay caused by bad weather, for example, or problems with air-traffic control. As a result, it is often difficult to know if a complaint is the result of an isolated event—perhaps one crew just having a bad day— or a systemic problem.

How can a service company overcome such formidable obstacles?

By creating an organization that excels in listening to its most valuable customers. By creating data that enable you to measure the kinds of performance that create value for those customers so you can improve performance and spot and correct any weaknesses. And by recognizing that the people on the front line are the ones who ultimately create value since they are the ones who determine the kinds of experiences that the company generates for its customers. We focus intensively on the customer, and our marketing, our operating philosophy, and our performance measures reflect that.

In several key places in our organization, we have created customer advocates: in our brand-management organization; in our marketplace performance unit, which is responsible for benchmarking our operations and collecting data; and in our customer relations department.

I guess the importance of brand management came home to me during my Norton Simon days, when I was responsible for Hunt-Wesson. That experience shaped the way I perceive service products. It helped me realize that instilling a brand culture is very important in a service business because a service business is all about serving people, who have values, ideals, and feelings. It helped me realize that we needed to see the product not simply as a seat but more comprehensively as an experience being orchestrated across the airline. That orchestration was the brand.

BA's seven brand managers are customers' main advocates within BA. They oversee the process of refreshing the brands and are among those responsible for thinking of ways to innovate and improve services. Each of our services—Concorde, First Class, Club Europe, Club World, Euro Traveller (European economy), World Traveller (long-haul economy), and domestic Shuttle service—has its own brand manager. We started to treat our categories of service as brands in the mid-1980s. We came to recognize that there is a wear-out factor in terms of the way we present our different categories or classes of service just as there's a wear-out factor for consumer products and their branding approach.

We recognized that delivering consistent exceptional service was not enough—that service brands, like packaged-goods brands, need to be periodically refreshed to reinforce the message that the customer is receiving superior value for the money. Refreshing your service is also a way to make sure you periodically reassess how the value you think you are delivering compares with the value customers think you are delivering. When we began, I thought the wear-out factor for a service brand was somewhere in the five-year range. Now I am pretty convinced that five years is about the maximum that you can go without refreshing the brand.

How does refreshing a service brand differ from refreshing a packaged-goods brand?

For consumer products, refreshing the brand may only require different labeling. But refreshing a service brand so the customer will really recognize the change requires something major. It can't be something superficial such as changing the color of the menus.

For example, when we relaunched our Club Europe service recently, we added some of the best short-haul cuisine anywhere in the world (to meet the needs of the numerous culinary cultures across Europe) and added nine new airport lounges throughout Europe. In addition, we created the most ergonomic short-haul seat around, a telephone check-in service, and a valet-parking service. Competitive pressure didn't force us to do this. We did it because we wanted to stay ahead so that we could continue to win premium customers.

Refreshing a brand also might mean a complete revamp of in-flight entertainment. For example, when we refreshed our World Traveller, or economy class, brand last year, we completely overhauled the audio and video channels. We are currently creating interactive video services for our new Boeing 777s. Customers will be able to complain to our customer relations department in-flight, order duty-free goods, gamble, get the latest news on business, fashion, and so forth. World Traveller's markets are, in general, very price-sensitive, but again, we're hoping to attract a greater portion of economy fliers who are willing to pay for value, which incidentally is one reason we don't reward frequent fliers with upgrades.

It always amazes us how U.S. airlines undermine the integrity of their products with upgrades. We have invested millions to research, develop, and deliver products to serve particular market segments and to build up brand equity. We need to get a healthy return on that investment so we can continue to reinvest. We also don't wish to alienate those customers who choose to pay for First Class or Club by degrading the brand. Conversely, upgrading people out of World Traveller would not add value to that service and would detract from our ability to focus on the needs of those customers, which are very different from the needs of those who travel Club. Upgrading people out of economy shouldn't be seen as relief. If getting an upgrade is the only way a customer feels he or she can get value, then our World Traveller brand is not doing its job, and we will have long-term commodity problems like our U.S. counterparts.

I've digressed. There's one additional large benefit that we reap by refreshing our brands: It motivates our employees. They see that management is genuinely committed to delivering high-quality service. Our employees want to be proud of their product and they want to feel that they are making a difference to customers. When competitors surpass our product, and especially when customers tell them so, our employees become upset. They are very vocal in letting management know about such situations. They really are committed to delivering quality. They want to be part of a winning team.

British Airways has a reputation for listening to customers more effectively than many other airlines. How do you listen?

Of course, we do many things that lots of companies do. Our senior managers, myself included, consciously try to talk to a lot of our passengers when we fly and move around London and the world at large. We also conduct customer forums to help us continually improve our current products and services and to help us identify services that we should consider developing over the longer term. In these forums, we ask customers to let their imagination, anger, enthusiasm, and ideas flow so we can capture their thoughts about current as well as emergent issues. But we think we've gone far beyond other companies—at least other companies in our industry—in developing additional methods for listening to customers. I'm specifically thinking of our market performance unit and our customer relations department.

Over the years, I have seen a lot of marketing people who had been very successful in the packaged-goods business fail in the service business because, as I said, it is so difficult to get reliable data. That's one of the first things I tackled when I joined British Airways. My attitude was, If the information does not exist, create it. So in 1983, we formed what we call our *marketplace performance unit*. The unit, which is charged with representing the customer's point of view, is completely separate from, and therefore independent of, the marketing, selling, and operating side of the business. Its role is to measure how we are doing relative to the standards we set for ourselves, relative to the way customers expect us to perform, and relative to competitors' performance. (See "Measuring Performance Through Customers' Eyes.")

Measuring Performance Through Customers' Eyes

Many service businesses suffer from a problem: the lack of comparative data to measure and benchmark operating performance. "If the information doesn't exist, create it," says Sir Colin Marshall, British Airways' chairman. That is exactly what Marshall set out to do when he created his company's *marketplace performance unit* in 1983.

The 10-member unit tracks some 350 measures of performance, including aircraft cleanliness, punctuality, technical defects on aircraft, customers' opinions on British Airways' check-in performance, the time it takes for a customer to get through when telephoning a reservations agent, customer satisfaction with in-flight and ground services, and the number of involuntary downgrades that have occurred in a given time period. It issues a monthly report, which goes to the chairman, the managing director, the CFO, and the top management team responsible for service and performance. Besides reporting on the *key performance indicators* (key operating data), the report typically has a section that focuses on a particular problem or issue. For example, it might examine a service, such as in-flight food, or it might address how British Airways is faring on a specific route, or it might evaluate the effectiveness of a particular ad campaign.

The unit's overarching mission is to act as a surrogate for customers in assessing the airline's performance. "That means using criteria that customers apply in judging how we're doing rather than those a manager might use to judge how he or she is doing," says Christopher A. Swan, the unit's head. "They're often quite different. Managers, quite naturally, tend to look at their operation's performance through rose-tinted glasses."

Take reservation agents' response time. The marketplace performance unit measures the entire time it takes for a customer to get through to an agent, including the time the phone is ringing and the time the customer is on hold until he or she is transferred to an available agent. "In addition, we measure how many people going through the process get so hacked off they hang up," Swan says. In contrast, airlines with a management perspective might measure only how many times the phone rings before the system answers it.

Waiting lines at check-in desks furnish another example. An airline with a management perspective might measure the number of minutes it took for customers to get to the front of the line. But when the marketplace performance unit asked customers, it found they were more concerned with the length of the lines and the rate at which they moved.

The marketplace performance unit also provides a critical means of measuring improvement in customer service. The unit's first assignment was to have staffers travel on British Airways' flights and submit regular reports on exactly what was done at what time during the flights. Soon after, it began benchmarking British Airways against competitors' flights.

"We look at everything down to when and whether the flight attendants served the packets of peanuts," Swan says. "It may seem small, but each customer comes away with an extremely personalized view of how a company served him. If a customer happens to be a peanut buff, the worse thing that can happen on a short domestic flight is for that person not to be offered a packet of peanuts. He'll remember that we didn't give him a packet while our competitors did."

This attention to detail led British Airways to overhaul the food service on its flights between Britain and Japan. The airline had prided itself on providing proper Japanese food, but when the marketplace performance unit investigated how Japanese customers perceived the food, the polite response was, "For Westerners, you're doing quite well." It turned out that details that British Airways had not realized were important—such as the shape and color of the dishes holding the food and how they were arranged on the tray—mattered significantly to Japanese customers. The unit also learned that the Japanese prefer to eat small amounts of food relatively frequently and that what they really love in the middle of the night are pot noodles, a kind of noodle stew.

The top 20 executives of British Airways can call on the marketplace performance unit to help explore issues, but the unit also can take the initiative when a competitor introduces a new service or when the unit's data or data collected by the customer relations department suggest that a problem or threat exists. When the unit has identified a problem, it presents its findings to senior managers, who then debate the possible solutions and create a plan of action. "The unit is not just a mystery shopper or a market-research department that produces numbers and then is ignored. It has the ear of the entire top management as an honest broker of customer information," says Marshall, whom the unit's members call "our champion."

In many instances, the marketplace performance unit's customer perspective has caused British Airways to take the less obvious path. For example, when a competitor began offering free limousine service to business-class and first-class customers arriving on long-haul flights, management asked the unit to determine whether British Airways should follow suit. It discovered that British Airways' customers were ambivalent about such a service. What they really wanted on arrival after a long night flight, they said, was a place to freshen up and relax until it was time to leave for their business appointments. This discovery led British Airways to establish airport facilities to which overnight passengers arriving in Britain on intercontinental flights could go. "It's important to test whether something is what customers really want or is just what management thinks they want," Swan says. "Our unit is not supposed to fit comfortably with the rest of the organization. We're supposed to generate creative conflict. We're another reality check."

We also are trying to learn from customers by tapping a source of information that many service companies do not exploit fully: customer complaints, suggestions, and compliments. We have transformed customer relations from a defensive complaint department into a department of customer champions whose mission is to retain customers. (See part V, chapter 1, titled "Championing the Customer.") Our goal is to make BA as approachable as possible and to respond to customers as quickly as possible, which again fits into our value-driven customer strategy. Both approachability and responsiveness strongly influence customer loyalty. I ardently believe that customer complaints are precious opportunities to hold on to customers who otherwise might take their business elsewhere and to learn about problems that need to be fixed. Customers who make the effort to register a complaint are doing you a favor because they are giving you an opportunity to retain them, if you act quickly.

You mentioned that it is difficult to deliver a consistent experience in a service business because numerous interactions between individual employees and the customer shape the experience. You hinted that achieving such consistency can produce a significant advantage that will be hard for competitors to copy.

Delivering long-term and consistent value in a service business begins and ends with the way employees are trained, nurtured, and led. We have a rigorous process for selecting new employees. It includes résumé screening, psychological testing, group exercises, and one-on-one interviews in which we probe areas of concern. Just as important is leadership; our managers are continually trained in leadership and in techniques to provide high-quality service. Finally, we have established performance criteria—we call them *key performance indicators*—that each team must fulfill. They are based on research on the level of performance we must achieve to remain efficient and to win repeat business. They ensure a focus on facts as opposed to personal perceptions. These practices may not sound unique, but we think we take them much more seriously than many companies do.

We strongly believe that to deliver consistent service quality, our employees must understand their role in delivering superior service and must have the power and ability to deal with customer problems. Teams must receive constant feedback on their service interactions. Toward that end, we hand out survey cards to passengers on every flight, and every day we ask a random sample of passengers who have just finished their flights to comment on our service quality. The person in charge of the cabin crew, the customer service director, receives this information, as does the crew, and it is used to assess performance and to identify training needs.

How do you get employees to understand and then deliver superior consistent service?

By giving them the freedom to act within specified boundaries. I try to impress upon our people that in a service business the customer doesn't expect everything will go right all the time; the big test is what you do when things go wrong. If you react quickly and in the most positive way, you can get very high marks from the customer. Recovery matters as much as trying to provide good service, since occasional service failure is unavoidable in a business like ours.

We want every employee who interacts with customers to listen to them and to be able to address issues that arise immediately. Consider the following incident: An aircraft door was left open in a rainstorm before takeoff, and a passenger near the door unfortunately got showered. The flight attendant not only did everything that was routine— offered to have the customer's garments cleaned or replaced and made sure that a customer relations representative contacted the customer later to demonstrate that we genuinely cared—but also made a special gesture by offering the passenger a complimentary choice of certain tax-free goods.

We try to make it clear to employees that we expect them to respond to customers on the spot—before a customer writes a letter or makes a phone call. It's an important focus in our training. We created a series of training programs on the importance of good customer service and how to provide it. My objective from the day we launched our initial program, Putting People First, at the end of 1983 was to give all our employees the opportunity to go through a motivational program on customer service at least once every three years. That may not sound very frequent, but given the size of our workforce, it was the best we could do because it takes us about 2 1/2 years to get all our employees through one. Responding to service failure was the focus of the most recent program, which was called Winning for Customers. The program's message was that employees have the freedom to act. But the program doesn't just tell them that, it puts them through a series of simulations and exercises that show them how they can help customers when problems occur.

How does British Airways ensure that managers encourage employees to take the initiative in providing good service, including helping to resolve customers' problems?

We realize that employees—all of us—won't always be right, but it is better that they make mistakes than not try to solve customers' problems. We discourage our managers from coming down on an employee like a ton of bricks if the decision the employee made was wrong. Instead, we want managers to explain why the decision was wrong and what the right decision would have been, so that the next time the employee is confronted with a similar situation, he or she will get it right.

We want our staff to know that management genuinely does care about the problems that our staff encounters. It is not an easy thing to achieve, but we keep hammering away at it. We're trying to reinforce that kind of management behavior constantly with our compensation and performance-measurement systems, with training (each of the customer-service programs had a parallel program for managers), and with a 360-degree feedback program we're now installing, which will provide feedback to managers from subordinates, peers, and superiors. Managers who are merely paying lip service to supporting subordinates will have nowhere to hide.

Last but certainly not least, our senior managers demonstrate their commitment to looking after the customer. At many companies, senior managers say it's very important to look after the customer but don't demonstrate their commitment when they're interacting with customers and their own people. I'd like to think we're different. We strive to practice visible management. When we put everyone through the original Putting People First program, I tried to take questions at the end of as many sessions as I could. If I couldn't make it, another senior manager closed the session and reported back to me about any big issues that came up. That's a practice we continued with the other programs in the series. In addition, we expect senior managers to attend the customer-listening forums regularly, to take calls or at least listen in on calls that come into the customer relations department's Care Line, and to discuss with our customer relations people the causes of and possible solutions to customer-service issues.

I also should mention profit sharing. One of the first things I did when I joined the company was introduce a profit sharing program. In the United States, such programs may be common, but they were quite alien in the United Kingdom at the time. We want our employees to understand that there is a direct connection between the service we deliver and the profits we earn. There have been 2 years in the past 12 when the program hasn't paid out because the profits weren't high enough. Those were the year of and the year following the Gulf War. In our financial year that ended this past March 31, we achieved record earnings, and every eligible employee received a profit-share bonus equivalent to just over three weeks' pay.

You have had a wide-ranging career. How did you come to hold your views on the importance of customer service?

To differing degrees, all the businesses I have worked in have been service businesses—or people businesses, as I like to call them. When I became a Norton Simon executive after it bought Avis, I still had overall responsibility for Avis as well as for Hunt-Wesson foods and a couple of other smaller subsidiaries. And Sears also had a service business—its retail stores. All those experiences have been invaluable in helping me to develop an awareness of the importance of the interrelationship between employees, customers, and shareholders. Employees need to understand why shareholder return is important, and shareholders need to understand the necessity of investments that produce a long-term payback. Customers must understand that in order to satisfy their needs ever more effectively, we need to have an enduring relationship with them.

Some people wonder how a company can not only contemplate but actually implement and maintain extensive training, motivation, and incentive programs such as ours. My response is that for a service business, they are not decorative embroideries but essential parts of the company fabric. From the customer's perspective, the quality and value of the product are determined to a great extent by the people delivering the service. We therefore have to "design" our people and their service attitude, just as we design an aircraft seat, an in-flight entertainment program, or an airport lounge to meet the needs and preferences of our customers.

I suppose my evangelistic determination to strive for customer-service excellence goes back to my career beginnings as a cadet purser with the former Orient Line shipping company. One day on a long voyage between Europe and Australia was much the same as another for passengers and crew alike. The trick, however, was to ensure that each day was like the first day at sea, with product polish and service sparkle at its brightest all the time. That way, both customers and staff derived a sense of real value. My philosophy evolved further in the intensely competitive car-rental business, where the automobiles are very similar if not exactly the same and the initial transaction and the after-sale service are what make the difference.

I have to say that working in the discerning U.S. consumer market for many years was an invaluable experience. It helped bring home to me the importance of emphasizing customer-service excellence in business strategy.

How do your extensive efforts to build a global network through alliances with other airlines mesh with your vision of what it takes to prevail in a service business such as yours?

In ten years' time, our industry will be much larger—probably twice its current size in terms of total traffic on a global basis. Clearly some markets, especially those in the Far East and Eastern Europe, will be growing much faster than the long-established markets of North America and Western Europe. And two other likely developments should lead to lower fares, thereby fueling worldwide demand: global deregulation and the introduction of an aircraft with a much larger carrying capacity and lower operating costs than the 747.

We don't think that the number of airlines will grow significantly, however. On the contrary, we think that deregulation will lead to consolidation. It is already happening, although it remains to be seen whether the consolidation of the global industry will be as drastic as the consolidation that occurred after the U.S. market was deregulated. We fully intend not just to survive but to be one of the major players, and the global network we are building is an integral part of our strategy. We are betting that this network will enable us to lower our costs. We will be able to share resources such as airport terminals and information systems, to buy and use aircraft more efficiently, and to use employees more efficiently. We also are betting that the network will increase our collective share of the world market, and that it will generate more business for our partners than they would be able to obtain on their own.

How do you maintain consistent levels of service throughout your network so that a customer identifies a partner's service with your brand? Conversely, how do you make sure that inconsistent service across the network does not under-mine your—British Airways'—brand?

I don't rule out our having a common name eventually, but that's a long way off. We wouldn't want to get rid of the individual names unless market research told us that it would benefit both the individual companies and the partnership as a whole.

In addition, there are different service expectations in different marketplaces. For example, business class, which falls between first class and economy, is the preeminent service on our international routes and our short-haul routes in Europe, but it is only beginning to emerge in the U.S. domestic market. The key is to make sure that even if each partner's service is different, it has the look and feel of a high-quality, value-driven product.

In situations where one partner is starting a service from scratch that another, say British Airways, already offers, we will at least explore whether it makes sense to make the partner's service similar to the one already established. For example, we did this with USAir when we helped it redesign its business-class service.

But overall, our aim for the network at this point is twofold: to create seamless service and to create a common public identity in the market over time without adopting a single name. We believe we can create a common identity through frequent-flier programs and by sharing frequent-flier lounges—steps we have already taken. Perhaps over time we will be able to move toward the adoption of a similar uniform and logo styles. By "creating seamless service" I mean dovetailing our route networks and our flight schedules, sharing codes to make it easier for customers to book a trip that involves legs flown with two or more of us, and making it easier and more pleasant to transfer between partners.

With our partners, we're beginning to work our way through these things. Our marketplace performance unit now tracks how our partners perform, so we have the data we need to compare services and decide where changes are in order. We also are working on a joint approach to information technology, which should provide the underpinning for a greater uniformity of customer service. For example, Qantas is switching over to BABS, British Airways' reservation system; USAir and BA are combining their frequent-flier databases; and we're exploring taking similar steps with TAT and Deutsche BA. This technology integration will allow us to share information on customers and costs, which will then allow partners in the network to take a network perspective when they make decisions about investments ranging from aircraft purchases to catering.

When you have an alliance, with whom is the employee supposed to identify?

It's very important, at least in these early years, that employees clearly identify with the company for which they work. It is also important that they recognize the existence of the alliance, see it as a good thing, and talk about it in a positive way.

I hope that, over time, we shall be able to engage in a larger degree of employee exchange. In fact, we already have some. For example, some of British Airways' North Atlantic routes have been flown by leased USAir aircraft painted in our livery, and operated by USAir pilots and cabin staff wearing our uniforms and delivering the authentic British Airways product. Obviously, this has meant teaching the USAir employees British Airways' methods and training them to perform to our standards; it also has required a great deal of interairline cooperation. The arrangement has been very successful as far as the customer is concerned—and tremendously mind-expanding for us.

What is the alliance's overarching objective?

It is the development of an integrated global air-transport system in which consistency of product, service standards, and operational integrity is implicit throughout. Our multinational combine will be able to be at the forefront of technological development, whether in the introduction of new large aircraft to succeed the existing jumbo jets or in the implementation of advanced ground-handling systems that will render the check-in queue, the delays in clearing immigration and customs, and the unseemly scramble for baggage upon arrival things of the past.

There is immense scope for invention, innovation, and pushing out the competitive frontier. Not the least exciting aspect of the future will be that as staff become freed from the existing mechanical humdrum of air-travel procedures, a whole new dimension in personal customer service will open up. For me, this, more than the application of new technology, forms the great challenge of the future.

4

Letter to the Editor in Response to "Competing on Customer Service: An Interview with British Airways' Sir Colin Marshall"

Frederick F. Reichheld

Kudos to Sir Colin Marshall and his team at British Airways! What a wonderful demonstration of how a company can grow its bottom line by focusing intensely on strengthening the loyalty of its best customers. And what a stark contrast it provides to those airlines that, faced with the same financial pressures, responded by cutting legroom, meals, and frequent-flier benefits as well as staff levels, training, and pay scales.

BA's strategy of investing to earn targeted customers' loyalty may seem radical in the airline business but has worked impressively in a wide variety of other industries. At Bain & Company, we have spent nearly a decade studying what we call *loyalty leaders*—companies that place the loyalty of customers and employees above profits. We have discovered that such companies not only earn superior loyalty but also generate astonishing levels of growth and profits—far greater than traditional accounting methods (and economics as taught in business schools today) can explain.

British Airways fits the patterns that we have observed among those loyalty-based competitors. For example, loyalty leaders work very hard to get and keep the right customers. As Marshall says, "Even in a mass-market business [like airlines], you don't want to attract and retain everyone." Loyalty leaders see customer service as a way to retain good customers. They invest heavily in the training and technology that helps their people serve customers more effectively. And they share the benefits of superior profitability with their employees. BA seems to have taken many of the initial steps that lead to loyalty leadership.

However, most of the loyalty leaders—companies such as John Deere, State Farm, Toyota/Lexus, MBNA, and Leo Burnett advertising—have been practicing loyalty-based management for decades. Those companies have learned to take additional steps to build enduring track records of customer and employee loyalty and would probably offer Marshall and his team the following four pieces of advice.

- Develop creative measures to capture a greater share of customers' spending; simply measuring satisfaction or retention is not enough. Thus, for at least a sample of individual targeted customers, BA might be able to partner with a credit card company or travel bureau to determine what share of city-pair flights they are really earning each month. BA probably would be surprised to learn how much *more* business it could be earning from its apparently "retained" customers.

- Don't rely on traditional market research techniques and customer satisfaction surveys to learn what you must change to earn 100% of your targeted customers' business. Once you have developed the real purchase-pattern data for key customers, you need to probe into the root causes of defection and loyalty with the fact-finding intensity of an investigative reporter-but without losing the strategic perspectives of your senior managers.

- Share the surplus earnings generated by customer loyalty with your most productive employees generously enough to win and keep *their* loyalty. Broad-based profit sharing is just one part of the equation. It is even more important to break up the organization into smaller teams whose productivity can be measured and rewarded separately. All loyalty leaders have built systems that attract and retain the best employees. As a result, their people achieve greater productivity, earn higher compensation, and have longer careers. It is impossible to perpetuate a customer loyalty advantage without a loyal base of employees.

- Finally, and perhaps most important, link customer loyalty to your financials so that board members and investors can understand the connection between loyalty, profits, and cash flow. To institutionalize the loyalty-based approach and to continue to make rational investments in customers, the management team must be able to measure the net present value of customers with the same rigor it applies to financial assets. Otherwise, the company's decision making will revert to a focus on short-term earnings, and the enormous gains created by forward-thinking managers like the ones at British Airways will eventually fade away.

PART

V

Tools for Building Customer Loyalty

1
Championing the Customer

Charles R. Weiser

When I joined British Airways' customer relations department in 1991, I found an operation virtually untouched by the quality revolution that had caused the airline's reputation and fortunes to soar. The department took more than 12 weeks on average to respond to customer correspondence, it lost 60% of calls from customers on any given day, and the cost of compensating customers with grievances was rising rapidly.

The company required a radically different approach to customer relations: to champion the customer as opposed to defending the company. The new management team that was brought into customer relations decided to take a proactive role in retaining customers. The best way to pursue that goal, it decided, was by making quick amends when a service failure occurred and by focusing the airline on spotting and eliminating the operational weaknesses that can cause service failures. The team subscribed to W. Edwards Deming's views that merely satisfying customers is not enough to retain their business and that customer retention is crucial. As Deming put it, "Profit comes from repeat customers—those that boast about the product or service."[1]

One of the first steps we had to take was to improve our understanding of why customers defected. Our research found that approximately 13% of customers who were completely satisfied with British Airways' service nevertheless did not intend to continue to fly with us; their reasons ranged from a job change to the draw of another airline's frequent-flier program. Of much greater potential importance

Exhibit I.

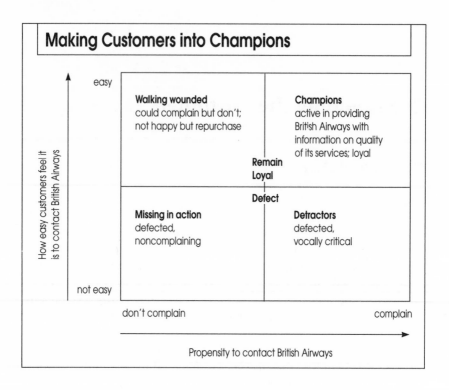

Making Customers into Champions

(easy / not easy — How easy customers feel it is to contact British Airways)

Walking wounded
could complain but don't;
not happy but repurchase

Champions
active in providing
British Airways with
information on quality
of its services; loyal

Remain
Loyal

Defect

Missing in action
defected,
noncomplaining

Detractors
defected,
vocally critical

don't complain   complain

Propensity to contact British Airways

was what we learned about customers who had experienced problems. Although 50% of those who chose not to tell the airline about
their experience defected to other airlines, the vast majority of those
customers with problems who did contact someone at British Airways—87%—did not defect. The powerful conclusion was that those
"willing communicators" who wished to tell us about the poor service
they had received could be turned around.

Intrigued, customer relations conducted further research to find out
more about these customers and ultimately developed the model displayed in Exhibit I. Armed with this information, the division set out
to move all of British Airways' customers into the upper right-hand
quadrant. For customer relations to achieve this goal, however, it
would have to transform its culture and methods completely.

In its traditional defensive role, customer relations had served as an investigator and adjudicator and had pursued four basic objectives. The first was to insulate the company from unhappy customers. Accordingly, customer relations was highly centralized, conducted little analysis of customer data, and for the most part did not disseminate what it heard or learned. The second was to assign blame for poor service rather than to help the organization, including product development, learn how to prevent or fix problems. As a result, line functions saw the department as an adversary. Its third objective was to buy dissatisfied customers' silence for the lowest possible price. Accordingly, the division had to adhere to detailed rules for compensation. The final objective was to maximize volume throughput—to process the largest possible number of customer complaints. Consequently, the department's performance measures focused on its backlog of work, not on its level of service to complaining customers or to other British Airways units. Customers certainly did not find customer relations easily accessible.

To champion the customer, the new management team instituted four objectives. Our first was to use customer feedback more effectively in order to improve the quality of the airline's service. To do so, we installed systems to collect and analyze customer data and then distribute the findings to British Airways' operations around the world. The second objective was to strive to prevent future service problems through teamwork. We tried to achieve this objective by having line operations join us in monthly reviews to discuss how customers were perceiving service quality, and by serving as active members of quality-improvement and product-development teams. A third goal was to change our approach to customer compensation so it would meet customers' needs, not the company's. Toward that end, we instituted a policy of dealing with all cases individually and began holding internal reviews each month to identify the most effective means of retaining customers. A related fourth objective was to practice customer retention, not adjudication. Accordingly, we changed how we measured the division's performance, assessing it on the basis of customer-retention rates and return on investment—that is, on the basis of the division's effectiveness in retaining customers with the resources available.

The bottom line became preventing customer defection. It was translated into a modus operandi of retain, invest, prevent, which was incorporated into all training programs, coaching sessions, and performance criteria.

Retaining the Customer is Job One

First and foremost, we had to retain the customer's business. Debating whether the customer was correctly perceiving the facts was a nonstarter. We had to deal with their perception if we were going to hold on to them. In training, we tried to help staff understand the following:

> If the company replies to a customer and claims that events did not happen as the customer suggested, then the customer perceives the company to be calling him or her a liar.
>
> If, after investigating, the company reports back to the customer that events indeed took place as the customer claimed, then the customer can become even more agitated because he or she infers that the company did not believe him or her at first.
>
> If the company relays information to the customer that he or she did not know, the customer may think that the company is trying to make excuses for poor service.

To deal with these issues, customer relations developed a four-step process that we incorporated into all our technical and human systems.

1. Apologize and own the problem. Customers do not care whose fault it was or who was to blame; they want an apology and they want someone to champion their cause.
2. Do it quickly. Aim to reply to the customer the same day, and if that is not possible, certainly do it within 72 hours. Our research showed that 40% to 50% of customers who contacted us with complaints defected if it took us longer than five days to respond. A speedy reply demonstrates a sense of urgency; it shows that the company really cares about the customer's feelings and situation.
3. Assure the customer that the problem is being fixed. Customers can be retained if they are confident that the operational problem that they encountered will truly be addressed.
4. Do it by phone. We found that customers with problems were delighted to have customer relations call them.

Invest in People and Systems

Because customer relations believed obtaining information and responding to complaints quickly were critically important for spotting and fixing systemic weaknesses, we invested in a reengineering effort that included the following:

Installing Caress. An image-based computer system, Caress (for Customer Analysis and Retention System) eliminated all paper. All information received from customers is now either scanned or (if received by phone) manually entered into the system. Caress allows a customer's case history to be shared easily and quickly across the organization and makes it easier to spot trends.

Redesigning the Customer-Service Process. Conducted in conjunction with the design of Caress, this overhaul cut the number of administrative steps required to serve a customer from thirteen to three.

Throwing Out the Rule Book. Instead, each customer relations employee was fully authorized to use whatever resources he or she thought were necessary to keep a customer's business. The new measurement system for assessing the division's effectiveness in retaining customers ensured that expenditures did not skyrocket.

Building Interpersonal Skills. Whereas the focus of training previously had been on writing grammatically correct letters, the new emphasis was on coaching employees on how to allay customers' anger, how to negotiate a win-win situation for customer and company, how to listen and empathize, and how to be assertive without being defensive. In addition, employees were trained in ways to help each other cope with their emotionally grueling job so they wouldn't take it out on customers.

Encouraging Customers to Communicate. Our research found that less than 10% of customers ever communicated with the airline about service issues—good or bad. Of those with complaints, we found that only 8% contacted customer relations. These customers turned out to be our most loyal: They not only stuck with British Airways, they also provided invaluable information on the quality of its services. Of the remainder, 24% contacted someone else at British Airways but the information never reached customer relations (meaning that we did not have an accurate picture of the true state of service quality), and 68% didn't talk to anybody at the airline. The key, therefore, was to lower the "waterline," that is, to get more customers to communicate either directly or indirectly with customer relations. (See Exhibit II.)

Data told us that this pursuit was well worth it: For every £1 invested in our customer retention efforts, the company received £2 back. The return was made up of three components. First, expanding

Exhibit II.

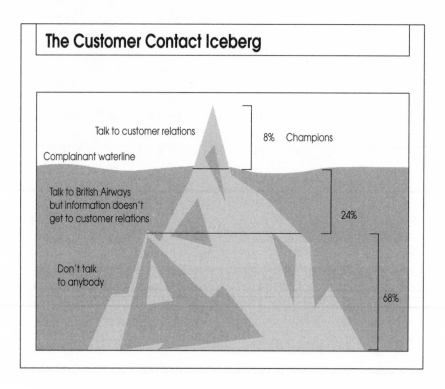

The Customer Contact Iceberg

Talk to customer relations

Complainant waterline

8%   Champions

Talk to British Airways
but information doesn't
get to customer relations

24%

Don't talk
to anybody

68%

the number of customers whose problems were resolved up front reduced the amount that British Airways had to spend overall on retaining customers. Second, those people whom customer relations retained then gave British Airways more of their business. Finally, those customers helped the airline win additional business by actively promoting it to others.

Customer relations employed two primary tactics to lower the waterline and thereby increase its approachability. The first was the establishment of 12 *listening posts.* These included an international, postage-paid card that customers could use to mail in comments; customer forums attended by British Airways executives where customers could air grievances; and our Fly with Me program, which arranged for customer-relations representatives and customers to fly together so that the representative could experience problems firsthand and discuss them with the customer.

Prevent It from Happening Again

Finally, the success of the customer-retention strategy required partnerships with customer relations' internal customers—our colleagues in other British Airways departments. Only with such partnerships could British Airways move from cure to prevention—by which I mean utilizing the information collected by customer relations to design out service failures and to design in early-warning mechanisms to pinpoint potential service failures, reducing the need for customer relations to act as a safety net.

In its previous incarnation, customer relations had had strained relations with many other departments. To persuade other departments that it genuinely wanted to work with them as a team player to eliminate causes of service failure, it had to cease trying to assign blame for such failures. To that end, it teamed up with a wide array of internal partners—from human resources to finance to information management to service delivery to sales—to champion a number of programs aimed at gaining factual information that everyone could use to identify and resolve service problems.

These programs included conducting monthly meetings with internal partners to review the "state of the nation" from the customers' viewpoint; sharing the results of market research that quantified the cost of customer defection; making available to the other departments all customer comments received by customer relations and the analysis of them (including information on trends and costs); reporting on the effectiveness of the company's various customer-retention efforts; and forecasting which service improvements would provide the greatest return on investment.

British Airways' customer relations department now can claim to be a true champion of the customer. The retention rate among those who complain to customer relations has more than doubled to about 80%, while its return on investment (the value of business saved plus increased loyalty and new business from referrals relative to the department's total costs) has risen 200%. We are never happy to have service failures, but we are eager to hear about them when they occur, because we know that ignorance is anything but bliss.

Note

1. W.E. Deming, *Out of the Crisis: Quality, Productivity, and Competitive Position* (Cambridge: Cambridge University Press, 1988), p. 178.

2
Do Rewards Really Create Loyalty?

Louise O'Brien and Charles Jones

Customer rewards have been reviled in the business press as cheap promotional devices, short-term fads, giving something for nothing. Yet they've been around for more than a decade, and more companies, not fewer, are jumping on the bandwagon. From airlines offering frequent flier deals to telecommunications companies lowering their fees to get more volume, organizations are spending millions of dollars developing and implementing rewards programs.

Company interest is justified. The theory is sound. Rewards can and do build customers' loyalty, and most companies now appreciate how valuable that loyalty can be. As Frederick F. Reichheld and W. Earl Sasser, Jr., documented in "Zero Defections: Quality Comes to Services" (see part IV, chapter 1), a company's most loyal customers are also its most profitable. With each additional year of a relationship, customers become less costly to serve. Over time, as the loyalty life cycle plays out, loyal customers even become business builders: buying more, paying premium prices, and bringing in new customers through referrals.

In practice, however, rewards programs are widely misunderstood and often misapplied. When it comes to design and implementation, too many companies treat rewards as short-term promotional giveaways or specials of the month. Approached that way, rewards can create some value by motivating new or existing customers to try a product or service. But until they are designed to build loyalty, they will return at best a small fraction of their potential value.

A rewards program can accelerate the loyalty life cycle, encouraging first- or second-year customers to behave like a company's most profitable tenth-year customers—but only if it is planned and implemented as part of a larger loyalty-management strategy. A company must find ways to share value with customers in proportion to the value the customers' loyalty creates for the company. The goal must be to develop a system through which customers are continually educated about the rewards of loyalty and motivated to earn them. Achieving sustainable loyalty, measured in years, requires a strategic sustainable approach.

The Rules of Rewards

Some of the best examples of building customer loyalty through value sharing can be found in traditional small businesses. For many years, successful neighborhood merchants and restaurateurs have understood intuitively the broader strategic purpose behind an effective rewards program. Such businesspeople make it a point to get to know their best customers personally and often reward them with special services and attention—notifying them when sought-after merchandise arrives, for example, or giving them a free drink or a special dessert. They know that delivering increased value to profitable customers turns them into loyal customers; and that loyal customers become even more profitable over time.

But as companies increase in size and complexity, their ability to detect which of their customers are the most valuable falls precipitously. High turnover of sales and customer service employees exacerbates the problem. Personalized customer relationships and the accompanying keen judgment on value sharing disappear.

Large companies striving for increased market share, scale, and efficiency try to compensate for the loss of personal relationships by using database marketing or sophisticated market research techniques to target valuable customers. For those investments to pay off, however, companies must also keep in mind the following principles of effective value sharing.

All customers are not created equal. Realizing the benefits of loyalty requires an admission that not all customers are equal. In order to maximize loyalty and profitability, a company must give its best value to its best customers. That is, customers who generate superior profits for a company should enjoy the benefits of that value creation. As a result, they will then become even more loyal and profitable.

For example, a company might consider offering better prices to loyal customers. Credit card companies often offer lower interest rates to customers with better credit profiles and superior payment histories. Taking into account long customer tenure and good accident history, State Farm Insurance provides individual discounts on its auto insurance policies. It also discourages business from problem drivers by not offering competitive prices for that customer segment. State Farm's competitors are thus put in the position of serving a less attractive base of remaining customers.

Unfortunately, most companies inadvertently treat all customers as equal, providing them with products of equivalent value regardless of how much they spend or how long they've been customers. A company that offers average-value products and services to everyone wastes resources in oversatisfying less profitable customers while undersatisfying the more valuable loyal customers. The outcome is predictable. Highly profitable customers with higher expectations and more attractive choices defect, and less desirable customers stay around, diluting the company's profits.

Value created must exceed cost of value delivered. Most companies launch rewards programs without assessing their own needs and the economics of cause and effect. They haven't thought through the links between the value delivered to customers and the value created for the company. A rewards program should not give something for nothing: The profits will be illusory, but the costs will be real.

Consider restaurant discount cards such as the one introduced by Transmedia in the United States two years ago. With this card, consumers are entitled to discounts of up to 25% at participating restaurants. Hundreds of restaurants in major metropolitan areas have signed on with Transmedia and similar programs, believing they could bring increased volume or a shift in share sufficient to offset the lower margins that accompany the deal.

A closer assessment of the real proposition for restaurants, however, reveals that the cards have more to do with cash management than with customer loyalty. Transmedia offers restaurants up-front cash in exchange for hefty discounts down the road. In effect, it is lending restaurants money at very high interest rates. Financially troubled restaurants find the offer appealing. Stable establishments, feeling intense competitive pressure, have joined as well.

But in the long run, neither the individual restaurant nor the industry as a whole is likely to benefit. Why? These discount cards represent a *transfer* of value from the restaurant owner to the consumer (and to Transmedia, which is now expanding globally) but no accompanying *creation* of value for the restaurant owner. In fact, by encouraging consumers to shop around, the cards discourage loyalty. The flaw is in the design of the incentives. Transmedia offers restaurant-goers the same discount at all restaurants regardless of how often they visit or how much they spend. Such discounts differ from traditional perks, which individual restaurateurs offer only to their regular customers.

Restaurants join discount card programs to attract new customers by shifting market share away from restaurants that don't participate. But the structure does not ensure either that customers will dine out more often than they used to or that they will focus their patronage on a single restaurant—the two acts required to create real value.

Customer behavior should drive value sharing. Rewarding—and thus reinforcing—desirable behavior may seem like an obvious tenet of program design, but the marketplace is full of companies that reward the talk instead of the walk. One credit card company, for example, recently launched a campaign that gives new customers 10,000 bonus points redeemable for airline miles and other rewards. That initial bonus puts customers well on their way to earning an airline ticket, so the value of the offer is quite high. Yet there is nothing to preclude customers from signing up, redeeming their points, and then defecting. That behavior does not benefit the company in the long run.

Such promotions are common today in consumer product businesses, and the results should sound a warning. Customers are so inured to offers promising everything from a free vacation in Florida to a free credit card that they either yawn when they see a new one or become experts at getting something for nothing. Long-distance phone companies routinely offer $50 checks or coupons for switching to their service. The strategy has brought to light, perhaps even created, a segment of chronic switchers, who routinely shop for the lowest price. No business should want those customers: The economics of loyalty ensure that no business can make money on them.

In order for a rewards program to be a profit center instead of a cost center, the payout must be inextricably linked to desired behaviors. The American Express Company learned that lesson with its Membership Miles program—a rewards system that allows Amex cardholders to earn points toward a variety of awards by charging purchases. Although Amex management had defined and communicated a companywide loyalty vision of achieving 100% share of customers' card spending, concern over program costs hindered rapid progress toward that goal. Because Amex originally developed Membership Miles in response to competitive pressures from other card issuers in the United States, many in the organization viewed the program as a purely defensive move. They didn't fully recognize its importance to the overall loyalty strategy. Until about a year ago, in fact, the organization treated its rewards program as a cost center, not a profit center: it cost Amex hard cash to purchase miles from the airlines, but many of the benefits of rewards were difficult to quantify.

Discontinuity between strategy and implementation is not uncommon. Tracking the benefits of loyalty requires new tools that go beyond traditional financial analysis. At Amex, quantifying the results of Membership Miles was an ongoing goal, but it wasn't easy to measure the full effect of value sharing on customers' behavior. Everyone acknowledged that customers who enrolled in the program charged more of their purchases to the card, but it wasn't until the company began tracking higher retention, incremental upgrades and purchases of Amex products, and acquisition of new customers that the true profitability was clear. Only when Amex understood these relationships did it begin to use the program more efficiently to encourage profitable customer habits such as referrals and to discourage unprofitable habits such as attrition.

Long-term perspective is critical. Onetime promotions can cost a great deal of money and do not, as a rule, generate loyalty. They do indeed change customer behavior but often in ways that are undesirable in the long run. Any positive impact is washed away as soon as competing companies launch their next promotions.

Many credit card companies have used lotteries, for instance, to increase response rates from potential new customers. A display of brochures urging people to "take one" may feature a chance at a free trip to London or a vacation in a luxury condominium. Such offers understandably generate more excitement than a standard description of a credit card product does. Yet once the lottery ends (with most customers turning out to be losers), people who signed up only to be in the drawing may defect. In the short run, the organization hits its numbers, but, in the long run, it is no better off.

The full potential of value sharing through rewards is realized only when customers change their habits to become *sustainably* loyal. And that shift occurs only when the company has developed and communicated a proposition that clearly has long-term benefits for the consumer.

Offers must target attractive customers. Progressive companies understand the superior economics of targeted marketing and the need for a segmented approach to developing products and value propositions. Many invest heavily in market research to generate elaborate demographic or psychographic segmentations. But too often these models prove unsatisfying because there is no practical way to identify a customer by segment. Defining a segment as "big backyards" or "personal-computer junkies" may call to mind a picture of the lifestyle or mind-set of people in those groups, but it does not provide a useful means of finding the customer.

In addition, as anyone familiar with market research knows, what customers say and what they do are two different things. The most sophisticated research methodologies in the world do not always yield accurate predictions of real-life behavior. For example, most people, when asked, will say they don't like companies calling them on the phone to sell products. Yet, in numerous situations, telemarketing has generated very high response rates.

A well-designed rewards program can target—and attract—valuable customer segments. At the same time, it can save the company money by discouraging those customers who would prove to be less valuable. Such a program is *self-selecting* and *individually correcting.*

MCI's Friends and Family is a good example of a series of self-selecting, individually correcting programs. It offers customers a significant incentive to enroll their friends and relatives with MCI. All calls within the specified network of friends and family members cost 20% to 50% less than other calls. The proposition is clearly most appealing to customers who use long distance heavily, a core segment with which MCI wants to build loyalty. In fact, Friends and Family has helped MCI lure away from AT&T a disproportionate share of profitable customers. In addition, the value to a customer individually corrects to match the customer's behavior. The more family members and friends a customer recruits for MCI, the more discounted calls that customer earns. Although the cost to MCI is substantial, there is no cost at all until the customer actually exhibits the desired behavior.

MCI shifted marketing dollars from sales-force expense to customer value by turning its customers into highly effective salespeople. It also provided pressure to keep customers from switching to competitors. At a time when most long-distance players were using competing coupon promotions to encourage switching, that was a significant accomplishment. (See "Customer Segmentation at Amex" for another self-selecting, individually correcting rewards program.)

Customer Segmentation at Amex

Self-selecting, individually correcting offers are new in customer segmentation. American Express is using the approach to reduce cost and shorten time-to-market when it tests new value propositions. One example is its recent *zero-spender stimulation test.*

Zero spenders are customers who hold the American Express Card and pay the annual fee but rarely or never use the card. Since those customers not only generate lower profits but also are more likely to defect than an average Amex customer, they are an obvious target for a loyalty program. However, not all customers in this segment are of equal potential value to American Express. Some are not using the card simply because they can't afford much discretionary spending, but others are using cash or a competitor's card instead. It is the zero spender in the second category that American Express wants to target. Easier said than done.

Although zero spenders consist of two different groups, the behavior of one is indistinguishable from that of the other. To identify the subsegments, Amex has begun testing a series of self-selecting offers designed to attract the customers who have the highest potential value.

One such offer, high in value and likely to appeal only to those with significant discretionary spending ability, is two airline tickets for heavy card use during a six-month period. The cost of the offer is high, but the cost of losing potentially valuable customers and acquiring new ones would be higher. And trying to identify valuable customers through market research could be expensive and time consuming, given the size of the company's worldwide base of customers.

Customer rewards at Amex are, in effect, a means of delivering mass-customized value. Most companies think of mass customization as it applies to packaging and delivery, but American Express is using rewards to mass-customize the value proposition itself. The approach allows the company to test an unprecedented variety of offers and products while lowering costs and speeding time-to-market. All products and offers are designed not only to appeal to desired target segments but also to allow the customers to select the relevant propositions, thereby identifying themselves and making targeted marketing easier in the future. As a global company, Amex can correlate lessons learned from one market with other markets—lessons showing which products and offers customers prefer and which behaviors and profits each proposition generates.

The Strategy Behind the Program

A rewards program is a competitive strategy and, as such, it must meet certain criteria. Does the program align with company capabilities? Will customers value the program? Can competitors offer a more desirable alternative? Would partnering make the program more competitive? Any rewards program that does not address such criteria is unlikely to succeed.

Does the program align with company capabilities? Just because your customers need something that you're not currently providing doesn't mean you should develop that capability. The need may already be satisfied with products your competitors are offering or planning, and your company may not be capable of meeting the need profitably, or as profitably as competitors can. Rewards programs do not exist in a vacuum; they must dovetail with a company's overall strategy and capabilities. The right question, therefore, is not What do our customers need? but Which of our customers' needs can we profitably and differentially meet?

For example, research that American Express conducted on one core segment, affluent business travelers, revealed that rewards offered by competitors were one of the major reasons why customers were defecting. A number of credit card companies had copied the airlines' frequent flier programs and had begun to offer their customers rewards ranging from airline miles to discounts on new cars. The offers represented a significant enhancement in the basic value proposition and were attractive to high-spending business travelers, who could earn rewards quickly and were already familiar with frequent flier programs.

When American Express decided to invest heavily in a rewards program, however, it considered not only customer demand but also its own capabilities and competitive advantages. Unlike the banks that issue credit cards through Visa and MasterCard and make money by charging interest on revolving balances, American Express must rely more heavily on the fees it charges merchants because its charge card customers pay their balances in full each month. However, since American Express is the leading payment product among affluent consumers and business spenders, it generally charges merchants higher transaction fees than credit cards do. As a result, increases in spending for customers who pay off their balances are more profitable to American Express than to its bank card competitors. In a world where customer rewards are based on dollars spent, American Express can afford to offer more generous value sharing to the cardholder.

Will customers value the program? Many of the rewards and loyalty programs in the marketplace today reveal a limited understanding of customer needs and desires. From a customer's perspective, five elements determine a program's value. They are cash value, choice of redemption options, aspirational value, relevance, and convenience. Few programs today offer all five, but companies that want to play the rewards game should be sure their value measures up to customers' alternatives.

There is more than one way to measure the first element, *cash value.* Although the Discover credit card offers a rebate in cash (up to 1% of all spending), most companies' rewards call for a yardstick other than cash, one that compares the underlying value of different redemption options. A simple rule is to think of the value of a reward (what the customer would have to pay in cash to acquire it) as a percentage rebate on what the customer spent to earn that reward.

Programs that offer airline miles as a reward are tricky because they require some assumptions about what an airline ticket is worth. Since airline seats are so often discounted, customers wouldn't take full retail value as the cash measurement. If, to earn a domestic round-trip ticket valued at $400, one must spend $25,000 with Citibank AAdvantage, the cash value of the reward is 1.75%. That is considerably higher than Discover's cash value, but there are other elements at play. With Citibank AAdvantage, *redemption choice* is limited to tickets on American Airlines.

The success of Citibank AAdvantage and other programs with single redemption options—the General Motors card, for one—demonstrates that although customers value choice, they also respond well to rewards that have *aspirational value.* Rewards that motivate a customer to change his or her behavior have as much to do with psychology as with economics. A discount on a telephone bill does not have the same aspirational impact as exotic free travel or a hot new car. The key is offering the right choice of aspirational redemption options. American Express is trying to address choice by converting Membership Miles into Membership Rewards and by adding more redemption options, such as hotels, resorts, entertainment, and discounts on automobiles.

AT&T has spent millions to launch and promote its True Rewards program. With True Rewards, customers have a choice of redemption options, including free minutes of calling, a 5% cash rebate, and airline miles. The program offers choice, aspiration, and competitive cash value, but customers can earn rewards only on their long-distance spending. For all but a few heavy-volume long-distance customers, it will take many years to earn an airline ticket. Thus, for most consumers, the program lacks *relevance.*

The bottom line is that customers don't want to play in 20 different games or wait 20 years to accumulate airline tickets. Even though frequent fliers have the option to participate in ten or more airline programs, they tend to focus their purchases. If they were to spread their purchases out evenly, it would take them ten times as long to attain rewards. That's too long to wait.

The final factor in determining customer value is *convenience*. To understand its importance, one need only observe Air Miles' different levels of success in different markets. Air Miles, an independent company founded in the United Kingdom, put together networks of wholesalers and retailers offering customers rewards for purchases within the participating network. The cash value of the program (5% on spending at most participating partners) was highly competitive when it was launched in 1990.

In the United States, however, the Air Miles membership card had no transaction capability (it was neither a charge card nor a credit card), and therefore tracking rewards required an entirely new infrastructure at point of sale. Customers wearied of mailing in receipts and redeeming coupons. Merchants resisted additional signage and tedious paperwork. Air Miles in the United States was not only inconvenient for consumers and participating merchants but also costly for the company to administer. As a result, the company folded its U.S. franchise within two years. Air Miles franchises in both the United Kingdom and Canada took the lesson to heart, subsequently partnering with banks for the critical transaction capability.

Rewards linked to a charge card or credit card have a clear convenience advantage because neither the customer nor the merchant needs to exert any incremental effort. Another advantage is that customers can accumulate rewards in a single program based on all their card spending. In fact, one of the reasons rewards programs work so well for card issuers is that they motivate customers to consolidate all their spending onto a single card rather than use two or three cards.

Would partnering make the program more competitive? To make value sharing work, the value a company delivers to its best customers should be competitive in all five dimensions: cash value, choice, aspiration, relevance, and convenience. Although few companies have all those capabilities in their own arsenals, that shouldn't prevent a business from attaining access to the full set.

Take the GM card, for example. General Motors, on its own, would not seem a likely candidate to offer a rewards program. Car companies are trying to influence a major but infrequent purchasing decision, whereas the typical loyalty-building program gives customers rewards for frequent spending on one company's products. But General Motors, accustomed to offering costly purchase incentives in the form of rebates, saw a better opportunity to shift share through a rewards program that locks in customers who might not otherwise purchase a GM product.

GM can't offer customers a free car for every ten cars they buy. But the company wanted to encourage repeat purchases and attract new customers. So it entered into a partnership with Household Finance. By launching a cobranded credit card that put 5% of spending toward purchase or lease of a new car, GM was able to share value with loyal customers and attract new customers as well. GM estimates that it will make money on the card if one of six cars sold through points redemption would not have been sold otherwise.

General Motors clearly understood that as a single entity, it could provide aspiration and cash value. It also understood that, to be competitive, it needed convenience, relevance, and, ultimately, choice. Household Finance saw an opportunity to acquire new customers, who would be attracted by the 5% rebate on spending toward a new car.

But sharing value through cobranding is not the only way a company can join with other organizations to create value through a rewards program. Moreover, customers do not want a wallet full of cobranded credit cards today any more than they wanted a wallet full of retailer charge cards 20 years ago. Recognizing that, some companies have chosen to become part of a rewards network, such as a credit card program, through which customers can earn one or more of a host of rewards provided by different companies. In a network, each company brings different capabilities to the table—and each may take away a different form of value. For example, a card-issuing partner might be building loyalty through the program in a straightforward way: customers like the rewards offered, so they use the card more frequently. But auto or entertainment partners might use the program to encourage consumers to try out their services. Identifying potentially profitable customers who can be turned into loyal customers is worth a lot. Exactly where companies plug into the loyalty equation matters less than the value that participation creates. (See Exhibit I.)

Consider the American Express Membership Miles network, through which participating companies with differing capabilities and needs gain access to Amex's base of affluent members. Across 19 international markets, including the United States, the program has generated a bank of billions of redeemable points. To companies in the

Exhibit I.

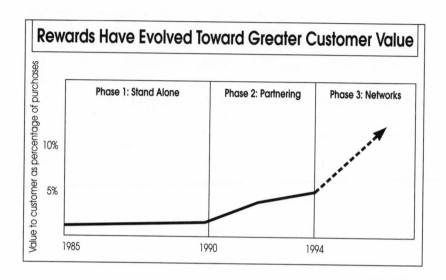

Rewards Have Evolved Toward Greater Customer Value

network, that bank represents purchasing power. American Express, in a sense, serves as a broker, lining up valuable offers for its cardholders while simultaneously creating value for its rewards partners.

The partners also benefit from the network's flexibility. For example, auto partners, being in a highly cyclical industry, can't afford to have too many points redeemed for rebates at a time when capacity utilization is tight. A network such as Membership Miles has the flexibility to steer customers toward the product that will generate the greatest value for a partner company at any given time.

Partner companies in Membership Miles also have access to detailed data on customers' spending habits that they never had before. That data allows partners to identify potentially valuable customers and differentiate the value proposition through rewards, service, and a range of value-sharing, loyalty-building options.

Undoing Flawed Value Sharing

Designing and implementing an effective rewards program that encompasses every internal and external factor is not an easy process, and some businesses must first undo past damage. In retailing, for example, bankruptcies, mergers, and inroads from large-scale discounters have ended the heyday of large department stores. What has happened to stores such as Macy's, which for so many years were both profitable and esteemed by their customers? The creation of value for customers has become unlinked from value sharing.

Macy's begins a season selling high-priced merchandise to its most profitable, loyal customers, who pay full price because they want to ensure a full selection of sizes and styles. At the end of the season, Macy's marks down merchandise by as much as 80% in a desperate attempt to clear excess inventory before the start of the next season. Some might argue that markdown sales are an effective application of customer segmentation: they cut prices for the price-sensitive. But the customers who are extracting the most value from the system aren't the loyal, highly profitable shoppers who frequent Macy's year-round. They are bargain hunters who feel little or no commitment to Macy's or to any other store.

The first step toward realigning the customer value proposition and turning around the profitability of chains such as Macy's is better information. Discounting has become a fact of life in retail clothing partly because the stores do not know enough about their customers to predict demand accurately. If they knew their most profitable customers and those with the potential to become highly profitable, they could maintain a database on their style preferences and sizes. They could reduce the costs of excess inventory, while offering superior value to their loyal customers in the form of selection, recognition and service, and perhaps price.

Retailers have begun to recognize the importance of improved information in achieving the profits of loyalty. Programs such as Neiman Marcus In-Circle and Saks Fifth Avenue SaksFirst offer rebates and rewards as incentives to use proprietary-label credit cards. Although department stores have had their own charge and credit cards for years, most traditionally focused on generating more profit through finance charges and have not used the information created to share value with their best customers.

These retail rewards programs are a step in the direction of value sharing, but, to be competitive, they must overcome gaps in customer value and restructure their incentives to create new customer habits. SaksFirst, for example, links the rewards customers can earn on their spending to their level of spending. A customer who spends more than $2,000 per year receives a certificate worth 2%, or $40, toward future services. At $5,000 per year, the reward increases to 4%. The tiered system motivates customers to spend more (and, in all probability, generates additional profits through interest on revolving balances).

The problem is that the level of discounting is still very modest compared with alternatives such as the GM card's 5% rebate on all purchases. And, when you consider that end-of-season shoppers are offered discounts of 50% or more, it's clear that these loyalty programs don't go far enough.

For the most profitable customers, retailers should be willing to provide even stronger incentives to encourage specific customer behaviors such as referring other customers, buying items not ordinarily purchased (or private-label items with higher margins), or paying full price rather than waiting for end-of-season markdowns.

Anyone who has attempted to get an organization to focus on customer loyalty and to design and implement an effective rewards program is already aware of the barriers. Each functional department views loyalty differently and is likely to promote its own set of solutions. And since customer loyalty is still a new concept to many companies, many managers are prone to use familiar but inappropriate measurement systems and incentives in their new programs. In addition, growth is a top priority at many companies and can lead to an emphasis on acquiring new customers at the expense of retaining current ones or building loyalty.

We've laid out the steps required to break this cycle. But for a company to commit to the steps that build loyalty, senior managers must agree that loyalty pays. Then they must be unrelenting about focusing the organization and all their marketing programs on the goals and measures that will develop a loyal customer base.

3
Do You Want to Keep Your Customers Forever?

B. Joseph Pine II, Don Peppers, and Martha Rogers

Customers, whether consumers or businesses, do not want more choices. They want exactly what they want—when, where, and how they want it—and technology now makes it possible for companies to give it to them. Interactive and database technology permits companies to amass huge amounts of data on individual customers' needs and preferences. And information technology and flexible manufacturing systems enable companies to customize large volumes of goods or services for individual customers at a relatively low cost. But few companies are exploiting this potential. Most managers continue to view the world through the twin lenses of mass marketing and mass production. To handle their increasingly turbulent and fragmented markets, they try to churn out a much greater variety of goods and services and to target ever finer market segments with more tailored advertising messages. But these managers only end up bombarding their customers with too many choices.

A company that aspires to give customers exactly what they want must look at the world through new lenses. It must use technology to become two things: a *mass customizer* that efficiently provides individually customized goods and services, and a *one-to-one marketer* that elicits information from each customer about his or her specific needs and preferences. The twin logic of mass customization and one-to-one marketing binds producer and consumer together in what we call a *learning relationship*—an ongoing connection that becomes smarter as the two interact with each other, collaborating to meet the consumer's needs over time.

In learning relationships, individual customers teach the company more and more about their preferences and needs, giving the company an immense competitive advantage. The more customers teach the company, the better it becomes at providing exactly what they want—exactly how they want it—and the more difficult it will be for a competitor to entice them away. Even if a competitor were to build the exact same capabilities, a customer already involved in a learning relationship with the company would have to spend an inordinate amount of time and energy teaching the competitor what the company already knows.

Because of this singularly powerful competitive advantage, a company that can cultivate learning relationships with its customers should be able to retain their business virtually forever—provided that it continues to supply high-quality customized products or services at reasonably competitive prices and does not miss the next technology wave. (Learning relationships would not have saved a buggy-whip manufacturer from the automobile.)

One company that excels at building learning relationships with its customers is named, appropriately enough, Individual, Inc. This Burlington, Massachusetts, company, which competes with wire, clipping, and information-retrieval services, provides published news stories selected to fit the specific, ever changing interests of each client. Instead of having to sort through a mountain of clippings or having to master the arcane commands needed to search databases, Individual's customers—which include such diverse companies as MCI Telecommunications, McKinsey & Company, Avon Products, and Fidelity Investments—effortlessly receive timely, fresh, relevant articles delivered right to their desks by fax, groupware (such as Lotus Notes), on-line computer services, the Internet, or electronic mail.

When someone signs up for Individual's *First!* service, the company assigns an editorial manager to determine what sort of information the client wants. The editorial manager and the client reduce those requests to simple descriptions, such as articles about new uses of information technology in home health care or about new products developed by Japanese semiconductor companies. The editorial manager enters the requests into Individual's SMART software system (for System for Manipulation and Retrieval of Text). Then SMART takes over. Every business day, the system searches 400 sources containing more than 12,000 articles for those pieces that will most likely fit the client's needs, and it delivers them by whatever method the client has chosen.

Every week, Individual asks a new client (by fax or computer) to rate each article as "not relevant," "somewhat relevant," or "very relevant." The responses are fed into the system, making SMART even smarter. In the first week of service, most customers find only 40% to 60% of the articles to be somewhat or very relevant. By the fourth or fifth week, SMART has increased those ratings to a targeted 80% to 90%. Once it has achieved that level, Individual reduces the frequency of the ratings to once a month, which still enables it to keep abreast of customers' changing needs.

Individual also responds constantly to clients' requests for new sources and ways of receiving information. Sun Microsystems, for example, asked the company to place *First!* on its internal Internet server. Once Individual provided this service, it discovered that many other clients that also depended on the Internet for sending and sharing information wanted to receive the service in the same way. Such responsiveness is undoubtedly one reason why Individual, which has more than 30,000 users and more than 4,000 accounts, enjoys a customer-retention rate of 85% to 90%. But there is also another reason: because of the time and energy each client expends in teaching the company which articles are relevant and which are not, switching to a competitor would require the client to make that investment all over again.

From Mass Production to Mass Customization

Although Individual uses information and interactive technology to its fullest, most managers fail to understand that variety is not the same thing as customization. Customization means manufacturing a product or delivering a service *in response* to a particular customer's needs, and mass customization means doing it in a cost-effective way. Mass customization calls for a customer-centered orientation in production and delivery processes, requiring the company to collaborate with individual customers to design each one's desired product or service, which is then constructed from a base of pre-engineered modules that can be assembled in myriad ways.

In contrast, product-centered mass production and mass marketing call for pushing options (and inventory) into distribution channels and hoping that each new option is embraced by enough customers to make its production worthwhile. It requires customers to hunt for the single product or service they want from among an ever growing array of alternatives.

Consider grocery stores. According to *New Products News,* the number of new products, including line extensions, introduced in grocery stores each year increased from less than 3,000 in 1980 to more than 10,000 in 1988 and more than 17,000 in 1993. And *Progressive Grocer* reports that the number of stock-keeping units in the average super-market doubled to more than 30,000 between 1980 and 1994. The same trend can be seen in many service industries: witness the prolif-eration of affinity credit cards and the numerous options offered by telephone companies.

Companies are also deluging consumers with a wider variety of messages. And, of course, there is a greater array of media for carrying them: direct mail, telemarketing, special newspaper supplements, and a larger number of television channels, among others.

For example, the average newspaper weighs 55% more today than it did just ten years ago, mainly because of supplements designed to carry specially targeted advertising. The problem with such supple-ments is that they are distributed to every subscriber. Nongardeners still receive the gardening supplement, and people reading the paper before heading to the office still get the work-at-home supplement. So the supplements really aren't so special after all.

Mass marketers use information technology to define the most likely customers for the products they want to sell. For the most part, the information comes from simple transactional records (such as cus-tomer purchases and invoices) and public information (such as vehicle registrations, address-change forms, and census data) compiled by companies like R.L. Polk and Donnelley Marketing. From those data, the mass marketer generates a list of the most likely prospects and solicits them with offers or messages that the marketer has attempted to customize by guessing their tastes. By contrast, the one-to-one marketer conducts a dialogue with each customer—one at a time—and uses the increasingly more detailed feedback to find the best products or services for that customer. Although many companies are moving toward this model, few have fully implemented it yet or combined it with mass customization.

Take Hallmark Cards and American Greetings, the leaders of the va-riety-intensive greeting card industry. Both companies have installed electronic kiosks in stores and other public places to enable people to create their own greeting cards. Consumers can touch the screen of either company's kiosk, quickly select the type of card they need (for example, anniversary or birthday card), browse through a number of selections, and then modify them or compose their own wording to express exactly the right sentiment. The card is printed in a minute or so.

Both companies seem pleased with the performance of their mass customization businesses, but neither has fully exploited its potential. The graphics for the cards are all preset (so only the wording can be customized), and there is little organization (so browsing through the choices can be time consuming). The greatest weakness of the electronic kiosks, however, is the absence of a system for recording individual customers' preferences. Each time someone uses the system, he or she must start all over again.

If a greeting card company were to harness the full power of mass customization and one-to-one marketing, it would be able to remember the important occasions in your life and remind you to buy a card. It would make suggestions based on your past purchases. Its kiosk would display past selections, either to ensure that you don't commit the faux pas of sending the same card to the same person twice or to give you the option of sending the same funny card to another person—appropriately personalized, of course. Perhaps the company would mail your cards or ship them across the Internet for you so they would arrive at the appointed time. Maybe the company would be able to remind you to send a card, allow you to design it, and arrange for its delivery on your personal computer through an on-line service that would let you incorporate your own graphics or photographs. It might even find your design so good that it would ask your permission to add it to its inventory.

Certainly, not every customer would want to invest the time that such a relationship would require. Neither would every customer buy enough cards to make such a relationship worthwhile for the company. But the advantages to a greeting card company of establishing and cultivating a learning relationship with customers who buy cards frequently are immense. Because every card sold to those customers will be tailored precisely to their needs, the company will be able to charge them a premium and its profit margins will increase. And because the company will be equipped to ensure that the customer never forgets an occasion, it will sell more cards to that customer. The company's product development will become more effective because of the expanded ability to understand exactly who is buying what, when, and why—not to mention the ability to use new ideas that customers could provide.

But, most important of all, the company will retain more customers, especially the most valuable ones: frequent purchasers. The more customers teach the company about their individual tastes, celebration occasions, and card recipients (addresses, relationships, and so forth), the more reluctant they will be to repeat that process with another supplier. As long as the company fulfills its end of the bargain, a competitor should never be able to entice away its customers. The battle will be limited to attracting new ones.

When Are Learning Relationships Appropriate?

As compelling and powerful as the benefits of learning relationships are, this radically different business model cannot be applied in the same way by everyone. Companies such as home builders, real estate brokers, and appliance manufacturers—which do not interact frequently with end users—cannot learn enough to make a learning relationship with those customers work. But they might find it beneficial to develop such relationships with general contractors. Similarly, makers of products like paper clips, whose revenue or profit margin per customer is too low to justify building individual learning relationships with customers, might find it advantageous to cultivate learning relationships with office-supply chains, which interact directly with end users.

Even producers of commodities such as wheat or natural gas, which cannot be customized easily, and of commodity-like products bought mainly on the basis of price have much to gain from this approach. Learning relationships can enable such companies to design services that differentiate their offerings. This is the strategy that Bandag, which sells truck-tire retreads to more than 500 dealer-installers around the country, is pursuing.

Bandag's retreads are essentially a commodity because they are comparable in price and quality to those of competitors. To break out of the pack, Bandag is providing additional services. For example, it assists its dealers in filing and collecting on warranty claims from tire manufacturers and will soon begin offering comprehensive fleet-management services to its largest national accounts.

Bandag plans to embed computer chips in the rubber of newly retreaded tires to gauge each tire's pressure and temperature and to count its revolutions. That information will enable the company not only to tell each customer the optimal time to retread each tire (thus reducing downtime caused by blowouts) but also to help it improve its fleet's operations.

Because of the current high cost of building such capabilities, many manufacturers, service providers, and retailers may find, as Bandag did, that it pays to establish learning relationships only with their best customers. But as advances in information technology continue to drive down the cost of building learning relationships, they will make economic sense in many more businesses and for a wider spectrum of customers. Many types of industries are already ripe for revolution. They include:

Complex Products or Services. Most people do not want to work their way through hundreds or thousands of options, features, pricing structures, delivery methods, and networks to figure out which product or service is best for them. One solution is for companies to collaborate with customers in custom-designing the product, as Andersen Corporation, the window manufacturer based in Bayport, Minnesota, is doing. It resolved the information-overload problem for its customers (individual home owners and building contractors) by developing a multimedia system called the Window of Knowledge. A sales representative uses a workstation that features 50,000 possible window components to help customers design their own windows. The system automatically generates error-free quotations and manufacturing specifications, which can be saved for future use. The resulting database of window configurations deepens Andersen's understanding of how its business is performing.

Big-Ticket Items. A company that succeeds in customizing all aspects of owning an expensive product or using a premium service stands to gain a competitive advantage over its rivals. Consider automobiles. A car buyer, over his or her lifetime, can generate hundreds of thousands of dollars' worth of business when financing, service, and referrals, as well as the original purchase, are taken into account. All together, they represent an enormous opportunity for companies that cater to customers' individual preferences. The same opportunities apply to big-ticket commercial offerings, including machinery, information systems, outsourcing, and consulting. (See "How to Gain Customers Forever.")

How to Gain Customers Forever

Industrial companies that sell to other businesses can benefit just as much from learning relationships as companies that sell products or services to consumers. Consider the case of Ross Controls (formerly the Ross Operating Valve Company) of Troy, Michigan, a 70-year-old manufacturer of pneumatic valves and air-control systems. Through what it calls the ROSS/FLEX process, Ross learns about its customers' needs, collaborates with them to come up with designs precisely tailored to help them meet those needs, and quickly and efficiently makes the customized products. The process has enabled the medium-size manufacturer to forge learning relationships with such companies as General Motors, Knight Industries, Reynolds Aluminum, and Japan's Yamamura Glass.

For example, Ross is currently supplying GM's Metal Fabricating Division with 600 integrated-valve systems. Based on a common platform but individually customized for a particular stamping press, each integrated system performs better than the valves it is replacing at one-third the price.

Two elements have enabled Ross to transform itself from a sleepy industrial manufacturer into a dynamic organization that cultivates learning relationships with its customers:

A Desire to Listen to and Collaborate with Each Customer. This involves spending time on the phone, faxing ideas back and forth, and often visiting plants to see how pneumatic systems are to be used in the customer's manufacturing process. And once a system is designed to solve the customer's problem, Ross gets feedback from prototypes and encourages the customer to make continuous upgrades to its valve designs, yielding more precisely tailored designs over time. Ross then stores them in a library of design platforms, components, and computer instructions for its manufacturing equipment so it does not have to start from scratch every time it works with a customer on a new project.

The Capability to Turn Complex Designs into Products. Through the effective use of computer-aided design (CAD) and computer numerically controlled (CNC) machines, Ross can electronically transmit tooling instructions directly from engineering workstations to multimillion-dollar production equipment, which can turn around new designs in as little as a day. But obviously, computer-aided-design and manufacturing equipment alone does not enable a company to mass-customize. Information about each customer's needs is also essential. To obtain such information, Ross created a crew of "integrators," each of whom is assigned to a given customer. The integrator talks with the customer, produces the valve designs, and determines the manufacturing specifications, including the instructions for the CNC machines. Using the CAD system, the integrator draws from the library's contents whenever possible to create a customized design and the computer coding required to make the product.

The ROSS/FLEX process has helped Ross boost the custom portion of its business from 5% to 20% of its revenues in the past four years. But the company is not yet satisfied with its ability to build learning relationships. It intends to add an interactive audio and video communications setup that will include a "what you see is what I see" CAD system so that an integrator and a customer do not have to be in the same place to collaborate on a design. And it plans to automate the access to its library so that integrators and customers—even on their own—can generate a wider range of designs and execute each one more quickly.

When Ross started down this road eight years ago, its primary goal was to gain customers for life by expanding the company's capabilities to meet each one's changing needs. It is clearly making a lot of progress. At a time when GM is reexamining virtually all its supplier relations, its Metal Fabricating Division won't go to any company but Ross for pneumatic valves and won't let its suppliers, either. Knight Industries, a supplier of ergonomic material-handling equipment, gives Ross 100% of its custom business and about 70% of its standard (catalog) business. When a competitor tried to woo Knight away, its president, James Zaguroli, Jr., responded, "Why would I switch to you? You're already five product generations behind where I am with Ross."

Digitizable Products and Services. Anything that can be digitized can be customized. If such products are purchased frequently, providing a discernible pattern of personal preferences, they may be ideally suited for one-to-one marketing as well. Obvious candidates include not only greeting cards but also software, periodicals, telecommunication services, and entertainment products such as movies, videos, games, and recorded music. Indeed, many companies in these businesses are working to develop learning relationships.

On-Line Services. Providers of on-line services already offer a broad spectrum of choices—including electronic shopping, special-interest forums, entertainment, news, and financial services—but few offer tailored convenience. Currently, the user must navigate through choice after choice. A competitor that learns a customer's wants and needs could navigate cyberspace on behalf of that customer and cull only the relevant choices.

Luxury and Specialty Products. Many businesses (such as apparel, perfume and cosmetics, athletic equipment, and fine wine) have customers with complex individual tastes. For example, people differ not only in their physical measurements but also in how they prefer their clothes to fit and look. Levi Strauss is capitalizing on these differences by mass-customizing blue jeans for women, using technology supplied by Custom Clothing Technology Corporation of Newton, Massachusetts. After a customer has her measurements taken in a store, she tries on a pair or two of jeans to determine her exact preference. The information is then sent to the factory for prompt production. Although Levi Strauss is currently limiting the program to one style of jeans, the approach offers the company tremendous opportunities for building learning relationships.

Retailing Services. In many industries, retailers have a big advantage over manufacturers in building learning relationships with end users, especially when customers want to touch, feel, and browse (clothing, shoes, and books) or when the product is immediately consumed (for example, in restaurants and bars). They also have the edge when individual customers do not buy a large amount of any one manufacturer's products (such as groceries and packaged goods). That is because the retailer is in a better position to see patterns in a customer's purchases and because it might be more expensive for the manufacturer to build learning relationships. Finally, many retailers offer consumers not products per se but service, and services can be mass-customized more readily than most products can. (See "How Peapod Is Customizing the Virtual Supermarket.")

How Peapod Is Customizing the Virtual Supermarket

One company that is exploiting learning relationships in retailing services is Peapod, a grocery-shopping and delivery service based in Evanston, Illinois. Its customers—currently in Chicago and San Francisco—buy a software application for $29.95 that enables them to access Peapod's database through an on-line computer service. They then pay $4.95 per month for the service and a per-order charge of $5 plus 5% of the order amount. Peapod's back office is linked into the mainframe databases of the supermarkets at which it shops for its customers (Jewel in Chicago and Safeway in San Francisco), allowing it to provide all the supermarkets' stock-keeping units and shelf prices electronically to its customers.

Rather than automating the trip to a retail store, as other on-line providers are doing, Peapod is using interactive technology to change the shopping experience altogether. It lets each customer create the virtual supermarket that best suits him or her. Using a personal computer, customers can shop in the way they prefer. They can request a list of items by category (snack foods), by item (potato chips), by brand (Frito-Lay), or even by what is on sale in the store on a given day. Within categories, they can choose to have the items arranged alphabetically by brand, by package size, by unit price, or even by nutritional value. Customers also can create and save for repeated use standard and special shopping lists (baby items, barbecue needs, and the like).

Peapod teaches its customers to shop so effectively in its virtual super-market that most of them discover that—despite the company's rates—they *save* money because they use more coupons, do better comparison shopping, and buy fewer impulse items than they would if they shopped at a real supermarket. In addition, they save time and have more control over it because they can shop from home or work whenever they want.

Peapod has found that every interaction with a customer is an oppor-tunity to learn. At the end of each shopping session, it asks the customer, "How did we do on the last order?" Peapod gets feedback on 35% of orders; most companies consider a 10% response rate to customer-satis-faction surveys to be good. And more than 80% of Peapod's customers have responded at one time or another. The feedback has prompted the company to institute a variety of changes and options, including providing nutritional information, making deliveries within a half-hour window (for an additional $4.95) rather than the usual 90-minute window, accepting detailed requests (such as three ripe and three unripe tomatoes), and delivering alcoholic beverages.

Peapod views delivery as another opportunity to learn about custom-ers' preferences. It asks its deliverers to find out where customers would like the groceries left when they're not at home and anything else that will enhance the relationship. They fill out an "interaction record" for every delivery to track those preferences (as well as entering basic service metrics, such as the time of the delivery).

Even with the rates it charges, Peapod has to be efficient and effective to make money in what is a low-margin business. That is why it mass-cus-tomizes all shopping and delivery processes. Each order is filled by a generalist, who shops the aisles of the store, and as-needed specialists, who provide the produce, meats, deli, seafood, and bakery items to the generalist. The generalist pays for the groceries, often at special Peapod counters in the back of the store. The order is then taken to a holding area in the supermarket or in a trailer, where the appropriate items are kept cold or frozen until the deliverer picks up a set of orders and takes them to the customers. At each stage—ordering, shopping, holding, and delivery—the processes are modularized to provide personalized service at a relatively low cost.

If a customer has a problem, he or she can call Membership Services, and a service representative will try to resolve the matter. Peapod treats each call as yet another opportunity to learn (and remember) each customer's preferences and to figure out what the company can do to improve service for customers as a whole. For example, service representatives found that some customers were receiving five bags of grapefruits when they really wanted only five grapefruits. In response, Peapod now routinely asks customers to confirm orders in which quantities might be confused.

Peapod's results stand as a testament to the power of learning relationships. The four-year-old service, which has 7,500 customers and revenues of about $15 million, has a customer-retention rate of more than 80%. And the service accounts for an average of 15% of the sales volume of the 12 Jewel and Safeway stores where Peapod shops for its customers.

Vying for the End Customer

Retailers, insurance agents, distributors, interior decorators, building contractors, and others who deal face-to-face with the end customer can certainly make the case that they should be the ones who control the relationship with that customer. On the other hand, manufacturers and service providers have an advantage when a customer often buys the same type of product (toiletries, magazines, or office supplies); when products can be economically delivered to the home or office (personal computers, software, or services such as lawn care and plumbing); or when customers already value their relationship with the product or brand (as with premium Scotch, designer jeans, or luxury watches).

Obviously, those boundaries are permeable and constantly shifting: manufacturers and service providers can become retailers and vice versa. And advances in technology are making it increasingly easy for one member of the value chain to undermine another's natural advantages. Consider, for example, three basic reasons consumers go to retail stores: to obtain the information they need to make a purchasing decision, to pay for the product, and to take possession of it. Thanks to the same information-based technologies that make learning relationships possible, consumers increasingly will not have to visit stores for any of those reasons.

Today, consumers can get better information—information that is unbiased, comparative, accurate, and immediate—through on-line services, CD-ROM catalogs, and fax-response systems, and eventually they will be able to obtain it through interactive TV. As the continuing boom in catalog and home-TV shopping attests, consumers and organizations can buy goods and services over the phone and through dedicated on-line services as easily as, if not more easily than, in person, and security measures will almost certainly be in place soon that will make it possible to purchase products through the Internet. Finally, almost anything can be delivered direct to the home thanks to Federal Express, UPS, dedicated delivery services, and (for digitized products) fax and on-line services.

For retailers, the message is clear: if they want to maintain or increase their competitive advantage, they must begin establishing learning relationships with their best customers today. On the other hand, a manufacturer or a service company one or more links removed from the end user has a variety of options. It could build collaborative learning relationships with those occupying the next link, gaining knowledge about their wants, needs, and preferences over time, and mass-customizing products and services to meet their requirements. That is the approach ITT Hartford's Personal Lines business is taking with the independent agents who sell its automobile and home insurance. And it is also the direction in which Andersen— which realizes that individual home owners buy windows too infrequently to form a productive, long-term relationship with the company—is heading. Although Andersen plans to continue to mass-customize windows for consumers, it also intends to cultivate learning relationships with architects, home builders, and window distributors.

Another option for a manufacturer or a service company is to form tighter partnerships with retailers so that together they control the learning relationships with individual end customers. Such a partnership would require sharing information and knowledge (and maybe a common database), linking operations tightly so consumers' desires could be translated efficiently and quickly into tailored products and services, and possibly making joint investment and strategic decisions on how best to serve end customers over time. This option might make sense for companies such as automakers, which rely heavily on dealers to provide the touch, feel, and test drive necessary for consumers to make a buying decision.

How to Build Learning Relationships

If managers decide that their company can and should cultivate learning relationships with customers, how do they go about it? There are basically four components to think about: an *information strategy* for initiating dialogues with customers and remembering their preferences; a *production/delivery strategy* for fulfilling what the company learns about individual customers; an *organizational strategy* for managing both customers and capabilities; and an *assessment strategy* for evaluating performance.

The Information Strategy. Cultivating learning relationships depends on a company's ability to elicit and manage information about customers. The first step is to identify those individual customers with whom it pays to have a learning relationship. That is easy for businesses like hotels or airlines, whose customers make reservations in their own names and whose transactions and preferences are easy to track.

In industries whose customers are anonymous, such as retailing, a company may have to use one of two approaches to persuade them to identify and provide information about themselves: show them that it can serve them better if they do or give them something of value in return, such as a gift or a discount. For example, Waldenbooks offers a 10% discount on all purchases if customers identify themselves by becoming Preferred Readers. The program allows the company to track the purchases of those customers at any Waldenbooks store. Learning about customer preferences enables the bookseller to let a particular customer know when, for example, the next William Styron novel will be out or when an author whose work the customer has purchased will be in a local store, signing books.

Few companies will want to have such relationships with all customers. Waldenbooks' program, for example, is aimed at people who spend more than $100 a year at its stores. As a screening device, the company charges a $10 annual fee for Preferred Reader status.

As with any new program, it is often best to begin with a company's most valuable customers. When the company sees that the value of a learning relationship with them exceeds the costs, it can gradually expand the program to other customers.

Once a company has identified the customers with whom it wishes to have a learning relationship, there are a number of ways in which it can conduct a productive dialogue. A rapidly expanding array of interactive technologies—including electronic kiosks, on-line services, and database-driven mail—are making such dialogues easier and less costly. (See "How to Interact: A Sampler of Today's Technologies.") Businesses that naturally involve personal contact with customers, either on the phone or in person, have golden opportunities to learn about them.

How to Interact: A Sampler of Today's Technologies

Interactive media that allow marketers to send specific messages to specific consumers and to conduct a dialogue with actual and potential customers already exist. One is the Internet, which now boasts more than 15 million users. Using it simply to prospect for customers remains problematic owing to the hostility of many users to commercial advertising on the Internet. But many companies have found the Internet to be a good way to obtain information from or about customers through bulletin boards, direct connections, and company-specific information services.

Other on-line services, such as those provided by Prodigy, America Online, and CompuServe, are much more advanced than the Internet in providing a full-fledged, structured medium through which customers and companies can interact. And several company-specific on-line services, such as grocery deliverer Peapod's, have proved useful for facilitating dialogues with customers.

Electronic kiosks have a wide variety of applications for interacting directly with customers. Some are purely informational—like those that provide directions to local spots from a hotel lobby. Others dispense coupons or gift certificates. And an increasing number are being used to dispense mass-customized products, including greeting cards, business cards, and sheet music.

A variety of interactive telephone services exists already. Seattle-based FreeFone Information Network offers one on the West Coast that enables marketers to find consumers willing to participate in a dialogue. When people sign up for the service, they fill out a questionnaire that is used to determine which advertiser's message is sent to which person. Each time a consumer makes a personal call and listens to a sponsored message while waiting for the call to connect, FreeFone credits the household account a nickel. The household gets a dime if the consumer requests more information, a coupon, or a telephone connection to the advertiser. Companies that advertise through FreeFone, including Ticket-Master, the U.S. Postal Service, NBC, and the National Association of Female Executives, can learn a great deal about each household. But FreeFone will not divulge a caller's identity to an advertiser unless the caller chooses to reveal it.

"Cash-back telephone coupons" provide a similar way for companies and consumers to learn about each other over the phone. These services, offered by such companies as Chicago-based Scherers Communications, are essentially reverse 900 numbers. For example, a car manufacturer might credit someone $5 for watching a videotape touting some particular models and calling in with the personal identification number contained on the tape.

Fax response is being used by many business-to-business organizations and a small but growing number of consumer-goods manufacturers to give customers up-to-the-minute price quotations and product options. Fax response provides the marketer with the telephone-number identity of the individual who requested the information, which can be linked with transactional data as well as with mailing information.

R.R. Donnelley & Sons' selective binding technology, which enables printers to put different pages in different editions of a given publication, has made it possible for publishers to mass-customize periodicals. *Farm Journal*, for example, assembles information on individual subscribers—how many acres of what particular crops they have planted, how many head of cattle they own, and so on—and then uses Donnelley's technology to tailor the editorial content and the advertising of each edition for the particular subscriber.

In conducting a dialogue with customers, it is important that the database "remember" not just preferences declared in past purchases but also the preferences that emerge from questions, complaints, suggestions, and actions.

The Ritz-Carlton hotel chain trains all its associates—from those on the front desk to those in maintenance and housekeeping—how to converse with customers and how to handle complaints immediately. In addition, it provides each associate with a "guest preference pad" for writing down every preference gleaned from conversations with and observations of customers. Every day, the company enters those preferences into a chainwide database that now contains profiles of nearly a half million patrons. Employees at any of the 28 Ritz-Carlton hotels worldwide can gain access to those profiles through the Covia travel-reservation system.

Say you stay at the Ritz-Carlton in Cancún, Mexico, call room service for dinner, and request an ice cube in your glass of white wine. Months later, when you stay at the Ritz-Carlton in Naples, Florida, and order a glass of white wine from room service, you will almost certainly be asked if you would like an ice cube in it. The same would be true if you asked for a window seat in a restaurant, a minibar with no liquor in your room, or a variety of other necessities or preferences that personalize your stay at the Ritz-Carlton.

By retaining such information, a company becomes better equipped to respond to suggestions, resolve complaints, and stay abreast of customers' changing needs. Many companies make the mistake of treating customers as if they were static entities rather than people whose preferences, lifestyles, and circumstances are constantly evolving and shifting.

Some managers may wonder whether customers will see requests for in-depth personal information as an invasion of privacy. Most people don't mind divulging their shopping habits, measurements, and friends' names and addresses if they believe they're getting something of value in return. Consumers' fears also will be assuaged if a company states unequivocally that it will jealously guard personal information, which any company building learning relationships must do. Unlike mass marketers, who buy and sell customer data willy-nilly, companies seeking to build learning relationships realize that such information is a precious asset.

The Production/Delivery Strategy. Children can create an unlimited number of unique designs with Lego building blocks. Service and manufacturing companies that have successfully mass-customized employ a similar approach: they create modules—components or processes—that can be assembled in a variety of ways to enable the companies to tailor products or services for specific customers at a relatively low cost. (See B. Joseph Pine II, Bart Victor, and Andrew C. Boynton, "Making Mass Customization Work," *Harvard Business Review* September–October 1993.) Admittedly, there is more opportunity to adopt this approach in some businesses than in others. For example, the Ritz-Carlton is more of a customizer than a mass customizer. If it could figure out how to mass-customize its services, as Peapod has done, it would be able to cater to the preferences of more of its customers *and* increase its profits.

However, creating process or component modules is not enough. A company also needs a design tool that can take a customer's requirements and easily determine how to use its capabilities to fulfill them. Individual, Inc.'s SMART system and Andersen's Window of Knowledge system are examples of design tools that enable companies to be as effective as possible in ascertaining what customers need, as efficient as possible in production and delivery, and as effortless as possible in matching the two.

The Organizational Strategy. Traditional marketing organizations depend on product managers to push the product out the door, into the channels, and into customers' hands. Product managers are generally responsible for performing market research, specifying the requirements for a fairly standardized offering, and developing the mar-keting plan. And once the product is introduced, they are rewarded for selling as much of it as possible. While these techniques are ideally suited for mass marketing, they are ill-suited for learning relationships in which the reverse is required: extracting a customer's wants and needs from a dialogue and creating the product or service that fulfills those requirements.

To build learning relationships, companies don't need product man-agers; they need *customer managers.* As the term implies, customer managers oversee the relationship with the customer. While they are responsible for a portfolio of customers with similar needs, they also are responsible for obtaining all the business possible from *each* cus-tomer, one at a time. To do this, customer managers must know their customers' preferences and be able to help them articulate their needs. They serve as gatekeepers within the company for all communication to and from each customer.

In addition, companies need *capability managers,* each of whom exe-cutes a distinct production or delivery process for fulfilling each cus-tomer's requirements. The head of each capability ensures that appro-priate capacity exists and that the process can be executed reliably and efficiently.

Customer managers must know what capability managers can pro-vide and must take the lead in determining when new capabilities may be required to meet customers' needs. For their part, capability man-agers must know what customer managers require and be able to fig-ure out how to create it. For instance, when a Peapod customer in-formed his customer manager (a Membership Services representative) that he wanted to be able to order both ripe and unripe tomatoes, the company expanded the capabilities of its ordering software and cre-ated a new set of capability managers: produce specialists. These spe-cialists have the skills and experience to squeeze tomatoes and thump melons, for example. Similarly, a customer manager at four-year-old Individual asked the company's manager of information suppliers— the capability manager responsible for managing and acquiring new sources of information—to add the *New England Journal of Medicine* after learning that a client needed articles from the publication. Indi-vidual expands the number of its sources by 75 to 100 per year in this manner.

In contrast to the traditional product manager's role of finding cus-tomers for the company's products, the role of the customer manager is finding products for the company's customers. Often, a customer manager will learn of a need for some product or service component that the organization does not consider itself competent to produce or deliver. The capability manager might then arrange to obtain it from a strategic partner or a third-party vendor. For example, it would not pay for AT&T's computer hardware and software business, AT&T Global Information Solutions (formerly NCR), to write software for every conceivable customer need. When a customer-focused team (the unit's equivalent of customer managers) learns that a customer needs a particular application that is unavailable in-house, it often asks a capability-management team to acquire or license the software.

In all cases, however, the customer manager must be held accountable for satisfying the customer. At ITT Hartford's Personal Lines business, every time a customer (an independent agent) makes a request, Personal Lines forms an instant team composed of people from whichever service modules (underwriting, claims payment, or servicing, for example) are needed to satisfy the request. But the customer manager is the one responsible for guaranteeing the promised customized service. He or she specifies the commitment to the agent at the beginning of each transaction, and a tracking system ensures that it is fulfilled.

The Assessment Strategy. Obviously, the value of a learning relationship to the company will vary from customer to customer. Some customers will be more willing than others to invest the time and effort. Those willing to participate are going to have a wide variety of demands or expectations, meaning that the company will have a varying ability to contribute to and profit from each relationship. Companies should therefore decide which potential learning relationships they will pursue.

The ideal way to approach this task is to think about a customer's lifetime value. Lifetime value is the sum of the future stream of profits and other benefits attributable to all purchases and transactions with an individual customer, discounted back to its present value. In their article "Zero Defections: Quality Comes to Services" (see part IV, chapter 1), Frederick F. Reichheld and W. Earl Sasser, Jr., showed that the longer customers are retained by a company, the more profitable they become because of increased purchases, reduced operating costs, referrals, price premiums, and reduced customer acquisition costs. We would add one more element to the list: some customers will have higher lifetime values because the insights they provide to the company may result in new capabilities that can be applied to other customers. Although it is a daunting task, companies seeking to build learning relationships should therefore try to track as many of those elements as they can, using such information as transactional histories and customer feedback.

A company's *customer share*—its share of each customer's total patronage—is one of the most useful measures of success in building a learning relationship. To calculate customer share, a company must have some idea of what the customer is buying from the competition and what he or she might be willing to buy from the company. The best source of such information is the customer—another reason why dialogue is critical.

Yet another important performance measure is what we call *customer sacrifice:* the gap between what each customer truly wants and needs and what the company can supply. To understand individual customer sacrifice, companies building learning relationships must go beyond the aggregate customer-satisfaction figures that almost everyone collects today. That is why Peapod asks every customer at every shopping session how well it did on the last order. Understanding and tracking this gap will enable customer managers to demonstrate the need for new capabilities to deepen learning relationships and will give capability managers the information they need to decide how to expand or change their company's capabilities.

Becoming a Learning Broker

After a company becomes adept at cultivating learning relationships with its current customers, how might it expand? Two choices are obvious: acquire new customers in the company's current markets or expand into new locations. But there is a third option: deliver *other* products to *current* customers and become a learning broker.

Because Peapod's customers already know how to interact with its on-line ordering system, the company could easily broker new product categories. For example, if Peapod could gain entry into a chain of home-improvement centers (meaning on-line access to the chain's computerized list of stock-keeping units and prices, and Peapod shoppers' access to the stores themselves), its knowledge about its customers and its customers' knowledge about it would immediately transfer to a whole new set of "virtual aisles." And once again, it would be Peapod—not the chains or the manufacturers that supply them—that would control the relationship with the customers. By arbitraging the information between customers and companies that supply products and services that they could potentially use, Peapod would have become a bona fide learning broker.

Discussions of what life will be like in the information-rich, interactive future often focus on personal electronic "agents" that will watch out for each individual's information and entertainment needs, sifting and sorting through the plethora of channels, messages, and offerings. But the dynamics of learning relationships are such that learning brokers can provide that service today in a wide variety of domains. They could provide individual customers with products and services beyond those that their companies have traditionally supplied. They also could advise their customers about other offerings and be on the lookout for items they might want.

One of the best examples of a company that already serves its customers in this fashion is the United Services Automobile Association. Seventy years ago, USAA began providing automobile insurance to military officers. It now supplies its customers—whom it still limits to current and former military officers and their families—with a wide variety of products and services. They include all types of insurance, full-service banking, investment brokerage, homes in retirement communities, and travel services. USAA also offers a buying service through which it purchases and delivers other companies' products, including automobiles, jewelry, major appliances, and consumer electronics. The relationship with the customer, however, remains the sole dominion of USAA.

USAA members have learned over the years that the company stands behind everything it sells and looks after their best interests. As more than one member has said, USAA could sell almost anything to them. More than nine of every ten active-duty and former military officers are members. And since opening up its services to members' adult children in the 1970s, USAA has been able to attract more than half of them, showing that learning relationships can even span generations.

The role of a learning broker clearly makes sense for distributors or agents such as Peapod and Individual, two companies that make no products themselves. Such companies are relatively free to go to whatever company can provide exactly what their customers want and need. Whether to take the path of a learning broker is a more complex decision for a manufacturer or a service company. But it is not out of the question. A company can become a hybrid like USAA: it offers its members a wide variety of other companies' products, but, in its core business, financial services, it offers only its own products. While it may be difficult to imagine today, many companies could eventually decide that it pays to become a learning broker even of competitors' products. But adopting that strategy will make sense only if a company reaches the point where its knowledge of its customers and their trust in it yield a greater competitive advantage and greater profits than merely selling its own products can. When that happens, learning relationships with end customers will have become the company's primary competency.

4
Learning from Customer Defections

Frederick F. Reichheld

On average, the CEOs of U.S. corporations lose half their customers every five years. This fact shocks most people. It shocks the CEOs themselves, most of whom have little insight into the causes of the customer exodus, let alone the cures, because they do not measure customer defections, make little effort to prevent them, and fail to use defections as a guide to improvements. Yet customer defection is one of the most illuminating measures in business. First, it is the clearest possible sign that customers see a deteriorating stream of value from the company. Second, a climbing defection rate is a sure predictor of a diminishing flow of cash from customers to the company—even if the company replaces the lost customers—because new customers cost money to acquire and because older customers tend to produce greater cash flow and profits than newer ones. By searching for the root causes of customer departures, companies with the desire and capacity to learn can identify business practices that need fixing and, some-times, can win the customer back and reestablish the relationship on firmer ground.

But if so much useful information can be wrung from a customer loss, why don't businesses learn or even try to learn from customer defections? In ten years of studying customer loyalty, customer defec-tions, and their effects on corporate cash flow and profits, I have uncovered seven principal reasons:

> Many companies aren't really alarmed by customer defections—or they're alarmed too late—because they don't understand the intimate,

causal relationship between customer loyalty on the one hand and cash flow and profits on the other.

It is unpleasant to study failure too closely, and in some companies trying to analyze failure can even be hazardous to careers.

Customer defection is often hard to define.

Sometimes *customer* itself is a hard thing to define, at least the kind of customer it's worth taking pains to hold onto.

It is extremely hard to uncover the real root causes of a customer defection and extract the appropriate lessons.

Getting the right people in your organization to learn those lessons and then commit to acting on them is a challenge.

It is difficult to conceptualize and set up the mechanisms that turn the analysis of customer defections into an ongoing strategic system, closely supervised by top managers and quickly responsive to changing circumstances.

Loyalty and Profits

In general, the longer a customer stays with a company, the more that customer is worth. Long-term customers buy more, take less of a company's time, are less sensitive to price, and bring in new customers. Best of all, they have no acquisition or start-up cost. Good long-standing customers are worth so much that in some industries, reducing customer defections by as little as five points—from, say, 15% to 10% per year—can *double* profits.

CEOs buy the idea that customer loyalty matters; they would prefer to have loyal customers. But without doing the arithmetic that shows just how much a loyal customer is worth over the whole course of the customer life cycle, and without calculating the net present value of the company's present customer base, most CEOs gauge company performance on the basis of cash flow and profit. They rarely study the one statistic that reflects how much real value the company is creating, the one statistic with predictive power: customer retention.

What keeps customers loyal is the value they receive. One of the reasons so many businesses fail is that too much of their measurement, analysis, and learning revolves around profit and too little around value creation. Their CEOs become aware of problems only when profits start to fall, and in struggling to fix short-term profits, they concentrate on a symptom and miss the underlying breakdown in the value-creation system. They see customer issues as subsidiary to profits and delegate them to the marketing department. In the most egregious cases, years of continuing defection can mean that former customers—people convinced by personal experience that the company offers inferior value—will eventually outnumber the company's loyal advocates and dominate the collective voice of the marketplace. When that moment arrives, no amount of advertising, public relations, or ingenious marketing will prop up pricing, new-customer acquisitions, or the company's reputation.

Although some executives do realize that profits are really a downstream benefit of delivering superior value to customers—and that customer loyalty is therefore the best indicator of strategic success or failure—they lack the tools they need to focus their organizational learning on this most basic building block of profitable growth. They make the most of standard market research, including customer-satisfaction surveys, but such tools are simply not up to the task. (See "The Satisfaction Trap.") And yet the message that relative value is declining—and all the information a company needs to make sense of that bad news and design possible remedies—is available from the day trouble starts. Defecting customers have most of that information. They are always the first to know when a company's value proposition is foundering in the face of competition.

The Satisfaction Trap

Many companies that use satisfaction surveys to learn how happy their customers are with their products or services often mislead themselves. What matters is not what customers say about their level of satisfaction but whether the value they feel they've received will keep them loyal. As tools for measuring the value a company delivers to its customers, satisfaction surveys are imperfect. As tools for predicting whether customers will purchase more of the company's products and services, they are grossly imperfect.

Satisfaction surveys have two principal problems. The first is that satisfaction *scores* have become an end in themselves at many companies but scores mean nothing unless the satisfaction they purport to measure translates into purchases and profit. The second problem is that satisfaction surveys are often poorly conceived and conducted. They measure the wrong activity or the wrong customers; they are easy to manipulate;

they encourage companies and employees to invest time and money unproductively.

In many organizations, good satisfaction scores are considered a higher goal than profits and have a more immediate effect on compensation. The automobile industry pioneered the use of satisfaction surveys and probably spends more money on them than any other industry. When General Motors committed itself to reversing the inroads of foreign competition by concentrating on customers, it tied a portion of management bonuses to improvements in satisfaction scores. In the 1980s, satisfaction scores went up, as do most measures included in management bonus calculations, but market share and profits continued to go down. Nevertheless, most automakers continue to track satisfaction scores with great statistical rigor and use them in incentive and recognition programs for a wide range of employees. Today, as a result, more than 90% of industry customers report that they are satisfied or very satisfied. But repurchase rates remain mired in the 30% to 40% range. How can that be? There are several reasons, all having to do with the second problem, the way satisfaction surveys are designed and carried out.

Whenever rewards are based on satisfaction scores decoupled from repurchase loyalty and profits, the result is unproductive behavior. Employees naturally seek the easiest ways to improve scores, not necessarily the most profitable ways. One Toyota dealership offered a free auto detailing to any customer who agreed to return a survey marked "Very Satisfied" in all categories. The dealer even provided a printed copy of the survey showing how to check it off. At another dealership, a salesman pleaded with a customer to fill the form with favorable responses. "I'll lose my job here if I don't get high scores," he said. Auto companies like to advertise high marks on J.D. Power and Associates satisfaction surveys, so they've also learned how to manipulate the scores. Calling customers immediately after they've bought a car and asking about the experience is one way to keep scores high but probably won't lead to increased loyalty.

A second reason surveys don't work is that they almost never provide the information that managers need to pick the investments that will maximize customer value and, in turn, cash flow. Early successes with satisfaction programs are often a matter of picking low-hanging fruit. A car company's surveys might identify easily remedied sources of dissatisfaction—mechanics wearing dirty uniforms, customers not getting their cars on time. Once a company has made the obvious improvements, however, it's likely to find that the next level of satisfaction enhancement requires a real investment. Is it worth $10 million to retrain all the service managers? Is it worth $10 million to increase the average satisfaction score from

85% to 90%? Is it worth $100 million? These questions are basic to delivering the best value, but satisfaction surveys cannot answer them.

A third drawback is that surveys ignore critical distinctions among customer segments. Companies should pay less attention to what customers say and make a greater effort to track lifetime purchases. What makes this effort so important is that it forces a company to channel its consumer-satisfaction investments toward customers with the highest potential value, whereas satisfaction research conducted broadly across the entire customer base—the correct approach statistically—will necessarily show the influence of unprofitable customers. For example, a bank's branch manager might hear many complaints about long teller lines, but it's perfectly possible that the branch's most profitable customers do most of their business by phone, mail, and ATM. Investing in more tellers may inflate satisfaction scores but actually deflate profits by improving service levels and increasing costs in areas that the best customers don't care about.

The Baby Bells are another example of companies using satisfaction surveys as they grope for the right management tools in an increasingly competitive environment. Most have developed surveys to help focus their organizations on customer service. But few have built systems to analyze lifetime purchases and profits from different types of customers. Those that do this analysis find that the top 10% of their customers are worth 5 to 10 times as much in potential lifetime profits as the bottom 10%. Telephone companies that try to manage through increasingly refined customer-satisfaction systems are likely to suffer the automakers' fate. While they work at raising broad satisfaction scores, competitors will lure away their best customers by delivering outstanding value to precisely these most profitable segments. Diminished cash flows will then make it more difficult to deliver good value even to average customers.

Yet another weakness of satisfaction surveys is that an increasing number of customers are tired of being surveyed. A Cadillac dealer tells this story: "One of my customers cornered me at a charity board meeting and told me, 'I got a call after I picked up my car, asking if I was satisfied with the sales experience. Then I got a call after the car was serviced, asking if I was satisfied with the service experience. Finally, someone called to check if I was happy with the ownership experience. So when am I going to get a call asking if I'm satisfied with the satisfaction-survey experience?'" One leading auto company admits that customers can get as many as six surveys in a year. Imagine how much this costs the company, to say nothing of customers' wasted time.

Companies serious about measuring the value they deliver to customers do not rely solely on satisfaction surveys. They recognize that satisfaction is an inherently unstable and temporary mental state and therefore is tricky to measure. Instead they track repurchase loyalty to determine the true value of their products and services relative to competitors'. When customers don't return for service, or when they buy another brand—these are incontestable signs that they are unhappy with the value. In business after business, 60% to 80% of lost customers reported on a survey just prior to defecting that they were satisfied or very satisfied. Some companies respond by trying to increase the sophistication of their satisfaction measures. Most automakers have chosen this approach, but they still see 90% of their customers claiming to be satisfied and 40% coming back to buy again.

The exception is Lexus, a consistent winner of auto satisfaction awards, which refuses to consider surveys the best measure of satisfaction. In the words of Dave Illingworth, the first general manager of Lexus, "The only meaningful measure of satisfaction is repurchase loyalty." Illingworth knows that the gap between satisfaction scores and repurchase loyalty can be enormous. Drive by a Lexus dealership and you'll see a satellite dish on the roof. It keeps the dealer in constant touch with Lexus headquarters and maintains a steady flow of information in both directions about customers' auto and service purchases. Lexus knows which customers are coming back for more and which are not, and it can analyze the differences between dealers who are earning superior customer loyalty and those who are not.

In depending so heavily on broad-based satisfaction surveys, companies are letting too many defectors slip through the cracks. There is a better way. To know how much companies can afford to spend to satisfy specific customers, they need to measure the return on their investment. The only way to do that is to study lifetime purchase patterns. But since they have to track purchase patterns to determine customer profitability, why not simply use this information as their satisfaction index? Customers' repeat-purchase loyalty must become the basic yardstick of success. Companies can avoid the satisfaction trap if they remember that what matters is not how satisfied you keep your customers but how many satisfied and profitable customers you keep.

In Search of Failure

The lifeblood of adaptive change is employee learning, and the most useful and instructive learning grows from the recognition and analysis of failure. A first step in getting the people in your organization to focus on failure analysis—in this case, customer defections—requires overcoming their preoccupation with success. Of course, success has lessons to teach. But businesspeople today are obsessed with success—and sometimes more obsessed with other people's success than with their own. Benchmarking has become a feverish search for the nation's or the world's lowest costs, highest volumes, fastest growth. Academics, consultants, and executives scour the globe for approaches that have led to big profits in one situation so they can apply them in others. Yet this quest for best practice has created much less value than one might expect, and the people who study systems can tell us why: When a system is working well, its success rests on a long chain of subtle interactions, and it's not easy to determine which links in the chain are most important. Even if the critical links were identifiable, their relative importance would shift as the world around the system changed. So even if we could point to the critical links and more or less reproduce them, we still could not reproduce all the relationships or the external environment in which they operate.

What *can* help is the study of failure. The people who build, fly, and regulate airplanes understand this. Airline performance in the United States, as measured by the fatality rate, actually exceeds six sigma—3.4 defects per million opportunities—which is the demanding standard of quality many manufacturers pursue but probably don't reach. When a plane crashes, investigators retrieve the flight recorder and spend whatever it costs to find out what went wrong. The result is that in a vastly complex and extremely dangerous operating environment, accidents have become rare events.

One of the world's consummate investors, Warren Buffett, reached a similar conclusion in his very different field. In 1991, he gave a speech at the Emory Business School in Atlanta, Georgia. He told his audience, "I've often felt there might be more to be gained by studying business failures than business successes. In my business, we try to study where people go astray and why things don't work. We try to avoid mistakes. If my job was to pick a group of ten stocks in the Dow-Jones average that would outperform the average itself, I would probably not start by picking the ten best. Instead, I would try to pick the 10 or 15 worst performers and take them out of the sample and work with the residual. It's an inversion process. Albert Einstein said, 'Invert, always invert, in mathematics and physics,' and it's a very good idea in business, too. Start out with failure, and then engineer its removal."

In addition to their preoccupation with success, there is another reason companies make so little use of failure analysis. Psychologically and culturally, it's difficult and sometimes threatening to look at failure too closely. Ambitious managers want to link their careers to successes; failures are usually examined for the purpose of assigning blame rather than detecting and eradicating the systemic causes of poor performance.

Defining Defection

Some customer defections are easier to spot than others. Customers who close their accounts and shift all their business to another supplier are clearly defecting. But what about customers who shift *some* of their purchases to another supplier, and what about those who actually buy more but whose purchases represent a smaller share of their total expenditures (a smaller share of wallet)?

The story of MicroScan—then a division of Baxter Diagnostics and now of Dade International, recently acquired by Bain Capital—is illustrative. In mid-1990, MicroScan was neck-and-neck with Vitek Systems in a race for market leadership in automated microbiology. Both companies made the sophisticated instruments medical laboratories use to identify the microbes in patient cultures and determine which antibiotics will be most effective. Both companies were growing rapidly, converting customers from manual testing and edging out other manufacturers of automated equipment. MicroScan had worked hard to improve quality and was thinking about applying for the Malcolm Baldrige National Quality Award.

Perhaps because diagnostics was its business, perhaps because competition had heightened its quality awareness, MicroScan was intrigued with the notion of failure analysis. To make itself an even stronger, more profitable competitor, the company decided to seek out defectors and use them to uncover and correct shortcomings. It began by asking its sales force to identify customer defectors. The sales force assumed that the company's executives meant total—that is, complete—defections and responded that there were almost none. A few customers had gone out of business, but in automated microbiology as in many other industrial businesses, total defections are relatively rare. Once companies have purchased equipment, they continue to buy consumables and service for many years.

But the sales force was ignoring the fact that defections can be partial. A customer may buy *some* equipment, *some* consumables, *some* service from other suppliers, and these fractional defections have meaning. MicroScan was not getting 100% of subsequent sales on all its accounts, and given the hotly competitive environment in which the company found itself, management chose to use this more demanding standard to measure failure. As it happened, the sales force was ignoring another fact as well: Systematic analysis of billing records revealed that, in fact, there were quite a few total defections among *small* customers.

The company interviewed every one of the lost customers and a large number of the partial defectors, searching for the root causes of each defection, especially when customers had defected to alternative microbiological testing equipment. The picture that emerged was clear, instructive, and painful. The customers interviewed were concerned about the reliability of MicroScan's instruments. They had complaints about certain features of the equipment and felt the company was insufficiently responsive to their problems.

There is always a strong temptation to rationalize these kinds of complaints: Those weren't good customers to begin with; it's not our fault that the customer's technical staff is not sophisticated enough to use our instruments; customers that use our hot line all the time aren't profitable anyway. But rationalization is just a way of failing at failure analysis, and MicroScan's managers overcame their natural impulse to explain complaints away. Instead, they listened, learned, and took corrective action. They shifted R&D priorities to address the shortcomings customers had identified, such as test accuracy and time to result. Having learned that their line of instruments was too expensive for many small labs, they accelerated development of a low-end model and brought it to market in record time. They also redesigned their customer-service protocol to make sure that they gave immediate attention to equipment faults and delivery problems.

MicroScan's ability to learn from failure paid off. Two years later, the company pulled away from Vitek to achieve clear market leadership, and it now enjoys the bottom-line benefits that go with it. Tracking and responding to customer defections, however uncommon—and they are now less common than ever—have become central to the way MicroScan does business.

Core Customers

In the process of deciding how it wanted to define customer defections, MicroScan had to make two critical judgment calls. The first involved the size of the unit of failure. Managers tightened the definition of defection: It no longer meant the total loss of a customer but rather the loss of any portion of that customer's business. Then they defined just who the company's core customers really were, recognizing that small labs were indeed important customers. Giving core customers good reason to stay loyal was, in the long run, what made the decisive competitive difference between MicroScan and Vitek.

Unfortunately, identifying core customers is not always as easy as it looks, especially in industries where the competitive landscape is changing. But the effort is well worth it. In fact, defining core customers can be one of the most critical strategic processes a CEO ever sets in motion. Although it may uncover an unexpected well of uncertainty and inconsistency, it will lead to a deep, animated discussion of the company's basic mission and its ultimate goals.

The most practical way to get started is by answering three overlapping questions. First, which of your customers are the most profitable and loyal? Look for those who spend more money, pay their bills more promptly, require less service, and seem to prefer stable, long-term relationships. Second, which customers place the greatest value on what you offer? Some customers will have found that your products, services, and special strengths are simply the best fit for their needs. Third, which of your customers are worth more to you than to your competitors? Some customers warrant extra effort and investment. Conversely, no company can be all things to all people: Customers who are worth more to a competitor will eventually defect.

The answers to these three questions will produce a list of your most obvious core customers. Identifying that group will give your management team a head start on the much more difficult task of developing the larger definition of core customer that your company will use in screening its customer base to see which defections warrant analysis. The discussion should also involve close scrutiny of some measurements and statistics that you ought to make sure you have available, among them the life-cycle profit pattern and the net present value of each customer segment, your share of customer wallet, and average customer retention by segment, age, and source.

Mass marketers such as banks and insurance companies often believe they must serve and satisfy all customers equally, and they therefore give equal attention to finding the root causes of all defections. Many companies give equal weight to first-class and third-class defectors in allocating resources to counteract defections, and some overzealous customer-recovery units spend money to save unprofitable customers or customers with negative value. Companies with high fixed costs, such as automakers, airlines, and telephone companies, fall easily into this trap. Every customer brings in revenue that helps offset fixed costs, they reason, so every customer is a good cus- tomer. But the companies that have achieved extraordinary levels of customer loyalty have discovered they must concentrate their efforts on that subset of customers to whom they can deliver consistently superior value. State Farm Insurance, for example, which serves more than 20% of North American households, knows it must focus in- tently on its own kind of auto-insurance customer: the better-than- average driver who values agent service. Sir Colin Marshall, chairman of British Airways, put it this way in a recent interview (see part IV, chapter 3): "Even in a mass-market business, you don't want to attract and retain everyone. . . . The key is first to identify and attract those who will value your service and then to retain them as customers and win the largest possible share of their lifetime business."

This is a good place to point out that all the techniques of root-cause defection analysis are important not just for customer retention but also for new-customer acquisition. After all, your new customers are some other company's defectors. By interviewing them to find out why they left and came to you and by watching to see how much of their spending you earn and retain, you can learn a great deal about them and about how to improve your company's customer-acquisition strategy. What percentage of newly acquired customers fits your defi- nition of core customers? Are you effectively promoting your real strengths and attracting the kinds of customers your value proposition was designed to serve? How do your new customers compare with your competitors' new customers and how do they compare to your defectors? One of the secrets of sustainable growth is to find and keep the right customers—core customers. If your advertising, sales incen- tives, or marketing promotions draw unprofitable or marginal custom- ers, the sooner you know it—and fix it—the better.

Root-Cause Analysis

Getting to the root causes of human behavior takes a lot of time, effort, and experience. In a factory setting, where root-cause failure analysis has been perfected over decades, the process is known as the *five why's* because you usually have to ask why something happened at least five times to get to the root of a failure. For example:

Why did the product get returned as defective?

The connector came loose.

Why did the connector come loose?

The plug was out of tolerance.

Why was the plug manufactured out of tolerance?

The intermediate stamping machine failed.

Why did the stamping machine fail?

Routine maintenance wasn't done on schedule.

Why?

There is an attendance problem in the maintenance department.

After five why's, you begin to see what needs to be fixed, though it may actually take a few more questions to figure out the best solution. Since applying this type of rigorous analysis to every single defect a plant experiences would be absurdly expensive, smart companies first perform a statistical frequency analysis, so they can concentrate their efforts on the 20% of categories that account for 80% of defects (applying Vilfredo Pareto's 80/20 rule).

Understanding weaknesses in customer value is much more difficult than understanding why a part was stamped out of tolerance in a plant. Objective fact is a big part of the five why's. The plug did not meet the precisely defined specifications for all such plugs. But the specifications for customer value are individual and tend to be subjective, so the only way to assess them is to interview customers and ex-customers and learn what they want and their views of the value they have received. The level of value a customer perceives can be defined as the time-weighted sum (more recent experiences are weighted more heavily) of all interactions with the company. So a good place to begin the search for failure is by reviewing the history of those interactions. (See "Rooting Out the Causes of Defections: A Case Study.") Occasionally, a single event is so powerful it leads to defection all by itself ("your clerk swore at me"), but that is the exception. In most cases, a series of events leads slowly to a decision to seek better value elsewhere. To assess the root cause of a defection, the interviewer must typically identify three or four disappointing events and weigh them appropriately.

Rooting Out the Causes of Defections: A Case Study

Everybank, with roughly 2 million customers, was a typical superregional commercial bank. With a typical defection rate of about 20%, Everybank was losing some 400,000 customers each year; and, aware of the dire economic consequences of defection, it found ways of learning from its lost customers. (Everybank is also fictitious—a composite picture of several such banks and representative experiences.)

Everybank had administered a satisfaction—or in this case, dissatisfaction—survey to customers who closed their accounts, but the superficial information the survey yielded was not much help in pinpointing what was wrong with the business system. For example, more than half of the respondents listed price or interest rate as the primary cause of defection. But when the bank called some of them, it heard stories like this:

How long had you been a customer at Everybank?
   Twelve years.
What caused you to close your account and move it?
   Commonbank was right around the corner and they paid a higher CD rate.
Have Commonbank's rates long been higher?
   I don't know, I just noticed recently.
What made you notice?
   I was a little irritated at Everybank, and then I saw an ad in Thursday's paper.
Why were you irritated?
   Because I was turned down for a credit card.
Had you ever been turned down before?
   Yes, several times, but this time, the bank gave me this big come-on about being a preferred customer—and then turned me down with a form letter!

As it happened, the rates at Commonbank were almost identical to those at Everybank, except occasionally on Thursdays, because Commonbank changed rates on Thursdays and Everybank on Fridays. But of course price had little to do with the defection. The real root cause was the credit card division's failure to coordinate its marketing and qualification efforts. When interviewers pushed the questioning far enough, *most* defectors who named price on their surveys turned out not to be price defectors after all.

Everybank needed to find the real causes—or at least the 20% that produced 80% of defections—but even a good sample of the defectors is too many for in-depth, root-cause interviews that can take two hours each. The bank solved the problem with computers. Professional interviewers spoke to several hundred defectors, reviewed their interactions with the bank, created a series of questions that would permit any interviewer to uncover the real reason for a defection, then translated that series into a computer program that enabled relatively unskilled interviewers to get to the root causes of defections in an average of 20 minutes. For example:

Why did you close your personal account at our Pine Street branch last month?
  Your prices are way out of line.
Do you mean our interest rates on loans or the fees we charge for checking services?
  The fees on some of my automated teller transactions and your loan pricing. That's why I refinanced my mortgage with another bank.
Have you closed any other accounts with our bank over the past few years?
  Yes, I used to do all my banking with you because your branch was located next door to my dry-cleaning business, but you closed that branch three years ago.
Did you switch your business accounts to another bank when your branch closed?
  Not right away. But First National offered me a package product that combined everything into one statement and gave me a better value because they considered all my balances in determining my fees. But the real key was the convenient statement.
Would you have stayed with our bank if we could have offered a comparable package?
  Yes, I think so. I like long-term relationships. Anyway, I like the manager at the Pine Street branch. He goes to my church. He really wanted my business—it's over $100,000 in balances—but he told me he couldn't match First National's bundled account.
Thanks for your help. One last question. Does your current bank charge lower ATM fees?
  To be honest, I'm not sure.

The computer system helped the bank question a large sample of defectors, identify core customers—in this case, the 20% of customers who created 80% of profits—and dig deep enough to find solutions. Senior managers were impressed but then grew frustrated when defection rates did not come down fast or far enough. The problem was confusion about who needed to learn. Everybank's new methods produced reliable information, but branch managers had seen customer research before and doubted that these root-cause interviews could tell them much they didn't already know about customers they had worked with for years. When branch managers were asked to look at individual names and suggest root causes, they asserted confidently that most had left to get better rates or products, or because backroom processing had made errors in their accounts—all reasons conveniently beyond the control of a branch manager.

The interviews showed, to the contrary, that roughly half of all defections resulted from branch-level problems such as customer service and complaint resolution. Some skeptical branch managers insisted on listening to the interview tapes themselves. Others accepted the root causes identified by the study but refused to believe the defectors were profitable customers until they reviewed the records. Gradually, the evidence persuaded them to open their eyes.

Then other problems arose. Many critical changes affected several departments that needed to work together. But cooperation across units was not a company habit. Worse, the failure-analysis team was itself something of a problem. The junior executive in charge couldn't get the attention of other unit heads, who were his boss's peers. The bank found that failure analysis needed the leadership of an executive with the power to assemble cross-departmental task forces, as the following example shows.

Removing the Sources of Failure

Among the most profitable defecting customers, 25% named incidental fees as a critical root cause. Large balances in multiple accounts delivered so much value to the bank, they believed, that $35 for bouncing a check was unreasonable. Top management did the arithmetic, found that 0.2% fewer defections would more than offset lower fees, and reduced them. But a new failure-analysis team, led by a senior executive, discovered that the problem had several dimensions involving several units. One was that salespeople had steered clients into products inappropriate for high-balance customers. The right products—for example, a bundled checking/money-market/savings account—had no fees. A second was that the marketing department had failed to include balances from products like mortgages and credit cards in the pricing formula. A third was that budget constraints had led the data-processing department to postpone implementation of a computer program that would link all of a customer's accounts. The final resolution of the fee problem involved many constituencies—the entire branch sales force, training, marketing, data processing, and above all a failure-analysis team with the organizational clout to do effective root-cause detective work and implement solutions.

The bank also discovered that the efficiency of learning depended on incentives. Education's first rule is that the student must want to learn. To get branch managers to stay longer with the bank and do more business with their best customers, Everybank revised its reward system to include multiyear bonuses based on each manager's success in penetrating and retaining top customer groups. The bank also found it could evaluate defection-correction teams by measuring how often root causes recurred. When people realized their bosses really cared about defections, they decided their root-cause analyses needed to be more precise. For example, credit-collection problems were high on the list of root causes, but no one knew what was wrong or how to fix it. Was it that collections officers called instead of the branch manager, whom customers knew as a friend? Were the calls too brusque? Did collections always know that a customer had $200,000 in CDs in addition to a nonperforming loan? Or was it just that customers never talked to the same person twice and had to repeat their story again and again? Each explanation would require a different solution. The root-cause survey process needed to be more precise.

Everybank found it couldn't rely on interviews alone. Not even the most sophisticated survey technology will uncover every root cause, because some customers don't *know* why they defected. For example, branch managers knew that employee turnover affected customer turnover, but few defectors mentioned it. Statistical analysis showed that personnel turnover could explain almost half the differences in customer attrition from branch to branch. Customers couldn't put their fingers on it, but they clearly perceived that employees less familiar with their own jobs and with their customers delivered lower value.

Everybank also learned that it needed to look for customer categories with distinctive attrition levels. For example, customers whose initial purchase was a particular money-market account showed loyalty well above the average, so the bank redirected new-account promotions to feature that product. Customers who opened three or more different types of accounts simultaneously had the highest retention rate, so marketing created a new product that combined checking, savings, credit card, and an overdraft line—all with one account number. Conversely, the bank found that certain promotions—CD bonus rates, for example—brought in customers with lower retention rates, so it dropped them. And upon finding that certain mergers and acquisitions brought in customers with very high attrition rates, senior managers adjusted their acquisition strategy.

In case after case, Everybank identified failure and removed its source. The combination of root-cause analysis and systematic statistical study of customer segments improved the quality of the bank's customer base. In the first year, defections in the best customer group fell by a third. But among customers who failed to cover their own costs, defections actually increased—as managers had hoped they would.

Sometimes it is helpful to map out the whole life cycle of a customer's interactions with the company. You can think of this life cycle as a corridor. (See Exhibit I.) Imagine that customers enter at one end and that the arrows along the top of the passage represent doorways or interactions with the company. At a bank, the corridor might start with an account application. What determines customer value is the sum of relative benefits and drawbacks, advantages and disadvantages, that consumers encounter at each doorway. The model can also show the frequency of those interactions, and frequency combined with interview material can tell a company which interactions are the 20% driving 80% of the differences in loyalty and value.

In many businesses, including banking, insurance, and other service industries, the customer corridor has a second set of doorways made up of the major changes in a customer's private life, which, along with competitors' efforts to lure the customer away, are represented by arrows below the corridor. Career moves, relocations, lifestyle changes, and almost any family watershed—a marriage, birth, divorce, or death—are often occasions for delivering additional value to the customer. In fact, if a company does not gear its products and services to such events, family upheavals will almost certainly produce defections. Banks that have analyzed defection frequencies find that changes of this kind increase the probability of defection by 100% to 300%. For obvious reasons, relocation is a prime culprit; but root-cause interviewers looking only at the arrows along the top of the corridor would miss that cause.

Once you have mapped out the customer corridor for your business, it is time to begin interviewing defectors in earnest—probing customer behavior, uncovering the root causes of each defection, and testing various solutions to see which, if any, would have saved the relationship. One secret to this process is to have the right people take part. It can't be done with focus groups. Professional focus-group leaders from outside the company cannot have the deep knowledge of the

Exhibit I.

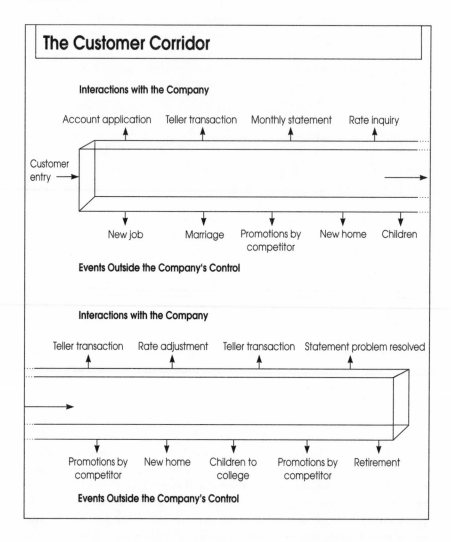

The Customer Corridor

Interactions with the Company

Account application   Teller transaction   Monthly statement   Rate inquiry

Customer
entry →

New job   Marriage   Promotions by   New home   Children
                               competitor

Events Outside the Company's Control

Interactions with the Company

Teller transaction   Rate adjustment   Teller transaction   Statement problem resolved

Promotions by   New home   Children to   Promotions by   Retirement
competitor   college   competitor

Events Outside the Company's Control

business they need to ferret out root causes, and asking groups why they made individual purchase decisions produces nothing but group-think. (If focus groups have a role, it may be to brainstorm solutions to specific root causes once they have been determined to have a high priority for core customers.) You can't contract the interviewing to a group of market research specialists, either, because they simply cannot know enough about your organization and its competitive situation, market and pricing strategies, cost position, and capabilities. Failure analysis demands a thorough understanding of the business system and its economics and a clear sense of what scale and unit of failure to scrutinize. In other words, failure analysis requires the guidance of senior managers. And if there is any uncertainty about precisely who the company's core customers are, or if the company needs to think about altering its value proposition or modifying its distribution channels, or if the defection data is incomplete, or if competitive conditions are undergoing rapid change, or if the organization is setting about failure analysis for the very first time—and there are probably very few businesses that meet none of those conditions—then senior managers must actually perform the failure analysis themselves.

The first step is to gather the senior management group (five or ten top executives) plus a sampling of respected frontline personnel—branch managers, say, or leading salespeople. Be sure to include people whose behavior will probably need to change. You must convince them that this diagnostic process has a top priority, and you must make it clear that they will not escape without making personal phone calls to defectors. Some will be very reluctant. Most people don't relish the idea of phoning strangers, let alone strangers who've been unhappy with the value they've received, and you will have to overcome that reluctance with leadership, peer pressure, and, if necessary, coercion. There is simply no substitute for having senior executives learn directly from defectors why the company's value proposition is inadequate.

Before making the calls, the group must determine which defectors are worth calling. You need to look at market research and satisfaction surveys, consider the opinions of frontline personnel about why particular customers behaved as they did, and identify differences between your company and your competitors with regard to business processes, structure, financial incentives, quality measurement, and value proposition. If your current information system is not up to the task of identifying key defectors, it is possible to assign telephone reps to call a large sample of apparent defectors and separate the wheat from the chaff by getting answers to half a dozen questions. You need to know something about their demographics—age, income, education, and so forth. You want to know how long they've been doing business with your company and to find out enough about their actual purchase history to determine whether or not they are core customers. And you need to make sure they have actually defected to a competitor, not simply stopped buying the product altogether. (The auto-insurance customer who sells the family car and switches to public transportation is not a defector but simply a former customer.) Phone reps are often a good investment because they not only collect basic data about each customer's demographics and true purchase history, they also can set up appointments for company executives to call back for a full root-cause interview. Most ex-customers will be so delighted at the prospect of a senior executive listening to their problems and complaints that they will leap at the opportunity. Sometimes, of course, you will need to offer them an incentive. Go ahead and spend what it takes to talk with a true representative sample of your target defectors.

When you've done all this, assign each executive (yourself included) 10 to 25 defectors. When you've interviewed a quarter to a third of your defectors, you should reconvene to discuss what everyone is hearing, resolve any problems with the process, share best practices, and most important, use these early interviews to develop a preliminary list of corrective actions the company might take. Additional interviews can then focus on the most important questions and test hypotheses.

The final step is the joint development of an action plan based, of course, on the results of the defector interviews. The group will probably come up with some remedies that require little spending or preparation and can therefore be tested at once. Others may require further research or analysis because of the size of the necessary investment. The frontline managers included in the executive group will help to ensure that your interpretations of customer behavior are reasonable and that your proposed improvements can be carried out.

One word of warning: The realization that every company has some customers it's better off losing poses a special hazard to companies engaged in defection analysis. The danger is that on the basis of inadequate information, the company will mistakenly identify potentially valuable customers as dispensable, ignore the lessons they have to teach, and make no effort to retain them. Such mistakes are easy to make because some first-class defectors are disguised as third-class. They were once outstanding customers and could be again, but by the time they're ready to leave, they've already moved a substantial share of their wallet to a competitor. As partial defectors, they look like unprofitable customers. But accepting the disguise at face value means accepting undesirable defections; it can tempt the company to underinvest in the kinds of improvements that make customers want to stay. These situations call for something resembling defection archeology—uncovering and analyzing several layers of historical and current data.

For example, one leading credit card company has built a computer system that lets its telephone reps instantly evaluate any customer who calls to cancel an account. The system is based on the potential profit from the customer's entire wallet, not merely on the company's present share, so a shift of spending to a competitor won't fool it. The phone rep can offer appropriate incentives to the best customers, and the company can watch to see whether the offers provide enough value to keep customers on board. Because of the inevitable tendency to dismiss all defectors as undesirable, knowing the true, sometimes hidden value of a defector turns out to be critically important in activating root-cause tracking systems.

In the case of a credit card company, information about a customer's entire wallet can be derived from credit-bureau reports. In banking, you can look at customers' mortgage applications to see where they keep their assets. In a few other industries, vendors make a business of collecting such data (the Nielsen ratings for television are one example). In most industries, however, the only way to determine share of wallet is to conduct a survey of your own and your competitors' customers. In other words, you have to ask.

Getting the Right People to Learn the Right Lessons

Unfortunately, useful learning is not closely related to the quantity of information available. If it were, we'd all be swimming in skills and expertise. Useful learning is instead a matter of getting the right information to the right people and giving them good reason to want to use it.

Market research with its customer questionnaires, satisfaction surveys, and focus groups was developed to give marketing departments the information they needed to set prices and design packaging, advertising, and promotions. It was not invented to help frontline employees provide better service or to give them better incentives or to solve the problems that cross departmental boundaries. Market research has the added drawback that those who learn most about customers are often the researchers, who usually are outside experts. They produce reports for managers (usually in marketing) who then interpret the findings for senior management. By the time information works its way back down the organization to frontline managers and employees in sales or service, it is too general to be at all useful.

The research we call root-cause analysis eliminates many of these weaknesses. When frontline managers and employees know the causes of customer dissatisfaction but cannot convince senior managers, the interviews that executives themselves conduct are nearly always persuasive. When frontline managers are mistaken about what is actually driving customers away, the immediacy, depth, and credibility of root-cause interviewing—they can often listen to taped interviews for themselves—overwhelms skepticism.

But although root-cause analysis enables people to learn, you still need some systematic way of getting them to want to learn. Therefore, the indispensable first step in unleashing the power of defection analysis is to make appropriate changes in measures, incentives, and career paths. In many organizations, the current incentives do little or nothing to make anyone care about fixing defections. Branch managers in a typical bank are paid bonuses on a variety of measures ranging from budgets to satisfaction surveys. Learning why customers defect takes time and energy, so unless it's clear to branch managers that their annual bonuses are tied to reducing attrition, supplying them with world-class failure-analysis technology won't improve their decision making.

Likewise, the marketing manager whose bonus is based on the volume of new deposit dollars generated through CD promotions doesn't really care if new depositors defect next year. And the credit-collections manager whose bonus is based on the balances collected from delinquent credit cards doesn't long to learn why customers defected from other bank products, such as savings and checking accounts. Often the most important barrier to learning from defections is that employees can't see how the learning relates to their own success.

Even in companies that care enough about retention to engineer effective incentives, it's sometimes necessary to remind employees how important it is to continue improving retention rates. Even though State Farm's agent-compensation structure was more heavily geared to retention than most competitors', managers at headquarters discovered that some of the company's agents had grown complacent. To shake them up a bit, the company calculated what would happen to an agent's income if he or she could achieve a one-percentage-point improvement in customer retention. The answer—a 20% increase in average annual earnings!—was just the tonic the company needed for its agents.

Lexus is another company that has cared passionately from the beginning about earning customer loyalty. The new carmaker chose dealers who had demonstrated a commitment to customer service and satisfaction. But like State Farm, Lexus has found it useful to let dealers know exactly how much their improved retention of customers is worth to them in dollars. The company has constructed a model that can be used to calculate how much more each dealership could earn by achieving higher levels of repurchase and service loyalty. These cash-flow calculations are important reminders, even for those who already believe in the importance of customer retention, because for some reason, raising annual retention rates just a few points doesn't impress people. Perhaps we should multiply all our numbers by 100 or 1000. Every baseball fan knows there's a world of difference between a .280 hitter and a .320 hitter, but the actual difference is only four percentage points. Business needs a similar way to dramatize the enormous potential of a four-percentage-point improvement in customer retention.

Making Failure Analysis Permanent

Once you have mastered the interviewing and analysis techniques, customer defections become such a rich source of information that you will want to make the system permanent. This is both harder and easier than it might seem. To begin with, you need to build a measurement system to monitor whether and how effectively the solutions you've arrived at are reducing defection rates. Share of wallet is one such measure, and to make it really useful you need to break it down further into the percentage of customers giving your business an increasing share of wallet and the percentage giving you a decreasing share. Another essential measure is the defection rate itself, calculated separately for separate groups of customers—your best core customers, the rest of your core customers, the rest of your customers, and, perhaps, the customers you wouldn't mind losing. You also need to monitor the frequency of various root causes to make certain that problems are actually being solved and that new problems don't arise undetected.

And you need to create an ongoing mechanism that keeps senior managers permanently plugged into frontline customer feedback. Lexus asks every member of its headquarters staff to interview four customers a month. MBNA, the credit card giant, asks every executive to listen in on telephone conversations in the customer-service area or the customer-recovery units. Some of those executives make the phone calls themselves. Every company benefits when executives can combine decision-making economics with lessons learned directly from customers and defectors. The alternative is to depend on research conducted by outsiders who will never really understand your business, your competition, or your customers, and who will never really care.

Deere & Company, which makes John Deere tractors and has a superb record of customer loyalty—nearly 98% annual customer retention in some product areas—uses retired employees to interview defectors and customers. USAA—the insurance and financial-services company based in San Antonio, Texas, that has come closer than any other U.S. company to eliminating customer defections altogether (it loses target customers at a rate of 1.5% per year, and most of that number are people who die)—treats customer defections very, very seriously and has pushed its analysis of them to a kind of pinnacle. The company recognizes that any event on the internal or external customer corridor that produces a spike in defection frequency highlights a dimension of customer value that needs improvement. USAA also tracks wallet share and retention rates separately by life-stage segment—for example, it knows when customers defect partially or entirely because their children have reached driving age and need auto insurance—so the company can spot problems and opportunities early and develop responses. In addition, focus groups of employees frequently review their customer interactions and draw up recommendations. Finally, to supplement its defector surveys, USAA has built an on-line system called Echo that enables telephone sales and service reps to input customer suggestions or complaints as they occur. Managers analyze all this data regularly to look for patterns, and they review problems and potential solutions at a monthly meeting with the CEO. The CEO then makes a formal quarterly report on customer retention to the board of directors. This careful, thorough, methodical approach to customer loyalty makes a striking contrast to the practice at most companies, where customer defection is either ignored, undervalued, or misunderstood.

The key to customer loyalty is the creation of value. The key to value creation is organizational learning. And the key to organizational learning is grasping the value of failure. As Vilfredo Pareto said more than 70 years ago, "Give me a fruitful error any time, full of seeds, bursting with its own corrections." Customer defection is a unit of error containing nearly all the information a company needs to compete, profit, and grow.

Executive Summaries

Loyalty-Based Management

Frederick F. Reichheld

Despite a flurry of activities aimed at serving customers better, few companies have systematically revamped their operations with customer loyalty in mind. Instead, most have adopted improvement programs ad hoc, and paybacks haven't materialized.

Building a highly loyal customer base must be integral to a company's basic business strategy. Loyalty leaders like MBNA credit cards are successful because they have designed their entire business systems around customer loyalty—a self-reinforcing system in which the company delivers superior value consistently and reinvents cash flows to find and keep high-quality customers and employees.

The economic benefits of high customer loyalty are measurable. When a company consistently delivers superior value and wins customer loyalty, market share and revenues go up, and the cost of acquiring new customers goes down. The better economics mean that the company can then pay workers better, which sets off a whole chain of events. Increased pay boosts employee morale and commitment; as employees stay longer, their productivity goes up and training costs fall; employees' overall job satisfaction, combined with their experience, helps them serve customers better; and customers are then more inclined to stay loyal to the company. Finally, as the best customers and employees become part of the loyalty-based system, competitors are left to survive with less desirable customers and less talented employees.

To compete on loyalty, a company must understand the relationships between customer retention and the other parts of the business—and be able to quantify the linkages between loyalty and profits. It involves rethinking and aligning four important aspects of the business: customers, product/service offering, employees, and measurement systems.

257

Competing for the Future

Gary Hamel and C.K. Prahalad

Is your company a rule maker or a rule follower? Does your company focus on catching up or on getting out in front? Do you spend the bulk of your time as a maintenance engineer preserving the status quo or as an architect designing the future? Difficult questions like these go unanswered not because senior managers are lazy—most are working harder than ever—but because they won't admit that they are less than fully in control of their companies' future. In this adaptation from their book, Hamel and Prahalad urge senior managers to look toward the future and ponder their ability to shape their companies in the years and decades to come.

If the future is not occupying senior managers, what is? Restructuring and reengineering. While both are legitimate tasks, they have more to do with shoring up today's businesses than with building tomorrow's industries. Restructuring tries to correct the mistakes of the past; reengineering mostly involves catching up to competitors.

Creating the future, as Electronic Data Systems has done, for example, requires industry foresight. Since change is inevitable, managers must decide whether it will happen in a crisis atmosphere or in a calm and considered manner, with foresight about the future of the industry; whether the agenda for change will be set by company's unique point of view about the future or by its more prescient competitors. Too often, profound thinking about the future occurs only when present success has been eroded. To get ahead of the industry change curve, senior managers must recognize that the real focus for their companies is the chance to compete for the future.

Trust and the Virtual Organization

Charles Handy

The technological possibilities of the virtual organization are seductive. But its managerial and personal implications require rethinking old notions of control. As it becomes possible for more work to be done outside the traditional office, trust will become more important to organizations. Managers need to move beyond fear of losing efficiency, which makes some cling to expensive and deadening "audit mania."

Handy proposes seven rules of trust. Trust is not blind: It needs fairly small groupings in which people can know each other well. Trust needs boundaries: Define a goal, then leave the worker to get on with it. Trust demands learning and openness to change. Trust is tough: When it turns out to be misplaced, people have to go. Trust needs bonding : The goals of small units must gel with the larger group's. Trust needs touch: Workers must sometimes meet in person. Trust requires leaders.

Virtual organizations call for new forms of belonging. A desk of one's own has been a security blanket for generations; a sense of place is important to people. What happens when that disappears? If workers get membership rights in an organization, a sense of belonging to a *community* can substitute for the sense of belonging to a *place*.

Virtuality's Three I's (information, ideas, intelligence) can improve quality of life. The question Handy asks is, Will they be for everyone? He believes the potential exists for the Three I's to benefit not just organizations but also those with whom they do business and society as a whole.

If businesses let virtuality turn them into mere brokers or boxes of contracts, then they will have failed society. Their search for wealth in the end will have destroyed wealth.

Service Comes First: An Interview with USAA's Robert F. McDermott

Thomas Teal

In an industry notorious for its indifference to service, insurance executive Robert McDermott has spent the past 22 years building customer responsiveness into the very fiber of the company he heads—USAA of San Antonio, Texas. His successful service recipe has three principal ingredients: a niche market that the company strives to understand and serve more and more effectively, progressive employment practices, and an aggressively innovative use of technology.

The niche consists of active and former military officers, a market that dates back to the company's founding in 1922 by 25 army officers who couldn't get property and casualty insurance commercially. USAA has since expanded its membership base to include the children and grandchildren of military officers. More important, it has expanded its range of products to include cradle-to-grave financial services—banking, life insurance, mutual funds, and more.

Employment practices include a four-day workweek; continuous education and promotion; physical amenities such as health clubs, tennis courts, and jogging trails; and a spirit of service injected into every nook and cranny of the organization on the theory that doing better work and helping others makes life more satisfying.

Technology, finally, seeks to achieve the paperless workplace in an industry too often choked by paper. Since the company does not sell through outside agents, it works by phones and mail (90,000 calls and 150,000 pieces of mail daily). The company has spent well over $100 million on computer systems such as document imaging and has more computer terminals than employees. Every service representative has weeks of training and instant access to every customer's policy file.

The Power of Predictabililty

Howard H. Stevenson and Mihnea C. Moldoveanu

When the primary human activity was hunting, people quickly learned that their lives became more predictable when they pooled their experiences and efforts. Thus were formed the first organizations. With the industrial revolution, not only did the people within organizations depend on one another, but organizations also depended on other organizations to perform in predictable ways. In the mid-twentieth century, global organizations began to promise employees economic security, personal fulfillment, and respect in return for performing clearly delineated activities. Employees were willing to make sacrifices, and employers were willing to invest in training in the mutual expectation of future reward.

But now, intense competition and rapid change are destroying predictability. Virtual organizations and many current managerial practices, such as reengineering, continuous improvement, matrix management, and "rightsizing," ignore this human need. Such tools are in fact destroying what holds organizations together. As a result, employees keep their résumés up to date and their commitments to a minimum.

The best way to approach organizational change is with the realization that dire predictions are better than no predictions at all or positive predictions that no one believes. Managers must make few promises and keep those they do make. The more managers make clear to employees which courses of action will improve their lives, the more employees can focus on creating value.

Capital Disadvantage: America's Failing Capital Investment System

Michael E. Porter

The U.S. system of allocating investment capital is failing, putting American companies at a serious disadvantage and threatening the long-term growth of the nation's economy. The problem, says Michael Porter, goes beyond the usual formulation of the issue: accusations of "short-termism" by U.S. managers, ineffective corporate governance by directors, or the high cost of capital. The problem involves the external capital allocation system by which capital is provided to companies, as well as the system by which companies allocate capital internally. America's system is marked by fluid capital and a financial focus. Other countries—notably Japan and Germany—have systems with dedicated capital and a focus on corporate position. In global competition, where investment increasingly determines a company's capacity to upgrade and innovate, the U.S. system does not measure up.

These conclusions come out of a two-year research project sponsored by the Harvard Business School and the Council on Competitiveness. Porter recommends five far-reaching reforms to make the U.S. system superior to Japan's and Germany's:

1. Improve the present macroeconomic environment.
2. Expand true ownership throughout the system so that directors, managers, employees, and even customers and suppliers hold positions as owners.
3. Align the goals of capital providers, corporations, directors, managers, employees, customers, suppliers, and society.
4. Improve the information used in decision making.
5. Foster more productive modes of interaction and influence among capital providers, corporations, and business units.

Reckoning with the Pension Fund Revolution

Peter F. Drucker

Fifteen years ago, Peter Drucker chronicled the "unseen revolution" transforming corporate ownership—the rise of pension funds as major shareholders of large companies. Today the revolution is clearly visible. The

20 largest pension funds hold 10% of the equity capital of the largest U.S. companies. In total, pension funds have assets worth 2.5 trillion.

In this article, Drucker offers new perspectives on one of the most startling power shifts in economic history. Pension funds, he argues, must address two critical issues: For what should corporate management be held accountable, and how should accountability be structured? The outlines of the answers can be found in Germany and Japan—two countries where ownership is even more concentrated than in the United States.

How do institutional owners of German and Japanese industry define performance and results? They maximize the wealth-producing capacity of the enterprise. This may sound vague. In fact, all the elements that go into the concept can be quantified with considerable rigor—and are so quantified by the Japanese and the Germans.

Drucker also foresees the rise of formal "business audits" as a new mechanism for accountability. Independent agencies, perhaps the auditing arms of the big accounting companies, will evaluate the mission and performance of business enterprises in rigorous detail. In ten years, pension funds may not invest in the shares of companies that refuse to submit to such audits.

Zero Defections: Quality Comes to Services

Frederick F. Reichheld and W. Earl Sasser, Jr.

Companies that want to improve their service quality should take a cue from manufacturing and focus on their own kind of scrap heap: customers who won't come back. Because that scrap heap can be every bit as costly as broken parts and misfit components, service company managers should strive to reduce it. They should aim for "zero defections"—keeping every customer they can profitably serve.

As companies reduce customer defection rates, amazing things happen to their financials. Although the magnitude of the change varies by company and industry, the pattern holds: profits rise sharply. Reducing the defection rate just 5% generates 85% more profits on one bank's branch system, 50% more in an insurance brokerage, and 30% more in an auto-service chain. And when MBNA America, a Delaware-based credit card company, cut its 10% defection rate in half, profits rose a whopping 125%.

But defection rates are not just a measure of service quality; they are also a guide for achieving it. By listening to the reasons why customers defect, managers learn exactly where the company is falling short and where to direct their resources. Staples, the stationary supplies retailer, uses feedback from customers to pinpoint products that are priced too high. That way, the company avoids expensive broad-brush promotions that pitch everything to everyone.

Like any important change, managing for zero defections requires training and reinforcement. Great-West Life Assurance Company pays a 50% premium to group health-insurance brokers that hit customer-retention targets, and MBNA America gives bonuses to departments that hit theirs.

Why Satisfied Customers Defect

Thomas O. Jones and W. Earl Sasser, Jr.

Most managers rejoice if the majority of customers that respond to customer-satisfaction surveys say they are satisfied. But some of those managers may have a big problem. When most customers are saying they are satisfied but not completely satisfied, they are saying that they are unhappy with some aspect of the product or service. If they have the opportunity, they will defect.

Many managers assume that there is a simple linear relationship between satisfaction and loyalty. But in exploring that relationship in a broad range of industries, Thomas O. Jones and W. Earl Sasser, Jr., made a startling discovery: In markets where customers have choices, the difference between the loyalty of completely satisfied and merely satisfied customers was tremendous. The rules of competition can change quickly, so managers who do not strive to satisfy their customers totally are taking a risk. Providing customers with outstanding value may be the only reliable way to achieve sustained customer satisfaction.

Companies that excel in satisfying customers excel both in listening to customers and in interpreting what customers with different levels of satisfaction are telling them. They realize that the actions required to turn neutral customers into satisfied customers are different from those required to turn satisfied customers into completely satisfied customers. They understand the importance of having systems for making amends to customers when something goes wrong. If companies are good at recovery, would-be defectors can be transformed. They can become apostles—customers who are so completely satisfied that they feel inspired to spread the word.

Competing on Customer Service: An Interview with British Airways' Sir Colin Marshall

Steven E. Prokesch

Just because the competition is tough, that's no reason to be tough on customers, says Sir Colin Marshall, chairman of British Airways. Even in a cutthroat, mass-market business such as air travel, he argues, many people will pay a premium for good service—even those who travel economy. Marshall's views may be unconventional, but so is his company's performance: While the world airline industry has racked up billions of dollars in losses, British Airways has remained solidly profitable.

Under his leadership, British Airways has striven to go beyond providing the basics (flying people from point A to point B on time, safely, and at the lowest cost). It has striven to provide customers with a high-quality, highly personal *experience.* Creating a service with "a global scope but a homey feel" as Marshall puts it, is no easy feat in a business where dozens of human interactions shape each customer's experience. But besides being hard for competitors to copy, this capability will help British Airways minimize customer churn and maximize its share of each customer's business, Marshall insists.

Championing the Customer

Charles R. Weiser

In "Championing the Customer," British Airways manager Charles R. Weiser describes the lead role that the airline's customer relations department plays in reducing customer defections. It encourages customers to report their problems, strives to make quick amends when service failures occur, and helps spot and eliminate operational weaknesses that cause service failures. The approach has attracted new customers, reduced the cost of retaining customers, and helped increase the airline's share of customers' business.

Do Rewards Really Create Loyalty?

Louise O'Brien and Charles Jones

Although reviled in the business press as short-term fads, rewards programs are gaining popularity. Rewards can and do build customers' loyalty. Unfortunately, they are widely misunderstood and often misapplied. A rewards program needs to share value in proportion to the value the customers' loyalty creates for the company.

A company must first make sure that its rewards align with company capabilities, then take into account the five elements that determine value to a customer: cash value, choice, aspirational value, relevance, and convenience. Any company can attain access to the full set of capabilities. Some businesses choose to band together with others in a rewards network.

Louise O'Brien and Charles Jones, developers of the customer loyalty practice at Bain & Company, explore principles that companies should keep in mind when trying to develop effective value-sharing programs: All customers are not equal; value created must exceed value delivered; customer behavior must drive value sharing; long-term perspective is critical; offers must target attractive customers. The authors detail the ways American Express, General Motors, State Farm, Neiman Marcus, Saks Fifth Avenue, MCI, Air Miles, and others are building customer loyalty.

The full potential of value sharing through rewards is realized only when customers change their habits to become *sustainably* loyal. And designing effective rewards programs often requires overcoming barriers raised by functional departments. Senior managers must agree that loyalty pays and be unrelenting about focusing their organizations and all their marketing programs on the goals and measures that will develop customer loyalty.

Do You Want to Keep Your Customers Forever?

B. Joseph Pine II, Don Peppers, and Martha Rogers

Customers, whether consumers or businesses, do not want more choices. They want exactly what they want—when, where, and how they want it—and technology now makes it possible for companies to give it to them. But few companies are exploiting that potential. Most managers continue to view the world through the twin lenses of mass marketing and mass production. To handle increasingly turbulent and fragmented markets, they try to churn out a greater variety of goods and services and to tailor their messages to ever finer market segments. But they end up bombarding their customers with too many choices.

A company that aspires to give customers exactly what they want must use technology to become two things: a mass customizer that efficiently provides individually customized goods and services, and a one-to-one marketer that elicits information from each customer. The process of acquiring those skills will bind producer and consumer together in what the authors call a learning relationship—an ongoing collaboration to meet the customer's needs over time that will continually strengthen their bond.

In learning relationships, individual customers teach the company about their preferences and needs. The more they teach the company, the better it gets at providing exactly what they want and the harder it becomes for a competitor to entice them away. A company that can cultivate learning relationships with its customers should be able to retain their business forever, provided that it continues to supply high-quality customized products or services at competitive prices and does not miss the next technology wave.

Learning from Customer Defections

Frederick F. Reichheld

U.S. corporations lose half their customers every five years. But most managers fail to address that fact head-on by striving to learn why those defectors left. They are making a mistake, because a climbing defection rate is a sign that a business is in trouble. By analyzing the causes of defection, managers can learn how to stem the decline and build a successful enterprise.

Companies often aren't alarmed by defections until it is too late. Why? For one thing, studying failures is painful. For another, they find it extremely hard to unearth the root causes of defections or to get the right people in the organization to do what is necessary to eliminate the causes.

But there are mechanisms for learning from defections and turning failure analysis into an ongoing strategic system. The author explains how to define core customers, how to ascertain what share of wallet the company receives from them, and how to get to the real reasons for defections by asking the *five why* questions. A group of managers heading the failure-analysis program should include the CEO and others whose behavior will probably have to change to eliminate the causes of core-customer defections. Everyone must understand that the diagnostic process is a top priority, and each member of the group should talk to 10 to 25 defectors. Eventually, failure analysis should be made permanent, with employees' financial incentives tied to retention of core customers.

The longer customers stay with a company, the more they are worth. The key to customer loyalty is value creation. The key to value creation is organizational learning. And the key to organizational learning, says Reichheld, is grasping the value of failure.

About the Contributors

Scott D. Cook is the cofounder and chairman of Intuit, responsible for driving Intuit's strategy of revolutionizing financial automation. Prior to founding the company, Cook managed consulting assignments in banking and technology for Bain & Company, Inc. Before that, he was a brand manager with consumer products giant Procter & Gamble.

Peter F. Drucker is a writer, a teacher, and a consultant specializing in strategy and policy for both businesses and non-profits and in the work and organization of top management. Dr. Drucker is the Clarke Professor of Social Science and Management at the Claremont Graduate School, an editorial columnist for the *Wall Street Journal*, and the honorary chairman of the Peter F. Drucker Foundation for Non-Profit Management. He has published 28 books that deal with society, economics, politics, and management, and two novels, *The Last of All Possible Worlds* and *The Temptation to Do Good*.

Gary Hamel is a professor of strategic and international management at London Business School and chairman of Strategos, a strategy consulting company. As a consultant, Professor Hamel has worked in companies around the globe, including Ford, Motorola, EDS, Nokia, and Dow Chemical. He serves on the board of governors of the Strategic Management Society. He and C.K. Prahalad have coauthored seven *Harvard Business Review* articles, including "The Core Competence of the Corporation," one of the most reprinted articles in the *Review*'s history. Their book, *Competing for the Future* (HBS Press 1994), has sold over 200,000 copies.

Charles Handy describes himself today as a philosopher. He has been an oil executive, an economist, and a professor at the London Business School. His books on organizations and the future have now sold over one million copies worldwide.

Charles Jones is a vice president of Bain & Company, Inc. and leads its financial services practice. As a founding member of Bain's loyalty practice, he serves as an advisor to clients and internal teams in creating and implementing loyalty-based strategies. Prior to joining Bain, Mr. Jones was a CPA with Price Waterhouse.

Thomas O. Jones is the president and CEO of Elm Square Technologies, a company specializing in the strategic integration of large scale customer information systems. He was also a cofounder of Epsilon, a company that provides data based marketing services to many Fortune 500 companies and specializes in the use of customer information systems to build and maintain customer loyalty. Dr. Jones has served as a senior lecturer in service management at the Harvard Business School, and is a frequent speaker at executive seminars and conferences worldwide.

Mihnea C. Moldoveanu is a research associate at the Harvard Business School.

Louise O'Brien is a vice president in Bain & Company, Inc.'s Chicago office and leader of the customer loyalty practice. Ms. O'Brien has managed numerous projects assisting clients in developing customer loyalty strategies and implementation programs. She has also done extensive international work in both marketing and operations, as well as customer segmentation and loyalty.

Don Peppers is the founder and president of *marketing 1:1, inc.,* a management consulting firm specializing in relationship management and marketing technology issues. He has delivered speeches, conducted seminars, and led brainstorming sessions in one-to-one marketing with clients around the world. Mr. Peppers is the coauthor, along with Martha Rogers, of *The One to One Future: Building Relationships One Customer at a Time,* and the author of *Life's a Pitch—Then You Buy.*

B. Joseph Pine II is a Ridgefield, Connecticut-based speaker, consultant, and author. He is the founder of Strategic Horizons LLP, a management consulting company dedicated to helping companies create and embrace new competitive strategies and overcome the inevitable obstacles of business transformation. He is the author of *Mass Customization: The New Frontier in Business Competition* and several articles for the *Harvard Business Review, Wall Street Journal, Planning Review,* and others.

Michael E. Porter is the C. Roland Christensen Professor of Business Administration at the Harvard Business School. Dr. Porter is the author of 14 books and over 50 articles. His book, *Competitive Strategy: Techniques for Analyzing Industries and Competitors,* is widely recognized as the leading work in its field. He has served as a counselor on competitive strategy to many leading U.S. and international companies and to community organizations. Dr. Porter also serves as a counselor to government, playing an active role in economic policy with Congress, business groups, and as an advisor to foreign governments.

C.K. Prahalad is the Harvey C. Fruehauf Professor of Business Administration and professor of corporate strategy and international business at the Graduate School of Business Administration, University of Michigan. He is coauthor, along with Yves Doz, of *The Multinational Mission: Balancing Local Demands and Global Vision.* He and Gary Hamel have coauthored seven *Harvard Business Review* articles, including "The Core Competence of the Corporation," one of the most reprinted articles in the *Review*'s history.

Steven E. Prokesch is a senior editor at the *Harvard Business Review* in the areas of operations management, product development, manufacturing, and R&D. Prior to joining the *Review,* he worked for the *New York Times* and *Business Week.* Mr. Prokesch is the recipient of the John Hancock Award for Excellence in Business Journalism and two *New York Times* Publisher's awards.

Frederick F. Reichheld is a director of Bain & Company, Inc. He is the leader of the firm's worldwide loyalty practice, and his pioneering work in the area of customer, employee, and investor retention has quantified the linkage between loyalty and profits. His recent publications include *The Loyalty Effect: The Hidden Force Behind Growth, Profits, and Lasting Value* (HBS Press 1996) and articles in the *Harvard Business Review* and the *Wall Street Journal.* He is a frequent speaker to major business forums and groups of senior executives.

Martha Rogers is a founding partner of *marketing 1:1, inc.,* and co-author, with Don Peppers, of *The One-to-One Future: Building Relationships One Customer at a Time.* A former copywriter and advertising executive, Dr. Rogers is also the Professor of Telecommunications at Bowling Green State University. She has authored or coauthored articles in a diverse set of publications, including *Journal of Applied Psychology, Journal of Advertising, Harvard Business Review, Wired,* and *Marketing Tools.*

W. Earl Sasser, Jr. is a professor and former chairman of the MBA program at the Harvard Business School. He is a coauthor, with James L. Heskett and Christopher W. L. Hart, of *Service Breakthroughs: Changing the Rules of the Game,* which explores how specific firms in a variety of services industries are constantly able to set new standards for quality and value that force competitors to either adapt or fail. Dr. Sasser also serves as a consultant to a number of companies in both North America and Europe.

Howard H. Stevenson is the Sarofim-Rock Professor of Business Administration at the Harvard Business School and former senior associate dean and director of financial and information systems. Specializing in the field of entrepreneurship, Dr. Stevenson has authored, edited, or coauthored five books and over forty articles, which have appeared in the *Harvard Business Review, Sloan Management Review, Journal of Business Strategy,* and elsewhere.

Thomas Teal is the senior editor at Bain & Company, Inc. His previous experience includes seven years as an editor at the *Harvard Business Review,* five years at *The New Yorker,* two years as managing editor of the White House speechwriting office under President Carter, and two decades as a translator from Swedish, Danish, and Norwegian for American book publishers.

Charles R. Weiser is head of the consumer financial services division of British Airways. Mr. Weiser specializes in change management, and has been involved in significant business process reengineering roles at British Airways, including setting up the airline's executive club frequent-flyer program and turning around the customer relations division.

INDEX